North Star Country

The Fesler-Lampert *Minnesota Heritage Book* Series

This series is published with the generous assistance of the John K. and Elsie Lampert Fesler Fund and David R. and Elizabeth P. Fesler. Its mission is to republish significant out-of-print books that contribute to our understanding and appreciation of Minnesota and the Upper Midwest.

The Gift of the Deer by Helen Hoover

The Long-Shadowed Forest by Helen Hoover

North Star Country by Meridel Le Sueur

Listening Point by Sigurd F. Olson

The Lonely Land by Sigurd F. Olson

Of Time and Place by Sigurd F. Olson

Open Horizons by Sigurd F. Olson

Reflections from the North Country by Sigurd F. Olson

Runes of the North by Sigurd F. Olson

The Singing Wilderness by Sigurd F. Olson

Voyageur Country: The Story of Minnesota's National Park by Robert Treuer

MERIDEL LE SUEUR

North Star Country

University of Minnesota Press

MINNEAPOLIS · LONDON

First University of Minnesota Press edition, 1998

Published by the University of Minnesota Press
111 Third Avenue South, Suite 290
Minneapolis, MN 55401-2520
http://www.upress.umn.edu

Printed in the United States of America on acid-free paper

Library of Congress Cataloging-in Publication Data

Le Sueur, Meridel.
North Star country / Meridel Le Sueur.
p. cm. — (The Fesler-Lampert Minnesota heritage book series)
Originally published: New York : Book Find Club, c1945.
Includes index
ISBN 0-8166-3252-9 (alk. paper)
1. Minnesota History. 2. Minnesota—Social life and customs.
3. Wisconsin—History. 4. Wisconsin—Social life and customs.
5. Great Lakes Region—History. 6. Great Lakes Region—Social life
and customs. I. Title. II. Series.
F606.L56 1998
977.5—DC21 98-21093

10 09 08 07 06 05 04 03 02 01 00 99 98   10 9 8 7 6 5 4 3 2 1

For my Mother and Arthur

Contents

Preface   ix

THEY SHALL COME REJOICING
The North Star   3
Jest Lookin' fer a Home!   12
Honey in the Horn   17
Big State Fair   24

THE LIGHT IS SWEET
Back of Beyond   33
Sweet Waters   42
Pelt and Pelf   57
Freedom Roads in the Wilderness   73

WOE TO MY PEOPLE
Traverse des Sioux   83
Sun Dance   91
Treaty   96
Massacre   102

THUNDER ON, DEMOCRACY
Bred in a Cabin   115
Refuge Seed   125
Man Alive   136
Corn and Wheat   153
Oh Susannah, Don't You Wait for Me!   167
I Rent Sky Space   177
Civil War   187

Contents

RISE, O DAYS

    Hayseeds Like Me   199
    One-eyed Watcher   208
    They Shall Live   217
    Work Ritual   226
    I Been Working on the Railroad   237
    Good-by to Bay Shalore   243

STRUGGLE

    Folks Say   253
    Drought   261
    The Farmer Is the Man   271
    Old Andy Comes to the North Star Country   275
    Industrial Struggle   281
    Strike   289

STRIDE ON, DEMOCRACY

    Cradled Hercules   301
    Milk Train   308
    The Shapes Arise   316

    Afterword
      Blanche H. Gelfant   323
    Index   335

Preface

This is a history of the people of the Midwest, told from their dimension in their language. The Homestead Act opened for landless Europeans a rich earth—fourteen feet down to bedrock—and made possible the first democracy in the world, a common aggregate of workers and farmers, inventors and poets. The proximity of work and land, the encroachment of power structures, and the mix of immigrants brought about a new speech, new folk ways, in the wheat and corn belt, in the mills, mines, villages, and factories; new forms of labor and ownership summoning new collectives of workers. Among the creators of a new underground culture, ignored by the establishment, were roistering lumberjacks, gandy dancers, wheat farmers who lost everything every four years, and heroic immigrant women. To survive, the people formed new social organizations—the Grange, the Alliance, the Populist party, the Cooperative movement, the utopian colonies, the IWW, the Socialist party, the singing societies. They spoke in long sentences against the wind, in wheat fields, at picnics, in village newspapers and farm almanacs, creating dreams of cooperation and coalition.

There was some bitter criticism of this book when it came out in 1945. Howard Mumford Jones asked who the people—the folk—were and, in effect, why their history should be more than folk ways, why the teamsters' strike should be a folk way. Another reviewer said the book should never have been written. Many attacked it because they saw history as made by leaders, not by the people. Why, they asked, should I talk of an Irishman dead under every tie on Jim Hill's railroad and not of the great fellow himself?

This Preface was written for the Bison Book Edition of *North Star Country*, published in 1984.

But the book survived. It was a Book Find selection and was read widely and is still read, although it has long been out of print.

I have waited for younger historians to continue this history of the people beyond the end of World War II. Even the negative, perhaps dated, and injured parts of the book have not been rewritten or revised. They appear as I perceived them then and their very distortions, half truths, or misapprehensions serve to gauge the change and growth that have occurred since.

The Indian section was very hard to research because most of the formal history was a downright lie and the Indians themselves were silent or ignorant of their own history, robbed by law of learning and speaking their own language and performing the rites of their religion, driven into protective silence. Reading that section now reveals how the true history has finally become visible, how the Indians have become visible. They can now do the sun dance legally and demand their rights at the United Nations.

Many of the passages of history and oral telling were like grains of corn that are now sprouting in global heat and light. The small place opens to a world where communication makes instantly visible unseen people articulating their hunger and need. Everywhere such folk poets are being heard and we can identify with a vast warm fraternal democracy that we recognize in our own roots. This book, despite or because of its age, is being reprinted to show that our true history and future action lie not in the static, linear preservation of an elitist past. We must now invoke the living history, the true history of the courage and chemistry of our people, consistently and heroically maintained.

There is an interesting relationship between *North Star Country* and the government projects of the 1930s. A part of Erskine Caldwell's series American Folkways, the book was inspired by the WPA and federal programs in writing, art, theater, design. To get on them, all one had to be was hungry. For the first time there was a base for a true people's culture. One could study art free, the theater for less than a dollar. One was part of it all, not just a consumer.

The Federal Writers' Project in Minnesota consisted of editors whose papers had folded, free-lance writers of science fiction, advertising copywriters—a wonderful, motley crew who worked together toward the final goal, the state guide. There were about eighty on the project and we went amongst the people to find the true history of every county in the state. There was a project just to record the "folk-says," the model for this being instigated by B. A. Botkin in Oklahoma. We interviewed people who had lived to tell it in their own words without fancy grammar.

American culture was changed by these projects; a buried and ignored culture was made visible, and the people gained courage and boldness to express their own experiences. The Writers' Project produced and nourished many writers who might have been buried. I got ninety dollars or so a month, but this was the first time in my life I had rent and food paid and could write. Not a small matter. Many of the well-known artists today also came from that moment of being able to work.

Although this book ended in 1945, its message continues, thanks to sophisticated electronic media, in vaster unimagined multiplicity and synthesis. Now there are recorders, witnesses, and participants everywhere. For the people compose a story that never ends, a river that winds and falls and rushes to the sea. The people are a story that is a long and continual coming alive from the earth into better wheat, Percherons, babies, engines—persistent and inevitable. The people will always know that some of the grain will be good, some of the crop will be saved, some will return and bear the strength of the kernel; that from the bloodiest year some will survive to outfox the frost.

Meridel Le Sueur
April 1984

They Shall Come Rejoicing

The North Star

Men and the Earth

IN THE WESTERN REACHES OF THE NORTH
Star Country a human skull was found. The estimated time
of burial was placed in the early Tintah stage of Lake Agassiz, between eight and twelve thousand years ago. The body
of a young woman was found in an even deeper glacial drift,
an ax buried in her skull, murder ossified in the violent,
remembering earth. A pit of workmen with copper mallets
in their hands and a Norwegian ax were plowed up.

3

Interglacial plants found only in the Arctic have been unearthed, also the teeth of chaetopods, small marine worms; the fossils of elephants have been found at the edges of the glaciers, marks of their roaming; gastroliths have been identified—the stones which dinosaurs and other great bird-like reptiles carried in their crops as chickens and turkeys now carry gravel.

These are witnesses that the tide of frost and northern lights, the valley meeting of Arctic winds and tropical siroccos, has ebbed above two-legged man for an unknown number of years, leaving the record of his footprints—along with worm and dinosaur, the prairie bone, flint—the mark of his coming and going, the smoothness of his palm upon wood and copper. He has marked the land with the ruck of buffalo bones and made it a Golgotha of skulls. He has left songs, drumbeats, the sounds of work in the air, stories, folklore, and the sad wail of his tribal wanderings.

A lion does not write a book. The broken trail of the people must be followed by signs of myriad folk experiences in story, myth, legend, reflecting the struggle to survive; in the spore of old newspapers, folkway marking the rituals of birth, death, harvest, planting, in the embroidery on the pillow, the democracy quilt. These signs are not to be found easily or read lightly, measured like rock, estimated as metal. Folkways are malleable. They disappear as inland rivers do and reappear to flood a continent. They are submerged by time, shadowed by events, by sudden jets of power, changing into their opposite, a new harvest coming with a new tool.

Folklore is the hieroglyphics of all man's communication, both obvious and subterranean, as he struggles with growing society, changing tools, to create a place, a community, a nation. To read the meaning of the bones lying all one way in the buffalo wallow, the monuments erected by weather and by grief, requires a witch stick sensitive to deep channels. The weather erects monuments, but not at the place where a woman stopped in Wisconsin, after burying her first baby at sea, to give birth to the second in a shack before she and her husband went on over the frozen prairie into Dakota. The trail must be followed in the spore, in the bloodstains and the marks of struggle: the desolation of tar-paper shanties, windows gaping still like the eyes of mad women who could not stand the solitude; the fleeing man seen in the unshut doors he did not close after him as he fled from Wisconsin to Minnesota, to the Dakotas, and then back again, losing a year's work, a wife, but never hope; the masks discerned, essential and instinctive in a new country full of danger and sudden weather changes, where a poker face saved your life, a tall tale hid a gun, a joke played for time, and tenderness was twin of cruelty.

Many signs mark the middle border country, a frontier nation not a hundred years old, with no connected primitive past, no deep historic shadow, no feudal fumbling of dark gestation. A swift action has taken place, recorded from the first day in diaries, newspapers, pamphlets, in a mass impulse for expression scarcely equaled, except perhaps in the Soviet Union. Expression grew like corn. Newspapers sprang up like whiskey stills. Democratic man wished not to die, but to be perpetuated, to speak in meeting, to write to the papers.

It was a new society, unique, set down green in the wilderness, adapting rapidly to climate, animals, minerals, mutually safeguarding new institutions, sharing prohibitions and extensions of freedom, rearing a new culture from the blend of diverse strands, sharing strengths, confidence, and myth, all in the bright humus of one idea: that the dignity of man is inalienable, and that by his own effort on this earth he can subjugate nature for the good of all.

Without the haven of the middle border country, the opening of the West, this belief might have died at the

Cumberland Gap. Here it was given time, cradled and sustained in the Mississippi Valley and at the source of the great "Conception" River in the North Star Country.

The man and woman moving behind the westering sun wanted room to think fast and big, invent, speak, plant land and children with freedom's plow. They wanted new ways of being together. They hankered after something beside death and taxes. They wanted to see straight and live on earth. Like the growth of scientific thought, the twin of democracy, they wanted to examine the humus, look at decay, the minutiae of soil and society, honor the lowest labor and growth. Hard-headed, they wanted their pie in the "here and now," every man under his tree, no man a servant. Horse sense or common sense was "commin doin's"; they all had it together because without it they would not survive.

As de Tocqueville said in his time:

These very Americans who have not discovered one of the general laws of mechanics have introduced into navigation an engine that changes the aspect of the world. The social condition and institutions of democracy prepare men to seek the immediate and useful, practical results of the sciences.

The task of this enterprising people was vast. They faced a boundless territory inhabited by hostile nations of red men, a country rich enough to haunt a man's dreams. Radisson had said when he first laid eyes on the verdant meadows:

I liked noe country better, for whatever a man could desire was to be had in great plenty, viz.: fishes in abundance and all sorts of meat, corne enough. This I say that the Europeans fight for a rock in the sea against one another and contrariwise these Kingdoms are so delicious, plentiful in all things, the earth bringing forth fruit, the people can live long and lusty and wise in their ways. What conquest would that be at little or no cost, what labyrinth of pleasure should millions of people have, instead that millions complain of misery and poverty.

And the people flooded in at the opening of free lands, following the North Star, breaking the turf with four yoke of oxen, letting the daylight down into the deep wilderness—building, in the space of one generation, an Empire.

It was fast; it was big.

Every morning Paul Bunyan grew two feet. When he laughed the folks in the villages ran into their houses and hid in the cellars thinking it was a thunderstorm.

He was quick as lightning, the only man in the north woods who could blow out a candle at night and hop into bed before it was dark.

He said he planted a kernel of corn and in five minutes the corn sprouted up through the ground till it was fifty feet high, and Ole, the Big Swede, climbed up out of sight.

Even the crumbs that fell on the floor were so large that the chipmunks who ate them grew as big as wolves and chased the bears right out of the country. Later the settlers shot them for tigers.

Paul had to invent the double-bitted ax, with a blade on each side, so his men could work twice as fast. It was wide as a barn door and had a great oak tree for a handle, and he chopped so fast, it got red hot and had to be dipped into the handy lakes to cool off.

Paul and the Six Axmen logged off North Dakota in a single month, and Babe, the Blue Ox, walked around on the stumps, pushing them into the ground so that the Swedes could plow the next day.

Things were "opening up," they said then as now. Newspapers were printed every week, on presses brought down on river boats, set up in shanties and barns, with the latest news on science, political theory, translating the Declaration of Independence and the Communist Manifesto. Simultaneously with building the sod shanties, breaking the prairie, schools were started, Athenaeums and debating and singing societies founded, poetry written and recited on winter evenings. The latest theories of the rights of man were discussed along with the making of a better breaking plow.

Inventions, new roads, tools, voyages, explorations, scientific discoveries opened the horizon of man's brain. Excitement was high. Fourier, Marx, Rousseau, Darwin were discussed in covered wagons, along with electro-chemical equivalents. Knute, a woodsman, penned the following after a lone winter in a cabin, seeing Indians through his doorway as he wrote:

Having all my wood in and when I was thus alone I sent for a free thinker paper in Norwegian, Dagslyset, and the writings of Ingersoll and Spencer. And after long study I moved out of the orthodox faith and into the faith of Ingersoll and after him I later named my first son. It was a hard thing to do but a great relief to get rid of the hell and damnation. I then slept sound and better nights.

Emigrants crowded the ports of Europe, Mennonites, German revolutionists, the forty-eighters, French Communards who had swum the Channel to the Jersey Isles. Gamblers, speculators, Yankee peddlers, three-card-Monty men, whiskey-sellers, quacks, dreamers, hunters, planters, milled together on the river-boats.

As Emerson said at that time there were "madmen, men with beards, Dunkers, Muggletonians, Come-Outers, Groaners, Agrarians, Seventh-Day Adventists, Baptists, Quakers, Abolitionists, Unitarians, and Philosophers." All these and more lashed their oxen west to take part in Jacksonian democracy in a tide of farmers, mechanics, land-hungry frontiersmen, with the marks of the knout on their backs, the prison pallor, famine color, breeding many kinds of tough, wild love of freedom.

So they came to the sun-down bailiwick writing a few notes, a letter that might go out when the thaws came. Some wrote back to New England in a tiny hand:

Mama, you should come here. You can plow a mile straight and never turn a stone. Don't say I'm crazy.

At night over the prairie we see a splendid mirage, a vast territory arising around us, a village in the air, with hay-cocks like castles, mirrored in the sky with no division between real and unreal.

Depending upon who you were and where you came from were your comments about the North Star Country. Margaret Fuller spending a summer in Wisconsin wrote of "its bold and impassioned sweetness, I do believe that Rome and Florence do not compare to this capital of natural art."

Englishmen like Basil Hall, Mrs. Trollope, Josiah Quince were willing to accept Boston society but the raucous frontier did not please them. The people, they said, were "convinced of their sagacity and acumen and proud of their shrewdness and independence . . . corrupt with political licentiousness which is producing turbulent citizens, abandoned Christians, inconstant husbands, unnatural fathers and treacherous friends."

While Harriet Martineau had the opposite impression, regarding the people as:

. . . a great embryo poet, now moody, now wild, but bringing out results of absolute good sense, restless, wayward in action but with deep peace and a gentle heart; exulting that he has caught the true aspect of things past and the depth of futurity which lies before him, wherein to create something so magnificent as the world has scarcely begun to dream of. There is the strongest hope of a nation that is capable of being possessed of an idea.

What sextant can be used to shoot the sun of this people's migration; what spirit levels found to make their work live and hold? What delicate needle would indicate the flux of oppressed peoples into the free lands, opened as Utopia, a domain of rich earth bought by Jefferson from Napoleon, the North Star standing in the dark of that feudal night, inviting haven from the knout, the guillotine, the Bastille, shining as a beacon of the new, democratic man? What seismograph will chart such complex strains, beating the pattern, shifting like a reflection, full of antagonisms, despair and hope, mounting toward disaster, growth, and that great identity called a new nation?

Tradition was broken, relationships lost, the new man a green tendril full of loneliness, a bag of recollections: hair-braided portraits lost in Ohio, an old woman's fragmented memory, a child's horizon madness, a buck-and-wing, a mother with a harp, pictures in a rawhide trunk of people never seen again, the jokes of Abe Lincoln, songs of nostalgia—"We will meet by and by, in that beautiful land beyond the sky," "My old Kentucky home, good night," "They shall come rejoicing, bringing in the sheaves."

A man having no more than a desire to become a Montreal merchant, opened the river, key to a continent.

Three men stealing out at night only to get ahead of an officer, founded a city.

The people of the North Star Country, because of their hatred of slavery, sent the first regiment in response to Lincoln's call and helped insure the solidarity of the United States.

Walking on giant paths, and being small and frightened, the north countryman created giant myths, sang to cover fear and nostalgia for old lands and bends of rivers he would never see again.

The mechanics, lumberjacks, the lakemen, rivermen, wood-cutters, plowmen, the hunkies, hanyocks, whistle-punks; the women beating the chaff, the roof-raisers, the cradle-makers, the writers of constitutions, the singers in the evening along unknown rivers; the stone masons, the quarrymen, the high slingers of words, the printers and speakers in the courthouses, the lawmakers, the carpenters, joiners, journeymen—all kept on building. Every seven years they picked up the loans, mortgages, the grasshopper-ridden fields, the lost acres, the flat bank accounts, and went on, started over, turned a new leaf, worked harder, looked over new horizons.

The heritage they give us is the belief we have in them. It is the story of their survival, the sum of adjustments, the struggle, the folk accumulation called sense and the faith we have in that collective experience. It was real and fast, and we enclose it. Many unknown people lived and were destroyed by it. What looks to us grotesque or sentimental is the humor of the embryo, the bizarreness of the unformed, and the understanding of it is a prerequisite to our survival. It was real, and created our day. Perhaps it encloses us.

It is the deep from which we emerge.

Like a lion the people leave marks of their passing, reveal that moment of strength when the radicle plunged into the soil, in a fierce struggle on a strong day, and a nation held.

Jest Lookin' fer a Home!

Farewell now, O valley of Seljord; farewell to kith and kin and the lovely gardens of home.

—SLOOP FOLKSONG

To the West! To the West! Where the rivers that flow,
Run thousands of miles, spreading out as they go.
Where the great waving forests that echo our call,
Are wide as Old England and free to us all!
Where the prairies, like seas where the billows have
  rolled,
Are broad as the Kingdoms and Empires of old,
And the lakes are like oceans in storms or in rest,
Away, far away, to the land of the West!

—HASTINGS FRONTIER JOURNAL

This board and bark it is our own,
It grew around my feet, sir.
It's paid no tax to squire or crown
Which makes it doubly sweet, sir.

—VARIANT OF "YANKEE DOODLE"

One Day of Turkey, Six Days of Hash

ADVENTURERS, VOYAGEURS, HUNTERS AND
gamblers, who at first rode the rivers in canoes and rafts,

gave way to farmers and their women when steam came; the Erie Canal was built in 1825 and linked the Hudson River with the Great Lakes; later the Ohio Canal opened navigation on Lake Michigan down the Illinois River into the Mississippi. In 1856 a portage canal was built between the Fox and the Wisconsin Rivers, completing the opening of that ancient water route to larger vessels, opening navigation from salt to fresh water. When finally, with the building of the Sault Ste. Marie Canal, the lakes were open to Duluth and the way was clear to Buffalo, the tide of immigration burst in a colorful flow up the lakes, the rivers, into the vast uninhabited prairie. These were the home-makers with plows, tools, ax, hammer, and women, wheat and lilac seeds and the babies born and unborn.

In the space of ten years, travel had developed from the two-wheeled Red River carts, the ox caravans, the stage coach, to the steamboat and railway, and the way was opened to the development of agriculture and the coming of the people.

Looking west from the famines, the stolen fields, turning restless in their sleep, the people of Europe felt the mighty pull of the North Star, free land, education, no military service—Jeffersonian democracy, the first in the world.

Industry was driving the Irish into the mills so that the land could be used for sheep to feed the hungry spindles. In sixty years, four million left Ireland; only the old and helpless "stayed in the motherland keening for the dead and gone." It is reported that in 1849 in Kilrush thirteen thousand suffered evictions; five thousand were unhoused in Limerick, fifty homes emptied of occupants on the land of Kildymo, and the demolition proceeded at a rate so sweeping and rapid that on some properties forty farmhouses were dashed down and burned in a day.

The Irish came to America bringing a bit of sod with them, and stayed on the long prairie where the sun was a slow time setting. And in the Old Country "never a boat went down to Queenstown or Derry without tears following the sun down to the sea."

A girl in Norway tended cattle all year in the hills, for which she received a bolt of cloth, a pair of shoes, and two dollars and a half. When she went to church she heard the minister say that she should stay away from America, that the ocean was full of beasts. Every year she saved the two dollars and a half, and in twelve years she had enough money for the six weeks' journey across the Big Water and the four weeks' trip across the Great Lakes to North Dakota, where she married and started a dynasty of her own—with eight sons and three daughters and three hundred rich acres of wheat land.

The number of Norwegians who migrated was equal to the total population of Norway in the beginning of the nineteenth century.

The Lithuanians came, stirred by the tales brought back by General Kosciusko, who had come to the aid of America in 1777 and afterwards spread stories among his people of the fertile lands waiting for the plow. The Russians have a saying that a Lithuanian goes into the forest riding his horse and comes out with a carriage and hand-carved harness.

The Czechs and Slovaks came in 1847, fleeing the royal vengeance and the potato famines which drove thousands for their very lives from Bohemia and France. America needed them, and agents from the railroads, the timber, and the mines waylaid them at every port and flooded Europe with advertisements: "Come! All men are free and equal before the law. Religious freedom is absolute and there is not the slightest connection between church and state."

Finns, Croatians, Poles, Russians came to the Big Woods and the Mesabi. English remittance men rode flat saddle and hunted coyotes to hounds hoping to establish manors on free land. New England workers came escaping labor conditions in textile mills. The Yankee peddler became known and also the New England banker; delicate young men came from Boston and Oxford dons lived in sod shanties with embossed libraries on their shelves. Ladies came to teach French and McGuffey's Reader. The voice of culture was raised by men like Emerson, Bryant, and Greeley against the shouts of bidders for sky-high and soaring lots.

The clash of cultures became as vociferous as the county-seat wars which rivaled in ferocity the clashes between Scottish border chiefs. The Norwegians tried to buy whole regions away from the Irish who withdrew haughtily to the ridges and left the valleys to the hard-working. The Norwegians brought the polka, the schottische, the smörgåsbord, and the festivals of winter to the North Star Country, and a thrift which at first irritated the Yankees; their women and children gleaned the fields after the reapers and actually winnowed the mountains of chaff by hand. Yankees laughed at such small potatoes, but a bushel of wheat meant a dollar more in the pocket.

The Old Country people worked the land for a home, plowed deep, harrowed over and over, up and down. They recovered the pecks. They founded singing societies too, had not much use for saloons, but bought their own liquor—raw alcohol, which they diluted and drank as part of eating, singing, living, at festivals and weddings, not understanding the Yankee habits of imbibing. The Norwegians, also, with the Finns and Danes, started co-operatives which seemed alien to the Irish and the Yankees. The Germans thought the rest barbarians because they would not go to the theater on Sunday, and the rest thought the Germans were headed for perdition. So it went, in a grinding of racial glaciers as fierce as that of the natural glaciers that made the top soil of the North Star Country.

But the map that La Salle sent to Louis XIV, showing the

crawl of the Mississippi, marking the tin, iron and coal mines, was not as momentous to history as the faces of the men and women who flooded with hope into the new country, unmarked courses in their blood, the eye adjusting to space, disaster, to the amplitude and prodigality of the prairies, to terrors of space and quiet, idiotic monotony, extremes of weather, to plenty and poverty, feast or famine. The map was broken, sometimes lost, the line obscured, the speech unrecorded of men riding together at night toward a far horizon, of lone women fearful of the loon's cry—all the architecture and lineaments of the human face, of houses, barns like cathedrals, and the pointing fingers of corn.

Walt Whitman, traveling by Pullman over this country, wrote:

> When I mix with these intermingling swarms of alert turbulent, goodnatured, independent citizens, mechanics, young persons, at the idea of this mass of men, so fresh and free, so loving and so proud, a singular awe falls upon me. I feel with amazement that among our genius few or none have yet really spoken to this people, created a single image making mark for them or absorbed the central spirit and the idiosyncrasies which are theirs; or who has confronted the voracious but ever erect and active, pervading, indulging will and typic aspiration of the land in a spirit kindred to itself. . . .

An early country newspaper said, "This country should not only make its own hobnails but its own poetry. Truly the light is sweet!"

Honey in the Horn

I love the banging hammer, whirring plane,
The crashing of the buzz saw, creaking of the crane.
Ringing of the anvil, groaning of the drill,
The clanging of the turning lathes, whirring of the mill,
Buzzing of the spindle, rattle of the loom,
Puffing of the engines, fan's continual boom.
The clipping of the tractors, droning of the awl.
The ploughman's merry whistle, the reaper's evening call,
The drover's shouts, the thresher's evening notes,
And the husker's mirth and jokes.

—TERRITORY NEWSPAPER

He rolled the prairie up like cloth, drank the Mississippi
dry,
Put the Alleghenies in his hat, a steamboat in his eye.
And for his breakfast buffaloes, O, some twenty he did
fry.
He whipped the whole Comanche tribe, the day before
he died,
And for a walking stick he took a Big Wood tallest pine,
And when he frowned he was so black the sun it could
not shine.
He whopped a ton of grizzly bears, one weighing each a
ton,
And proved himself by all these feats—to be a western
man.

—NEWSPAPER POEM

Westward the Jug of Empire

BIPED MAN IN THE NORTH WAS FULL OF BRAG with "gold in the pocket, silver on the tongue, brass in the face and iron in the heart." As James Goodhue, editor of the *St. Paul Pioneer Press,* said, "Our blood is red."

Human history is work history. The heroes of the people are work heroes. Work, not money, has been the true genius of the North Star Country. In frontier society the possessor and the doer are one. The independent democratic frontiersman, with his own land and corn title, was a new man. The sons of bondsmen cried, "Give me liberty or give me death!" The activity of authority or the state was a matter of convenience with no danger or limit to it. "With the past we have nothing to do," said a Fourth of July orator. "Its lessons are lost and its tongue is silent. We are ourselves the head and front of all political experience."

So man stood on the horizon and threw no shadow. The least among them could write to the paper, speak in public, found a town, survey his own land, and by night draw up his own constitution, including provisions for rights for women and no saloons on Main Street.

Men like Lincoln began to emerge as folk patterns of this mixture—comical, bitter, melancholy, tall, tough, spitting a long shot at old traditions, with a new taut muscle, a yellow swamp skin, a burnt parchment over the bones, independent as a hog on ice, direct, hospitable, liking the plain uses of a plain life on this earth and basing chances of heaven on it. Laconic, insolent, men of the North Star Country wore their hats the way they pleased. An Englishman who opened a land office describes them:

These long, lean farmers come into the office in the coldest weather thinly dressed, frost-bitten hands, yet with the airs of royalty. Without speaking or sitting down they warm themselves fore and aft. There is no fancy talk or bowing to anyone. He seldom sits straight in a chair and either has to tilt back against the wall or his feet on the stove, or if there is a wainscotting he is sure to be up on that. His outside position when not in constant labor, is to sit or lean on something and whittle on a soft stick.

There was enough work for a continent of men; new tools to be made of wood, iron, and, later, steel; bridges to be built, miles of roads; and canals to be dug, trees felled, bonanza wheat threshed, ore wheel-barrowed to lake ships, all in the space of a few years by two-handed, two-legged, heart-dynamoed man, with his shoulders, elbow grease, his bantam earth-spanning legs, and the queer skull-piece that keeps his backbone from unraveling. Workers were shanghaied from New York boats, driven west by depressions and soup lines. Calls were sent out:

Wanted, twenty thousand feeble bodied scalliwags to bring on litters from the east, bundles of raw meat packaged loosely in original skin, for Minnesota to manufacture into full grown men. One hundred thousand pairs of decaying lungs, wrecked constitutions to be repaired that have been shaken to pieces by fever, ague, or abolitionists, made whole on the electric anvil of our blue sky.

Send us your paupers, except lawyers, have each bring at least one woman. We want girls to whip their weight in wild cats, outscream the cormorant, give the young badger heartache and grace a wild home.

In a new country there is always much talk. A new man with a new tool and a new horizon talks up in the evening, congregates after labor, talking bolder than he sometimes feels. Picking out speech against a wilderness silence he shouted across fields, orated at picnics, held forth at the country store on babies, crops, politics, prices, and slavery:

She's a nice old gal, liberty. I take her to my arms and say, old gal, you are for me.

It was all so big I feared I would fall into the sky!

You got to know how to hate an Injun, love a gal.

One man is as good as another, or a damn sight better.

We Yankees are tarnation cute rascals, make a fortune with the right hand and lose it with the left. I'm half fire, half love and a touch of thunderbolt. I'm the most tempestuous original and never-to-be-forgotten smash biler-bustin' free peddler as ever was raised. Go ahead!

What a man thinks here he is very apt to say, if he likes you it is easily known and if he thinks you're a damn fool he is not likely to qualify it much!

There are no fences, boundaries, all open pasture, free for all, no holds barred. Our chicken fixin's and common doin's are the same.

I like my fellow man best when he is scattered some. With my ax I'll cut a lane through this wilderness till I see daylight on the other side. I can do it!

This is a golden land, the grain threshes itself in the granary, Munchener beer runs in the creeks, and little roasted piggies rush about the streets, politely inquiring if you wish for ham, the clocks strike the hour like eight-day clocks!

> Sugar in the gourd, honey in the horn,
> I never was so happy since the day I was born!

Mark Twain said that following the jug of empire westward the missionary came after the whiskey; next came the immigrant, the trader, gambler, desperado, and then the smart chap who has an old grant on the land; this naturally brought the lawyers, which brought the vigilance committees, which brought the undertakers and all these combined brought the newspaper, which started politics and the railroads, and they all pitched in to build the church and the jail!

The robust West and the effete East had verbal clashes. A new language came with a new tool, new relationships and actions. Races poured words into the pot and stewed up a horsey speech, useful as an ax handle, plain and fancy, for Sunday and weekdays. Words sprang up out of whole cloth—cantankerous, rumagious, hifalutin, teetotaler, sock-dolager, honeyfuggle. Every nationality borrowed words from its neighbors, like eggs, and rarely returned them without colorful additions. When the rivers were frozen the whole countryside came to the rural courthouses for oratory and wit, which often led to mortal combat. There was high talk from salty frontier lawyers who set up with a kitchen table, one law book, in linsey-woolsey and a sawbuck vocabulary.

A pompous Eastern lawyer rebuked the frontier for its loose court procedure and its cud-chewing lawyers, and invoked the glory of learning, "the Thracian wit, the Macedonian courage, the Hellenic taste, the Mithradatic patriotism and the Pantheonic wisdom necessary for the right practice in our glorious land of law and equity." There was silence. Then the young whippersnapper lawyer of the West squared off for a good round with the hated East.

Hi, there, you downeaster, don't be so all-fired quick, don't go to runnin' down my steamboat. I can span three lengths of my ax helve and a hand breadth over it. Stand around me and let me git a fair sweep. I don't know nothin' about Mathra Datic or Tom Datic. Now these downeasters would like to tuck a bib under our chins and feed us with a wooden spoon made out of a Boston sapling. But they cain't come to it nohow you fix it. We lived so long on hog and corn, fish and suckers, to gape fer Yankee fixin's. Oh, horngunflints and wooden nutmegs, I aim to win this case hands down and hand runnin' on jest the words I got me.

All you had to do was throw a clod and hit an orator.

The American eagle, then as now, was the favorite fowl of eloquent speakers. After extolling the great land of his birth and its gigantic fruits, an orator raised an ecstatic finger to follow the flight of the miraculous bird through the heavens as he cried out in stentorian voice: "Don't you see him, fellow citizens, rising higher and higher and higher?"

Some future inventor, a yokel realist, sang out, "Wal, I'll be damned if I can see him."

"Hoss," said the orator, transfixing the matter-of-fact citizen with his gaze, without dropping his magnificent tone, and keeping his finger to the sky—"Hoss, I was speakin' in a figger!" And off he went again with his eagle.

An Englishman made a Yankee mad, telling the exploits of his countrymen. The Yankee told this one:

That ain't a prime to what Short Tom kin do. He undertook to swim the Mississippi but got aground in seven foot of water, and you see, Tom was only five foot high and eight foot through, most of it solid and whiskey-logged. Well, he stuck agin a sand bar and found out he couldn't git over, and bein' mighty tired, he had to back down.

You see, he drank whiskey for a living altogether, and thet thar made his body impervious to the water, which had to stand back away from him about a foot all around. He perspired so strong, the water couldn't tech him.

Thar was some fellers sailin' close by and they seed him goin' down, and as they wasn't acquainted with the rum deposits of Short Tom they jest naturally suspected he was a goner.

They hunted about atter him an hour or sich. At last they skivered the old fellow a-settin' on the bottom of the sand spit, smokin' his pipe and tryin' to make a catfish stand on his tail!

The frontiersman thought he had a right to speak, to write for the papers. It was part of the freedom of the new country. He might not be so all-fired elegant as the English poets; he might write a poem about a shabby guy whose pants fit him too soon, making love to a gal by the hogpen; it might be lonesome poetry like Lincoln's—whatever it was, you had a right to speak your piece in open meeting. Talk was high. Every poor season, every bank crash produced more talk, more writing, more fresh plans and green argument, discussion of the possible along with the fantastic; tough practical knowledge and invention and the tall tale.

The credo ran:

Monday I started my bank operations. Tuesday I owned a million by all calculations. Wednesday, my brown stone mansion began. Thursday I drove out a spanking bay span. Friday, I gave a magnificent ball. Saturday smashed with just nothing at all!

It was fast and still is.

After every crash, depression, drought, or panic, the pioneers subsisted on oat-and-acorn coffee, winnowed the chaff more diligently, tightened their belts, and spoke to each other in the evenings:

It says in the paper, "To the conscientious and industrious man a crash never comes." I'll swan we get a crash every six years to a day.

Talk is cheap; it takes money to buy whiskey.

When you get down to your last bean, your backbone and your navel shake dice to see which gits hit.

The soil was my only backer.

It's hard times in Dakota, our crops are rotting here, our taxes and our interest will not be met this year.

We were sure going to be a success.

I don't owe or own a thin dime.

And this was rapid, too, the devastation. In the village where I live there are not one hundred people where, in the span of man's memory, there was a metropolis, grist mills, sawmills; where thousands of workers, lumberjacks, rafters, farmers, gamblers put up big money on the Saturday races; where dynasties were being born, bonanza wealth accumulating from wheat and timber and ore.

The wood is felled, the land has blown away, ruined towns lie like slag on the prairie. Some of the bones of bullbuckers, cookies, fallers, farmers lie in the cemetery on the hill; and some whose bones have no marker went west again to hunt for a strike at the next stop, listening for the summons now farther away—something lost behind the range, something hidden, something missed, come and see!

Big State Fair

───────────

Millions of bushels we are bringing,
Our songs of corn march on.
Our feet will follow the furrows lead
To raise the food our allies need.

—VILLAGE POEM SPELLED IN CORN KERNELS, 1944

After the toils of the day, gathered in rural merriment
and festal glee around the old kitchen fireplace, right
glad to find one of its corners tenanted by some merry
neighbor who would partake of jokes, apples and boiled
cider. This was a goodly scene, for the fireplace was of
sufficient size to enclose the whole family in the warm
embrace of its jamb. There the joy-inspired tankard
passed, apples are named and the ballad sung.

—THE PLOUGHBOY, EARLY RURAL JOURNAL

I see in the people the strength and will of their river.

—IMMIGRANT SONG OF JONAS LIE

The Dern Crick's Rose

YOU CAN HEAR THE ROAR AS YOU APPROACH
the Fair grounds which lie in the hollow of the valley with
the lowlands stretching away to the truck gardens, to the

wheat, oats, and barley fields, and now to the munition plants which produce grenades where corn once grew.

You can hear the roar amid the pennants flying and the bright wheels and merry-go-rounds, signs of speed and thrills, but above everything you can hear the peculiar roar, singular among animals, like the roar of a mighty river that flows on unabated, the sound of the human voice congregated after work and harvest, in one rich cacophony of sound, blended with the call of beasts and cry of barkers, rising as it has risen here for a hundred years, with the odor of weather, animals, of teeming turds and hay.

Now, after settlement, after struggle with the earth, Indians, grasshoppers, drought, taxes, now war. But the cornucopia is full again at festival time, filled by relentless toil, this year rising as always from the conjunction of the year's fruitful and deathly, ruinous and productive energy.

There are men and women at the Fair who have lived on buffalo meat, in covered wagons, have fought Indians. In one generation they have gone from the sod hut and the tar-paper shanty to the skyscraper and back to the sod hut. They have seen cities rise and die. You can see now the flood, the energy here of the people both for life and to defend themselves against death. You can hear the sound of that energy in flesh and fowl, its tide moving in danger, now a new one, as they stand before the guns that would blow everyone to kingdom come on this autumnal afternoon.

In the farm exhibits the skill, craftsmanship, the undismayed spirit stand in the embowered mottoes made of corn kernels, of bunched wheat, flax, and soybean leaf. They say: *We can. We will. We must. United We Stand for Victory.* A corn marching-song is spelled out in corn kernels.

The words "Freedom" and "The Common Man" are spelled out in flax sheaves, and they are not new to the North Star Country. These are the words that stood with the North Star to oppressed peoples of the old countries, calling them in the dark nights over a darker ocean, and this feeling for democracy has remained as persistent as grass and lively as gophers.

The precise and patient energy that makes a country is shown in the work of the Ladies' Aid, in all the handiwork from church, farm, and village. The Democracy Rose quilt wins the sweepstakes. Crowds stand before the pies, cakes, drawnwork, the silhouette-cutters, signs of work, languors, odors of good rich corn-growing days, smell of clover in the hot sun, needlework snatched up before supper by ruminating milky women.

The fine flesh of farm women smells of summer, of the hot kitchen. Then the harvesters come and there is the odor of sweet summer hay cocked in the blazing sun, of wheat chaff blowing sweet, corn standing tall, wind over the ripe fields and the smell of many kinds of ripeness, seed, and the hurry of fruition before death.

Old-timers will tell you that once the wild strawberries were so plentiful that they stained the hooves of the horses.

The change of seasons is strong, with spring coming out of the tomb of winter, miraculous and delicate, the little flowers under the snow, the frozen ruts thawing, the river ice breaking with a great roar, cracking in the sun. In the old days the frozen dead were waiting for the ground to thaw, the horses and their driver frozen solid, standing as they stopped, released from the sweet bite of frost at last. The sudden warm days come, and then snow again and hail as big as hen's eggs. Dutchman's-breeches, arbutus, and the fuzzy faces of hepaticas show, and wild strawberries and marsh marigolds.

Summer ripens the fields golden with wheat, and rye; on a warm night when the bright moon is up after a shower has fairly wet the earth and waked up the drowsy corn, I will swear that you can see the stalk stretch and swell in its new sheath, rise through the contracted lips of the upper blade to crack and burst and murmur in green-tongued speech. You hear the green cry of growth and the potatoes murmur to each other "move over."

Autumn is a fine season with the blaze of swamp maple, the hills afire moving up the sky, the stooped back in the field gleaming, the fat quiet ripeness hanging under the sniff of smoke, the rising mists, the sudden frosts, the Indian summer haze hanging under the hills—grapes and chrysanthemums, shocks of corn, and the white hoar frost in the morning. At night there is the high wedge and honk of birds flying south, the sound of the saw making the woodpile grow; sudden and miraculous come the warm days again, after the fall equinox. These lost death days have the nobility of the death of a great and ancient man—after a good life and a fruitful time.

Then the cold winters begin; the low gray sky comes down, locked upon the earth. The sudden storm comes often in November, freezing the hunters still in the bottom lands, marooning automobiles, stopping city traffic, and workers spend the night huddled in hotel lobbies. In the country barrels have to be piled on the chimney to keep a smoke opening, and a guy rope is strung from house to barn, so you won't get lost two feet from your own door. The lumberjacks used to say the snow got so deep you had to dig a hole downwards, lasso the trees, and pull them up!

The bitter cold, standing at below zero, is very still with blue shadows. The trees pop and split, and you can freeze without knowing it. On a cold day you can hear a long way: a woman speaking over the slope, a wolf howling, or a fast through train sounding for a crossing far, far away.

The Territorial Pioneers meet every year at the Fair in their big log house, the trophies of their time flickering in the fire from the big logs, the wooden pestles, sawbucks, buckets, yokes, chairs, and cradles hewn from solid oak chunks. Medals of other wars are shown. A farmer says he is ninety and hayed this year because his boys were all at war, "Maybe altogether, counting grandsons, there are thirty-two of our men in the war." He says he is one of Lincoln's volunteers, a drummer boy, and was wounded at Gettysburg. He has a medal inscribed, "Awarded for brave and meritorious service," and signed by General Gilmore, but his son says, "Pa sets no value on it, never would wear it, left it lying around the house until we took care of it." His grandson wears the uniform of the U. S. Marines and came back for the Fair, which he says he wouldn't miss if he could help it. He also says his grandfather went out in the fields for the haying this year. The old man says:

We're short o' hands this year jest like my pa in the Civil war, so even if I'm ninety I done my share o' hayin' and there's a lot to be said fer it. I feel fit as a fiddle, aim to live out this war. I got a heap o' satisfaction ridin' the old sulkey rake agin, linin' up the windrows and watchin' the younger fry gather up the stacks. When it's all cocked and yer ridin' up to the big barn chewin' on a timothy stalk, and everybody lines up fer a swig of cold water, there ain't nothin' more comfortable to yer innards.

After a lively hoe-down they all go over to see the modern exhibits of war. There are huge worlds with minute maps of far places. Around these world maps cluster the thick mass of people of every nationality, their speech rising in questions; they mark now another time, the offspring of Scandinavians, Norwegians, Finns, Croatians, Germans, Irish, Danish, English, Italian, African, of the many and various migrations that have made this country, now speaking of another time, their faces lifted to the unfamiliar map of the world, to new frontiers:

Look at those maps! Look at where John is, that small spot!
I got me two sons in the Air Corps.
In my time you knew where you were going, what you were going to have for breakfast. You knew where your sons were going to be come morning. Well, a settin' hen never gets fat.

All we had to start from was a passel of kids. We trusted in the Lord and didn't expect much.

A human being has a right to stand like a tree has.

Ninety from my town lost at Bataan.

Yes sir, it's a different time, a mighty movin' time. We gone a long way from sunset to sundown, from can't see to can't see. We're movin' on. The big river has come over us.

I got me lost once in a big snowstorm with an ox. I expected to die then, couldn't see my hand in front of my face. I found the tail of that ox and held on for dear life. The ox wandered around and got us home. I was saved by the tiny tail of an ox. Just one tiny thing like that is keeping me optimistic forever.

Yes sir, it's like my grandpaw in the Civil War. He never saw the big drink and he was supposed to patrol along the beach of the Gulf of Mexico, walk up and down until he was relieved. Well, when the next patrol come my grandpaw had disappeared, they couldn't find hide nor hair of him. They halloed and halloed and pretty soon out from the water, they hears Grandpaw halloin' right back. They yells, "What in tarnation air ya doin' out there in the middle of the big water?" And Grandpaw yells back, "I ain't moved. I been walkin' up an' down in the same place, but the dern crick's rose!"

The Light Is Sweet

Back of Beyond

In the direction of the sunset the wind is blowing,
In the direction of the home of the giant.
Someone somewhere is speaking from the north,
Someone somewhere is speaking.

—INDIAN SONG

The vast prairie that we passed over was one of the most
beautiful countries in the world; for a distance of one
hundred and twenty miles it everywhere showed the
richest soil, and an abundance of good water which
flowed from a thousand living springs.

—GEORGE CATLIN

THE NORTH STAR COUNTRY, WITH MINNESOTA
as its center, occupies almost the exact geographical center
of North America and has three great drainage systems flowing in divergent directions through wide valleys of glacial
loess. The Alleghenies and the Rockies pushing up on both
sides of the continent form the magnificent Mississippi Valley. In this region it extends north to south through the
elbow of the Minnesota River, a rich basin left by glacial
invasion and occupied before the white man's coming by the
great Sioux nation. The surface then tilts down northward,

to the beaches of the dead Lake Agassiz whose dry basin makes the Red River Valley, the winter wheat area of North Dakota.

The ice ages left the rich soil that has been depleted so quickly by man. The first sheet, entering the northwest, carried the red drift from Lake Superior beyond the present course of the Mississippi. A later sheet advancing from the northwest and entering the Red River Valley spread a gray drift over the red. It is good farming on the gray drift. But the earth, like man, is moving. The earth is not everlasting, nor the hills. The soil—the living surface of the earth—dies, is replenished; the rivers run through it, take it along, the land returns in the wind, and the sun combines many kinds of energy in earth and man. The land moves. Man moves.

In a short space of time man has defaced and destroyed this earth, wounded the farm land, in what is called "accelerated erosion." The destruction of the prairie grass, which with finger-like roots clung to the rich topsoil, holding it to the skull of stone, has let the soil blow away. Natural prairie fires also once refertilized the earth with ash and humus every year; now no longer.

The glacial movement created abrupt transitions from the forests of the northern ridges and the great deposits of iron ore under the lake scalp down to the broad prairies with their rich residual soils. All the southern and western portions are treeless except along the streams. The driftless area and the bordering belt of loess covered themselves with hardwood, while the Big Woods themselves extend north—in their time the greatest forests of white, Norway, and jack pine in the world, from which the tall masts of the sea were taken until the big daylight came in. These abrupt transitions of the land contributed to the development of an empire within the period of fifty years; the new earth and the juxtaposition of forest and plain brought water power to

the mill, and made lumbering and farming complementary
industries.

Some rivers run south and some run north in the North
Star Country. This frightened many Norwegians. A river
running north to them had special and strange powers.

To the southwest rising four hundred and fifty feet above
the level of the prairie is the Coteau des Prairies, called by
Carver the "Shining Mountains," a wall of compact quartz
rising gradually from the prairie in swells and terraces, one
above the other, running from north to south for nearly two
miles, where it disappears at both ends again under the
prairie.

At the base of this wall stand five stupendous boulders,
leaning against each other like brothers, composed of feld-
spar and mica of an exceedingly ancient appearance. There
is not another boulder within fifty miles. The Indians regarded them with awe. Countless small groups of stones of
incredible variety and beauty are scattered about. Carver
said a man could travel the continent without being able
to find where they came from, and come at last to the con-
clusion that numerous chains of primitive rocks had reared
their heads on this continent, whose summits have been
swept away by the force of the diluvial currents and their
fragments strewn like foreigners in a strange land, the only
remaining evidence of their native ledges which have been
submerged and lost.

From the heights of this grass-covered mound you may
look over the most sublime and unbounded view of—nothing
at all, only the boundless ocean of prairie vanishing into the
far horizon, and above it the answering disk of sky swinging
upon it.

The low-pressure area created by the Mississippi digging
its way to the Gulf makes one of the finest skyscapes in the
world, with constantly veering winds passing from east to

west and back, sudden storms riding up from the southwest into the wide funnel with a roar, sometimes gathering up a cyclone.

Wide variation of temperature marks the climate. Great changes occur, ranging from 103° above to 60° below in winter. The Arctic Current often persists all summer, and sometimes hail falls in July and snow in May.

Striped Weather

Years of striped weather come along, with a mile strip of sun and a mile of rain. In one of these years, it is said, the sun shone on the corn fields until the corn began to pop, while the rain washed the syrup out of the sugar cane; both rolling into the valley made popcorn balls.

The pioneer was used to sudden changes, lightning disaster, years of drought when the frogs jumped into the pools backwards to keep from skinning their noses, siroccos that parched the corn and wheat, and years of rain and cold when nothing would ripen and years when the land lay under floods.

The Indians had a curious little god, Ha-yo'-ka, expressive of the perversities of prairie weather. He wore a green cocked hat, went naked in winter, and in summer wrapped his buffalo robe around him. The little prairie hills were his home. In joy he sighed and in sorrow laughed. He felt confidence when beset by dangers and quaked with fear in safety. You can see him now in those little whirlwinds that tear across the prairie with nobody in them.

The great thunderheads, birds of wind in the sky, were thought by the Indians to be giants who dug the ditches of the rivers, and when they died became thunderbirds, the lightning the flash of their eyes, the thunder the sound of their terrible song. Those that did not live in the sky became the lonely boulders found standing without reason upon the plains.

The prairie fires standing on the horizon in the wind every fall ran toward the firebreaks of the frontiersman. And suddenly, without warning, into the forest regions the timber fires came on the wind. Scarcely a town in the north woods that has not been burned to the ground many times, its continuity of life horribly severed. Fire and hurricane often mingle, standing like judgment in the sky, snapping trees like matches, engulfing men and women so they are charred running or baked in the clay they have rolled in: a hundred and thirty burned in a lake, an engineer took a burning train at full speed through the hurricane, lumberjacks have been found dead in the charred trees like blackbirds, whole cities destroyed in the wink of an eye.

Electric changes, violence, cataclysm have undoubtedly marked the people of the country, made them brothers of change, rovers, but if you survived you lived a long time, like the pines. A preacher drove up to a tavern where an old man sat amidst broken pipes, jugs, and chairs. "My friend," said the preacher, "you seem to have had company last night." "Yes, I had some of the boys here." "Boys!" said the preacher, "and how old may you be?" "Oh, goin' on a hundred." "A hundred—that is a very great age; you can't expect to stay with us long." "No," said the old man, "I was thinking as you rode up that next spring I would sell out here and go west!"

When man came upon the rivers and the treeless plains he had a startled expression of wonder, a sense of surprise, elation, pleasure.

In an early expedition of Major Long's party the Major wrote:

At last the valley widened and we found ourselves almost instantaneously in sight of the majestic Mississippi, in whose broadly extended valley nature displayed herself with gigantic features. The river, one of the largest in the world, rolling its waters with an undiminished rapidity in a bed decked with islands, was a spectacle which always filled the mind with awe and delight.

And another:

When we stood on the prairie, towards the close of the day a landscape was presented that combined grandeur and beauty in a way I never beheld; far as the eye could follow were traced two gigantic walls of the most regular outline, formed as it were, by successive faces of pyramids. Between them extended a level verdant prairie.

Ole Rynnings in his *True Account of America* sent back to Norway a factual yet lyric description:

The western part where the land is very flat and low. One can go two or three miles over natural meadows, which are overgrown with the most luxuriant grass, without finding a single tree. These natural meadows are called prairies. From earliest spring until latest fall they are covered with the most diverse flowers. Every month they put on new garb. The soil is usually rich and free from stones and roots. In order to break a field, therefore, only a strong plow and four or five yoke of oxen are needed; with these a man can plough up one or two acres of prairie a day. Without being manured, the soil produces corn, wheat, buckwheat, oats, potatoes, turnips, carrots, melons.

It is not strange that every nationality settling in the Northwest found country which seemed a replica of the homeland. The Finns in the extreme north thought the forests, the severe winters, the inland sea, the deep mines, like Finland. The Norwegians discovered middle-country pastures, forests, and deep streams like Norway's. The French found the St. Croix Valley and the Lake Pepin country as beautiful as the green forests and broad rivers of France. Even the Dutch found inundated swamps bad enough to rival their own poor land. On good land sometimes they failed. It was too good; they did not know how to till it. But on bad land, where they had to fight for every grain, drain the swamps, wrestle like Hercules with wind and weather—this was cream to them, this they knew, here they could succeed.

Prairie travel resembles that of the sea. The compass is the guide, the direct course is not always the best, and the probabilities of finding wood, water, grass, and a road compare with those of obtaining favorable and moderate winds and a smooth sea. At night when the wind is down, you can hear a scream for miles, and conversation is audible from a wagon coming over the horizon, so tiny you can blot it out by one finger. The silence is enormous; women whisper to each other afraid of breaking it; the insane asylums are full of women who could not stand it. You can see a storm far off raging in thunder and sulphurous light, while where you are standing a struck match will burn steadily in the open air.

Nowhere in the world, not even at sea, does the wind have such free play—the hot winds and the cold winds, the *blitzartig* hailstorms. The wind is part of the folk-say:

The wind does get up and blow here.
A splinter was driven clean through the log of our house.
It's three shirts colder today.
The wind blew the old man flat against the barn. I got a hoe and scraped him off and the same wind turned around and blew him up again!
When the wind starts blowing I have to go out and hold down every grain of my land.
My whole place dried up and blowed away.
I didn't sell out, I give out.
A latter-day Indian made a comment on the colossal vagaries of the weather.
He stood watching the earth sink into the abyss of the Mississippi. Flood water rushed through monstrous chasms. Giant trees

rocked and fell into the savage flood. The Indian stood gazing
upon the scene.

"What do you make of all this?" he was asked.

He sorrowfully replied, "Great spirit got whiskey—too much."

> Ө, I'm goin' where they don't shovel no snow,
> Lawd, Lawd, Lawd.
> I'm goin' where the chilly wind don't blow,
> Lawd, Lawd, Lawd.

The cold brought famine even to the Indians. Radisson,
one of the first white men to come to the North Star Country, wrote a vivid description of one of these terrible winters
which caught them without caches of corn or meat. This was
set down around 1674 and was probably read by Longfellow
before he wrote the description of the famine in the *Song of
Hiawatha*. He did not overdraw it.

The winter comes on, the snow begins to fall, soe we must
retire from the place to seeke our living in the woods. . . .

We must live on what God sends, and warre against the bears
in the meane time, for we could aime at nothing else, which was
the cause that we had no great cheare. We beated down the
woods dayly for to discover novelties. We killed severall other
beasts, as Oriniacks, staggs, wild cows, Carriboucks, fallow does
and bucks, Catts of the mountains, child of the Devill; the snow
increases dayly. . . .

We are come to a small lake, the place of rendezvous where
we found some company that weare there before us. We cottage
ourselves, and stayed 14 days in this place most miserable, ffor
there did fall such a quantity of snow and frost, and with such
a thick mist, that all the snow stooke to those trees that are so
ruffe, that caused that darkness upon the earth that it is to be
believed that the sun was eclipsed them 2 months; so the famine
was among great many that had not provided before hand and
live upon what they gett that day, never thinking for the next.
It grows wors and wors dayly.

Tall tales of the cold were told in the long winters around
the pot-bellied stoves:

The logging camp was buried under the snow and the men rode to the surface in elevators. The head sawyer slept under forty-two blankets, got lost, and was three days getting out and almost starved to death.

We ate with our mittens on and the hot biscuits froze before you could take a bite.

Our words froze and were thrown behind the stove and the next spring our ears burned when they began to thaw out!

Even the shadows froze to the ground and had to be pried loose with pickaxes.

Tom saw a bad storm coming and went on his pony down to the coulee before the blizzard broke to get the animals. Before darkness fell his horse stepped into a badger hole and broke its leg and he had to shoot the animal. It was doubtful if a human could live through the night in the snow and wind. He slit the belly of the horse open, ripped out its entrails, crawled inside the carcass, pulling the ribs together. Against his will he drifted into sleep. Daylight awakened him and he peeped through the jagged ribs to see the sun shining through Arctic cold on hard packed snow.

When he tried to pry the ribs apart he found the carcass had frozen solid and himself imprisoned inside, able only to get his hands and wrists through the narrow slit which he had not been able quite to close. As he pondered his imminent death from cold and starvation he heard a couple of coyotes sniffing about the carcass. That gave him an idea. He waited until the coyotes were close to the narrow slit in the carcass, then thrust his hands out like lightning and grabbed a tail of each.

The frightened animals took flight, pulling the carcass across the snow with Tom inside holding tight to their tails; he got his bearings and learned to guide them by pulling on the tail of one or the other. Within ten minutes they were hauling his odd carriage up the long slope to his farm. As the carcass came abreast of his front door, he let go of the tails of the coyotes, who vanished over the top of the hill, and as his craft skidded to a halt he shouted to his wife, who got an ax and chopped him out. After he'd had a cup of coffee, he went out and did the chores.—*Liar's Club*

Sweet Waters

The Mississippi was the ornriest, the worst-behaving river in the world; it was winding and twisting, making figure eights. You'd meet yourself coming back. It would run straight, turn somersaults, run downhill and then turn around and run uphill. For no reason at all, when you were floating logs down it, it would straighten out and become a mile wide and an inch deep and then when the men on the rafts would become accustomed to that it would suddenly turn over on its back and become an inch wide and a mile deep.

There were six Mississippis, then, and you couldn't tell one from the other. Some of them turned west and wandered around, and some flowed east and then doubled back and would finally empty logs into Lake Michigan just when you thought you surely must be to New Orleans.

Conception River

IN 1634 JEAN NICOLET ENTERED THE STRAITS of Mackinac and, looking westward, saw that the sea widened, and supposed that the wide sweet water met the ocean and the coast of China. He saw the reflecting lakes, the smoke fires far off, the sundogs on the horizon and two moons in the sky. He marked the shining sweet air that rose

42

from the cold waters, secretly rimmed with iron; and the long streamers of the northern lights, and the mirage of Isle Royale upside down in the air.

One mirage he dispelled forever—the illusion of the Northwest Passage—and it was simpler, from then on, for the mapmakers. His exploration closed the western shores of Lake Michigan to all speculation and wrote WILDERNESS across the map's breadth. It became known then that the Great Lakes were a shining waterway into the continent's heart. So men began to go down the rivers into the wilderness, running a race for possession, the French from the north, the English and Dutch driving from the Atlantic coast, and the Spanish trying to penetrate from the south.

Of the three great drainage systems made by the vast lowlands, the biggest—rivaling the Euphrates, the Jordan, and the Rhine—falls away south into the Gulf; a central one, including the Red River, the Saskatchewan, and the Churchill, discharges its waters into Hudson Bay; while the northern system, of which the Mackenzie is the chief artery, empties into the Arctic Ocean.

The Mee-zee-see-bee, born out of the north, flows through three climates, reflects many landscapes, draws snows through the Big Horn from the roots of the north country, from its tributaries, the Crow Wing, the Minnesota, the St. Croix, the Chippewa, the Wisconsin, flooding at St. Louis where the Big Muddy enters; and also the snows of the Appalachians, mixing with vast midland regions the soil, the torrential history of the West. It is a symbol of both space and unity.

An unknown man had named the giant Mississippi the "Holy Ghost." Another called it "Conception River," and Nicolet named it "Cradled Hercules"; many men were to be buried in it who rode down in piratical flotillas with their faces toward the receding western line, pushing it back on the King's map, landing with ermine robes and clanking armor, with Spanish hogs and horses, and in their hearts the rumors and the desire for silver cities, golden hills, and fabulous mines.

Excitement in the courts of Spain and France centered around the penetration and partitioning of these beautiful rivers, which gave into the rich earth deposits, the fertile prairies, from three directions. The nations were hurrying to get ahead of each other, toward the heart's vein of the great new country whose expanse they did not dream, never suspecting that the river ran down the center of a long, dark continent to emerge southward.

Names borne by lakes, mountains, rivers, forests, reflect this confusion of enterprise; they were named, renamed, and named again as they were lost, taken, stolen, ceded over, fought about. One set of names is applied by the Chippewas, another by the Sioux, a third by the French, and a fourth by the English.

Trade and religion entered the forest hand in hand, with greed and speed. In 1634 the Jesuits joined a party of Hurons who were returning from Quebec, and raised the first rude temple on the shores of Lake Huron.

The southern shore of Lake Superior was explored in 1660 by Mesnard, who was lost in the forest. Then Green Bay was occupied by the French. The mission of the St. Marys was founded on the river connecting Lake Huron with Superior, and a great congress of lake tribes gathered there, with delegates not only from the lake districts but also from the Mississippi and Red River nations; there the priests, listening, heard a tale that was to haunt the dreams of many men, of a large and beautiful river running thousands of miles to the ocean—of herds of buffalo, fertile plains, and many nations of people.

Marquette and Joliet proceeded west from Green Bay along the Fox and Wisconsin Rivers and reached the

Mississippi at the mouth of the Wisconsin. There were a hundred thirty-two years between the discovery of the lower Mississippi by the Spaniards and the upper by the French.

Men unrecorded and unnumbered entered the wilderness, some with wonder and some with greed, some set by the ears for unknown souls; and pirates and swashbucklers, and common men shanghaied from the streets of Quebec and Montreal, who went with a gun at their back, or because the wildernesss was more fearsome behind them than before.

Some also saw a new country, large, full of promise to take the sting from the old European shores. Some saw a great work to be done, opening the course not only of empire, but of life.

Men and the River

A boy in France learned to play the flute and the violin at the age of ten, became apprentice to a watchmaker, then grew to be a scholar and mathematician, an astronomer, speculating on magnetic forces, writing celebrated treatises on the probable duration of human life.

But he came to the wilderness and was the first white man to love the forests, the broad rivers flowing north and south; to see the green valley of the Fox and keep on into the wilderness like a lover, following the Indians to the portage path that led to the west-flowing river and thence—where?

He was Jean Nicolet, astronomer, geologist, whose magnificent maps link his name forever to this land. Driven by seven Huron paddlers and wearing a Chinese vestment over his buckskin, he met the Winnebagos in the Straits of Mackinac, thinking that before him lay the Orient. He stood up and fired his pistol in the air, and the naked Indians came out on the shore to see. Then he took off his robe and joined them in a feast of twenty beavers, named them the "stinking people," and later signed a treaty with them.

And they brought in thousands of furs to the French. He loved the Indians, and the native life and culture of their tribes. For sixteen years he lived among them, learned their languages, made notes on the flora and fauna, not caring for trade or evangelism but celebrating what he found here. The tradesmen, the whiskey-sellers came, but he was before them. Sailing down the Wisconsin for eight days, paddling through wild celery and rice, he was the first to see the bright light mingling in the flood, between shores widening to distances of half a league, the approaching rocky bluffs like towers and battlements of hostile cities; he saw the moose, the elk, the vast herds of buffalo in the sweet meadows, and turkeys crying from the wild woods, and on the seventeenth of June, 1672, "with a joy I cannot express," he saw the great river.

He loved the solitude and the broad light over it. The wilderness taught him, darkened his skin, deepened the guttural in his speech, and gave him an unknown burial.

Then there was the prince of the Jesuits, golden-haired Marquette, with his friend Joliet, who carried the line of the river on the map to the mouth of the Arkansas.

They went without grants or letters or crimson robes. With portable altars on their backs and flasks of communion wine they went into a wilderness five times the size of France. Marquette brought his harpsichord and played it, far from the courts of France or the bells of Rouen, in the filth of Indian camps amidst crying children, barking dogs, and fleas.

In the long cold winter nights he learned six languages and walked off into the solitude of tall pines to read his breviary.

He looked to the south. He thought such a river as the Mississippi could only rise in a continent midland, and in the night, alone, fearful of the thought, he entertained it:

this land was a solid vast continent, and the river dropped down to some sea—

He traced the map for La Salle, who did not like him, to the Arkansas, with a frail hand that trembled with its coming death.

He left his body in the wilderness he loved.

Louis Hennepin came from the wharves of Calais and Dunkerque to sail with La Salle on the *Griffin* from Niagara to Green Bay.

He claimed to have sailed down the Illinois to the Mississippi and to its mouth. But others contended that he was given to exaggeration, and La Salle called him a liar outright and said, "Exaggeration was his nature." Du Luth asserted that he stole his—Du Luth's—own story, lock, stock, and barrel. At any rate, Hennepin liked to write it all down and make a good story of it.

The truth was that he was captured by the Sioux and carried to their hunting grounds along Lake Pepin—named the "Lake of Tears" because, as he reported, his captors cried all night when their chief refused to let them kill their French prisoners.

They met Du Luth near La Crosse, and the man whose thunder he is said to have stolen had him released.

His account of the Falls of St. Anthony is exaggerated, but he saw them and named them, and the land gave him a sense of the future, and he said of the Great Lakes, "It were easy to build on these great lakes an infinite number of considerable Towns which might have Communication one with another by Navigation for Five Hundred Leagues together, and by an inconceivable Commerce which would establish itself among them."

He taught the Indian children to repeat the Ten Commandments. He bribed them to do it with beads, raisins, and prunes.

Mathieu Sageab was with La Salle and itched to discover something for himself, so he ascended the Mississippi with two Frenchmen and two Indians and they came back with a fine tale.

They saw lions, leopards, and tigers, they said, which did them no harm. They said that after a hundred and fifty leagues they found a great nation, that of the Ascanibas, governed by King Hagaren who claimed descent from Montezuma. The king and his subjects were gloriously clothed and worshiped idols of gold—one of these was the figure of an ancestor mounting a horse which carried a jewel large as a goose egg in its mouth, which Sageab thought might be a carbuncle.

He said they entered a magnificent vestibule of vast extent and made of solid gold, with bands of music stationed in its four corners. The king had an army of a hundred thousand men all riding black oxen, preceded by trumpeters with golden trumpets and drummers with golden drums.

When Sageab came back he impressed the French minister so deeply that he was sent to Louisiana to organize a party. Here, however, he unfortunately met friends who had known him in Canada and who rudely denied that he had ever been on the Mississippi. Nevertheless, he held fast to his story and always said that gold mines could be reached by the Missouri River.

Tradesman La Salle

He was a stern man with a hawk nose and a greedy eye for conquest, hoping to use the river as a wedge which would threaten the English beyond the mountains, push the Spaniards out of Florida, and extend the boundaries of France by an unknown and immeasurable distance west. He also saw himself the head of an inland empire, a bustling trading post, replica on a vast scale of his father's business at Rouen—himself a priest of commerce, the new and first Industrial King.

His first dream was exploded by Marquette; there was no China at the termination of the shining waters, and his earliest grant of land was derisively called "La Chine."

He was getting along all right with a partial monopoly on the fur trade at the head of the St. Lawrence. He gave one pint of brandy for a beaver skin. There are four pints of brandy to a tankard, a hundred tankards to a hogshead; ten hogsheads should buy, then, about four thousand beaver skins at four livres apiece, making sixteen thousand livres on an investment of one thousand, which is fifteen thousand livres' profit.

But he heard from the Senecas of a great river that arose in their country after a voyage of eight or nine moons, and fell into the sea; after that his profits seemed to him small. Lying by his fire along the cold lakes, he made notes, charted plans, took longitude and latitude never before put on hides. He rose alone at dawn and went along the wilderness paths, a stern lonely man without a friend except Tonty who accompanied him to his death.

Marquette stopped at the fort on Lake Ontario; he surmised also that the river fell into the Gulf, probably near Florida on the Spanish gulf where it would be strategic to have a French fort.

The difficulties of that journey were prodigious: creditors, jealous priests, court machinations, loans. The wilderness itself was inimical. Ships, forts, men were wiped out like tiny embattlements of ants. Father Hennepin set out alone with his altar to make friends with the Indians in advance of the voyage. Shipbuilders went to Niagara to begin a fort and docks in preparation for building the *Griffin*—first sailing ship on the Lakes, but doomed to disaster.

When La Salle reached Niagara he found that docks and ship had been wrecked in the night and all the stores in the hold wasted. He began to build again within two days. He believed that his bird-ship, the *Griffin*, would fly clear of intrigue, make a magic way down the fatal river, fly faster than "the crows"—the Jesuits.

The winter came, the ship was not finished; La Salle, itching to be gone, set out for Frontenac. During the spring he could get no word; the country was a thawing block and the Senecas were stirred up against him. They threatened to burn the ship when she appeared, and La Salle waited, his men hating him. They tried to poison Tonty but he did not die.

Finally there came, not the *Griffin* bellying in the wind, but Father Hennepin, tumbling out of his bark barefooted with two savage children and a basket of eggs, and the news that the *Griffin* was on the way but becalmed and would be along when the wind freshened. La Salle again could not wait and set out for his ship, and in eight days saw her riding at anchor, well-rigged, ready for sailing, with five small guns.

He got her on Lake Erie, where a ship had never before spread sail, and brought her into port at Michilimackinac, and the noise of her cannon shook the Indian villages and traders' huts ashore. But when they struck land the men deserted, debts settled on him like flies, and he had to send back accounts to Paris and leave the *Griffin* at the portage with supplies to meet her later at the mouth of the St. Joseph.

At the mouth again he waited. Again he built a fort, the men grumbling and close to mutiny. Even the priests were urging him to return; surely the *Griffin* had been lost in a storm. The river was freezing now. Hunger stalked them. La Salle had to stand behind his men to keep them from shooting him.

A buffalo mired in the mud saved them for a moment from starving.

January Epiphany. In Rouen the bells would be ringing,

people gay on the bridges, the ships snug in the harbor, in every house the King's cake and the merry toast. But La Salle crouched in the new country, his pale and frightened men around him, whispering to each other tales of beasts in the river and a bottomless abyss into which the whole party would undoubtedly plunge. The night was bitter. Six men ran away, among them two of his best sawyers, taking with them the best guns. His broth was poisoned.

He did not know what to do, so he built another fort and called it out of his sadness "Fort Crèvecoeur."

There was no answer and no report. His credit was gone as rumor spread that he was ill, bankrupt, derelict, and ruined. A winter, a spring, a summer, and another fall must pass with disaster and wanderings before he could get started down the river, and then not in his winged ship, which he never heard of again, but in canoes they had built and with the most meager supplies.

In that final spring La Salle went to Montreal, wangled supplies, dragged the baggage along the ice down the Illinois at the Chicago portage, and with twenty-three men, eighteen Indians, and ten women to cook, they set out, passing the ruins of Fort Crèvecoeur—the labor five years gone, the seed gone, rotted in the wild unspoken earth. The river opened and they made elm-bark canoes, and on February 6, 1682, they reached the great river.

A shout went up from the men and they threw their hats into the air and waited for the ice to go out, when they would set their frail canoes upon the waters and embark for the unknown.

La Salle slipped the ring of the brass astrolabe over a tree limb, adjusting the movable index sights, and took his bearing. He looked at the zodiacal charts that showed the sun's north and south positions for the calendar month, and estimated the latitude; the longitude even of Quebec at that time was not yet certain. He looked at the pale northern sun, whose relative position was unknown in the new world, and concluded that where they stood was thirty-nine degrees—as far south as Mexico. He marked this down and later King Louis, raking in his gambling money at Versailles, stopped long enough to take a look at it.

Father Membres had made an altar with paddles on forked sticks covered with the sails of the canoes; he placed it under the flying buttresses of the trees. And now before starting they gathered for Mass, the men behind the nobles, and the unaccustomed syllables fell in the snowy silence, the ancient forms of words dropping in the new air that blew so softly from the direction of the rising Dog Star. The tiny Mass bell tinkled and the men felt uneasy with the unknown forest at their backs and the thawing river beginning to gleam in the high sun.

Later the night fell thick and the men could not sleep. It is hard to come by sleep in the wilderness. Questions come into the mind. Why did we come? Where are we going? Talk begins to spread from one man to another. Where is the gold? Is it true there are cities of turquoise?

Is it certain that she falls into the Gulf? She might make a turn and come out in India or China yet—

And lands, whispered Prudhomme the armorer, where cities could be built and hammers clang, and that's the truth. Lands, like the Indians say, all lying ready for the plow, taking a man weeks to ride over. Where a man could be his own boss. Is it a fact?

Did you hear what the Chickasaws say, though? There are whirlpools and dangers, and a hot breath to scorch an army. What if there are no animals, no corn, no food?

Why don't we stay in this good climate, like Paris? You can see in your mind's eye even on this dark night a cluster of homes along these greening plains.

That's too far to look for me. Now I can't see a thing but that cursed river. Why did I come? It's woe to a man who happens down the streets of Montreal when that silver-tongued La Salle is looking with his hawk's mug for men to feed the belly of his schemes.

Why did I ever leave my girl?

Suppose this earth is deep and wide, and we never get back? Who knows if the earth is round or not?

Oh, for the warmth of her now, I say! I took her off a boat and wed her.

They've got you now going and coming. If you don't marry they take away your hunting license.

If you do they give you an ox, a cow, a hen and a cock, two barrels of salt meat, and eleven crowns. That's why I did.

That's only so you won't die of hunger before the first one's got.

I want to get back to the bed of my girl.

We can all make the Chicago portage and back to Montreal by Easter.

And the bells ringing, and the fun and good brandy, and no mysterious river turning round a bend every day of your life.

La Salle treading through the forest floor heard them. And when the figures darted together in clusters for secret leaving, he stood among them and said, "You are going down the river with me." Tonty held a torch above his head and a gun on the men. "You will die if you start back alone. I have waited thirteen years and now I am going, and you are going with me."

Without a cheer the men flowed back to their blankets in the dark, with the wilderness night over them like stone, miles deep.

Well, they went down the river and it was long, with the country shaking out in blossom before them, warm, as they rode into summer.

And all along the rich country they stopped, and La Salle donned his ermine robe, the seals and documents were unwrapped, and they took in the name of the King the copper country, even the silk worms in Arkansas—the prairie, the forests, the river broadening until you could not see a man across it.

It is a long story and you cannot tell it here. There was no record, no ledger, and yet they were creating it. The little clerk took out his notebook and wrote in it. La Salle put down every bend and even at night calculated what wealth might be accrued from an industry using the worms of the mulberry tree.

Then they felt the unmistakable pulse, the slow ebb and swell, of the tide coming up the river to meet them.

"The sea!" they all shouted.

La Salle, on the sand, made it twenty-seven degrees north on his map, which would make the mouth about thirty leagues from the Rio Grande, sixty from Rio de Palmas, and ninety or a hundred from the Tampico River on the Spanish coast. The country fooled him; he was defeated by not making it big enough. It was this miscalculation that led him later to pass the true mouth and enter Texas, a disaster for him and death by his own men.

The men were set to work hewing the King's Column, a task they were, by now, very weary of. And the smiths set to casting the King's Arms from a copper kettle.

La Salle opened his beaver bag, now full of speeches, commission grants, and legal tender. He took out his ermine robe, his speech, and his commissions from the King. He stepped up to the Cross and the Column. The men stood back, fingering their caps. The French nobles put on their gallant attitudes of court as they shouted, "Vive le Roi!" and the herons screamed. The *Te Deum* was chanted, the *Exaudiat*, the *Domine salvum fac Regem.*

Then the Sieur de la Salle, with his papers in his hands, spoke, and the men looked down at the unfathomable earth.

"In the name of the most high, mighty, and victorious Prince, Louis the Great, by the grace of God and the King of France this month of April, one thousand six hundred and eighty-two . . .

"I, in virtue of the commission of His Majesty, which I hold in my hand, and which may be seen by all whom it may concern, have taken, and do take, in the name of His Majesty and of His successors to the Crown, possession of this country, the sea, harbors, ports, bays, adjacent straits, and all the nations, people, provinces, towns, villages, mines, minerals, fisheries, streams, rivers . . ."

A turtle flopped into the water.

He read the paper he had prepared, finished speaking the *procès verbal;* the authentic act was drawn by the notary and it was signed and sealed amid the proper volley of musket shots, and together with the leaden inscription and the King's Arms, was buried at the foot of the King's Column.

The men who signed the document at the mouth of the river, taking possession in the name of the King, were, in the order of their signing: Jacques de la Métairie, notary public of Fort Frontenac, who went along for the sole purpose of carrying the precious seal and performing the necessary act of signing, sealing, and witnessing; Zenobe, missionary; five others who hoped to get land; Jean Michel, the surgeon; and the little clerk, a relative of La Salle, who kept an exact and accurate record of the trip. And of course there was Tonty.

The names were not on it of those who would settle the country: the sailors, joiners, blacksmiths, farmers; the rascals, traders, carpenters, armorers, who had no land and no seals to set and who signed nothing—who stood fingering their hats, their bellies rumbling from the poor fare of smoked fish that preceded further hungers. There were some Abnakis from Maine—shall we say, the first New Englanders?—who were later to come in droves and make a deep impression on commerce and culture in the Northwest. Also a few Mohicans.

And the pillar of the King was set in a shifting soil in the midst of a new world.

All that country would pass from the hands of Spain and of France. La Salle and his men would remount the river amid the friendly tribes now turned hostile; he would sail back in confusion and treachery, pass the river mouth he aimed at, his ships lost again, would be shot down in the tall grasses that had known no white man's blood.

Pelt and Pelf

Pelf

ANIMALS, BEFORE MEN, FOUND THIS COUNTRY
a rich source of life. Man later found the animals a source
of enormous wealth. New York tenements were built from
the wealth of the beaver, the buffalo, the bear, otter, mink,
and fox of the North Star Country. The standard value in
the forests was a prime beaver called *plus* by the French.
A plus was given for as much vermilion as could cover the
point of a knife, and the same price was paid for four charges
of powder or shot, or two branches of wampum. An otter,
three martens, a lynx, fifteen muskrats, were worth one plus;
a keg of mixed rum, thirty plus. An outfit of six bales of
goods worth two thousand dollars brought ninety-six bags
of beaver, worth thirty-five thousand dollars in the East.

Indians did not know why the white man wanted to kill
off the animals. An Indian said, "White people do not know
how to live: they leave their homes, they risk their lives on
great waters, among strange nations for the beaver. And of
what use is the beaver? Are they good for gunpowder? Does

the beaver preserve them from sickness or serve them beyond the grave?"

One of Major Long's guides in 1823 said that he purchased of an Indian two packs of beaver containing a hundred and twenty skins, for which he paid two blankets, eight quarts of rum, and a pocket looking glass. The beaver brought four hundred dollars in Montreal.

This is how the wealth grew.

In 1798 the Northwest Company alone took out 106,000 beaver skins, 2,100 bear, 1,500 fox, 4,600 otter and fox, and 3,200 mink.

This is how the animals disappeared from the country.

Peddler

An old man lay on the bed trying not to die. He wanted to know what the ledgers said; there was an old lady among his thousands of tenants in New York who had not paid her rent. He was so old, they had to wet-nurse him and toss him up in a blanket for exercise. To look at him, a phlegmatic man whose son dusted the moths out of the furs, it would have been difficult to recognize John Jacob Astor, a butcher's son, who had been in the past century the center of an orgy of bloodshed and plunder, and had amassed one of the great American fortunes.

He had been a peddler of cakes. He came to America with five pounds, seven flutes, and one suit of Sunday clothes. He lived above a fur store and saw that beaver skins were bought for a dollar from an Indian and sold for six in London. This was profit on any ledger, in any man's language.

So he stopped peddling cakes and started peddling furs.

He talked to the trappers who brought in the furs, and improved upon their methods of trade and barter to such an extent as to create a dynasty in the Northwest, with trading posts, forts, an army, his own constitution-makers and legislators.

The American Fur Company was in reality John Jacob Astor. It controlled a vast region extending along the Missouri River far north to the Great Lakes and west to the Rockies. It ran out all competitors, even the great Hudson's Bay Company which had set up a kingdom in the northland. It employed force and fraud, overawed and dominated everything—if not by murder, then by whiskey, skulduggery, land grabs, and debauchery.

Through the long winters the Indians hunted the forests for skins which would multiply Mr. Astor's wealth and adorn the royalty of Europe and America. They brought their furs in to the forts and the posts in the spring and were artfully made drunk and robbed by a sharecropper system of credit.

The Astor traders gave credit to the Indian at the rate of three hundred and four hundred per cent, demoralized whole tribes by rum, and traded with shoddy merchandise. The chicanery was so obvious that the books covering the business of the northern department of the American Fur Company were hidden for seventy-five years and found quite by chance. There are six folio volumes of about a thousand pages each in two stout traveling cases, under lock and key; one for British money and one for American. The governor of Michigan Territory was involved, and so the accounts covering the record from 1817 to 1835 were conveniently lost.

They are history. Those figures show the death of great nations—the Sioux and Chippewas, the extinction of millions of animals, the robbing of hunters and traders, destruction by famine, disease, and firewater.

Colonel Snelling said, when he took over Fort Snelling on the Mississippi River across from St. Paul, "He who has the most whiskey carries off the most furs. The neighborhood

where whiskey is sold presents a disgusting scene of drunken-
ness and debauchery and misery. I have daily opportunities
of seeing the road strewn with the bodies of men, women,
and children in the last stages of brutal intoxication."

John Jacob's greatest trading post at Mendota was directly
across the river.

Pelt

Traders of every nationality became cunning in their
understanding of how to rook the Indian. Radisson and his
brother-in-law, Groseilliers, came into the wilderness early,
setting up forts in the name of the English or the French,
whichever promised to be more profitable. His account of
the peace pow-wows at which he sold the Indians the idea
of the "Great White Father" is well told. He has just described the splendor of the arrival of the chiefs at one of
these meetings in the wilderness, called by himself to effect
an understanding between two warring nations so that the
fur company might operate peacefully. He continues:

They came to the biggest cabbans constituted for that purpose. There were fires kindled. Our Captayne made a speech of
thanksgiving which should be too long to write. They made
speeches, presenting us with guifts of Castor's skins, assuring us
that the mountains were elevated, the valleys risen, the way very
smooth, the bows of trees cutt downe to goe with more ease, and
bridges erected over rivers, for not to wett our feete, that the
dores of their village, cottages, of their wives and daughters,
weare open at any time to receive us, being wee kept them alive
by our merchandises. . . .

The speech being finished they intreated us to be att the feast.
They made a place higher and most elevate, knowing our customs, in the middle for us to sitt. Presently came foure elders,
with the calumet kindled in their hands. They present the
candles to us to smoke, and foure beautifull maids that went
before us carrying bears' skins to put under us.

Now we are together an old man rises and throws our calumet

att our feett and bids them take the kettles from the fire and
spake that he thanked the sun that never was a day to him so
happy, and sang awhile. Having ended, came and covers us with
his vestment, and all naked except his feet and leggs he saith:
"You are masters over us; dead or alive you have the power over
us, and may dispose of us as your pleasur." So done, takes the
callumet, brings it, so a maiden brings us a coal of fire to kindle
it. So done, we rose, and one of us begins to sing. We had the
interpreter tell them we should save and keep their lives, taking
them for our brethren, and to testify that we shott off all our
artillery which was twelve gunns. Which putt them in such
terror they knewed not what was best to run or stay. We throw
a handfull of powder in the fire to make a greater noise and
smoake.

The next day we gave them gifts of . . . 2 dozen knives, 5
gratters, 2 dozen awles, 2 dozen needles, 6 dozen of looking
glasses made of tine, a dozen little bells, 6 ivory combs, with a
little vermillion. Butt for to make a recompence to the good
old man that spake so favorably, we gave him a hatchett, and
to the Elders each a blade for a sword, and to the 2 maidens
that serves us 2 necklaces, which putt about their necks and 2
bracelets for their arms. The last guift was in generall for all
the women to love us and give us to eat when we should come
to their cottages. The company gave us great, Ho. Ho. Ho, that
is, thanks.

Radisson then traveled across country and ate and drank
and "sang" to the Crees, and made a union, thus maintain-
ing peace and loyalty to the French (for the moment) and
prosperity to the fur trade.

A vast system of trading posts and forts grew in the wilderness and centers of the fur dynasty held together by the highways of lakes and rivers. Traders lived like nabobs. Cargoes
of furs were brought up and down the rivers in the spring
by the voyageurs, the traders, the Indians and half-breeds,
and were counted by Scotch and English clerks and sent
yearly to France, and ladies of the court wore the beaver
and mink of the wilderness.

The palace corridors of Versailles waited impatiently for

the wealth of animals, as well as for news of lands taken in the name of Louis XIV: mines of copper, zinc, and lead; cities of gold; and exploration—the new line on the map the King had painted on the Easter egg he gave his mistress on Easter morning. There, delineated in bright colors, was the latest acquisition along the Mississippi.

North country animals went to the France of Madame de Sévigné and Molière, and the dried ears of tiny creatures of the forest can hardly have appreciated the music of Sully or the Fables of Fontaine.

In the name of these conquests by the French, Spanish, or English crowns, thousands of unknown men—private soldiers, workmen, builders—lived, built the forts, cut the timber, put up bakeries, blacksmith shops, ice cellars, sutler's stores, magazines, planted gardens and even gave plays in the long fort winters when the officers, nobles, and their cultured ladies longed for the refinements of the old country.

The forts grew, and a strange European culture was imported to live in them. Fine wines were brought in hogsheads. Music, set down in gold leaf on parchment, was played on lyres within the stockades. Classic French was spoken over the ledger, and in the evenings French court culture strangely flourished in the log houses, the wilderness savage at the window.

Some, a few, brought their richly clad women and kept them in the forts, and these brought with them the cookery of France and the embroidery and the parlor refinements.

In the spring race of water came the voyageurs, singing down the rivers, their narrow pirogues laden with furs. Indians and half-breeds made the compounds bright with their squaws and families, whole tribes making holiday in anticipation of rum trades for their winter's haul. The pelts were piled high and the recording and trading began.

Afterward the rum kegs flowed; violence made the night loud, unnatural murder issued from the firewater, Indian women were forcibly abducted by the traders. Inside the forts gigantic feasts were served, tall tales told, and the stacks of pelts lay ready to go up to Montreal.

When the traders assembled at Fort William to take the furs north there was more feasting on choice dainties, more drinking, hilarity, and violence. The wealthy owners in Montreal lived like the potentates they were: tradesmen kings of the new world.

It is recorded that in Wisconsin one evening *She Stoops to Conquer* was played entirely by soldiers wearing what Parisian gowns they could get over their buckskins; all done in the full glare of pitch pine-faggots on a homemade stage.

The mail came only once a year, or at most twice; some of the carpenters, joiners, masons, and blacksmiths never heard of their families again, and they must have been as good as lost and dead to the wives and children at home. The mail carriers when they did come were men of strong fiber and nerve, walking with their packs and muskets day and night through the deep snow, and when overcome with sleep, wrapping themselves in a blanket and lying in a snow-bank, figuring how close the howl of the wolf was getting.

They had to keep up appearances even in the wilderness. Parades were given with full regalia, flags raised and lowered with the snap of attention, there were morning and evening guns, and taps. And when they looked up they saw the faces of men who were later to be famous, so that they could say:

Big doin's in this country then.

The goose hung high. There was rich fixin's. I can recollect when we had venison, bear, porcupine, geese, and fish on the table at the same time.

The officers' ladies was mighty uppity. They brought out their Paris furniture. We up and dropped the piano into the river once, movin' it from boat to boat. They spoke pure French you couldn't understand, and dressed for dinner.

It took a heap of work to settle the wilderness. It filled up behind you. A fort you built one year would be lost the next when you went by it, the wilderness grown up around your labor. It was a long time. The sound of the ax was loud.

Judge Foster tells about a ball at the cabin of Joe Le Grue close to the mouth of the Willow River:

There were three ladies from Catfish Bar there, part Negro, part French, who were the leading belles, straight as Indians. Having long black hair, they appeared to realize their superiority, as the balance of the ladies consisted of the squaws and half-breeds. Women were scarce but squaws were plenty and dances must be had. The dark-eyed maidens of the woods were brought to grace the ballroom. The dancing went off lively, the ladies occasionally clipping the pigeon wing in their beaded moccasins; there was none of that rough coming down on the heel of the young buck of the present day. They danced reels and cotillions, but the most interesting dance was the one before the nut cakes and the black strap made of whiskey and maple sugar was served up—a sort of French dance.

Uncle Massey led to the middle of the floor an elderly half-breed lady, saluted her in the style of the French dancing master, the music struck up, and they commenced dancing at each other with all the force and energy they could throw into it. A ring was formed at once, the men on one side and the ladies on the other. Mears stepped in in front of Massey, made a bow to him, turned to the lady and got right down to work beautifully. In jumped one of the belles with the beautiful hair, curtsied low to the half-breed lady, turned to Mears and shook her beaded moccasins most beautifully at him. The excitement ran high; the sweat fairly ran off the fiddle. There was a half brother of Peter's present, a full-blooded Indian, and having some whiskey in him he was getting as excited as a regular war dance, and he gave a war whoop that made the cabin ring.

Afterwards the ladies and gentlemen ate nut cakes, drank black strap and shook hands all around to show that all was lovely.

The making of maple sugar was a festival.

The men placed a gauje or hoke on their shoulders, a bucket of basswood suspended on each side in which they carried the liquor. The bucket was made by sewing the seams of the inner bark of basswood, then gumming them over with pine pitch. The large vessels were barrels of oak. There were some good coopers came to the new world. Many stout barrels were needed. You learned also from the Indians. You didn't have to fight with them, not wanting anything, so they taught you how to make spouts for the trees out of basswood, and the macock—in which the sugar was packed—of birch bark, gathering the bark in the supper and never using pine because of the disagreeable odor it gave the sugar.

The women hung the kettle to boil for twenty-four hours, usually beginning in the morning and keeping the fire bright all day, watching with a branch of hemlock, and when the liquor threatened to boil over, stirring it quickly.

When the sugar was boiled down they had to transfer the contents quickly and sand and clean the empty kettles. It has to be brought in fast and kept boiling. For the sugar cakes you boil in a brass kettle, slowly, and pour it on a board of basswood with proper molds gouged out in the form of animals. Sugar gum is good poured into wooden bowls filled with snow.

There was not much law.

There was some. A roly-poly Frenchman, Charles Raume, once commissioned as justice of the peace by King George III, sat beside a rough wooden table with one law book and a jackknife, dressed in a scarlet frock coat faced with white silk, and dispensed the law. His territory was then about one half of Wisconsin and part of what later became Michigan.

When he wished to summon a person to court he would send his constable to fetch him, showing as his badge of authority the judge's jackknife. Raume took care of all complaints, marriages, and recording of births, and his legal judgments were worthy precursors of later law.

A fellow appeared before him with a present.

"Good morning," said the judge. "I have given jedgment agin' you."

"Coming along," said the miscreant; "I saw a coffee-pot hanging out and bought it for you, judge. Will you do me the pleasure to accept it?"

"Well, thank you kindly."

"Judge, I don't owe that fellow a thing; I overpaid him."

"You did. I reverse my jedgment and he shall pay the costs!"

Two men once appeared, one as plaintiff and the other as defendant, and he listened to both with rising indignation and then rendered his decision: "You are both wrong. You bring me one load of hay, and you bring me one load of wood, and now the matter is settled."

So there grew a great belt of French fortresses from Quebec to New Orleans, held together by the highways of the Great Lakes and the Mississippi and the smaller rivers, keyed by the stronghold of Fort Chartres.

Strongly armed forts were necessary, for the fur trade meant war. The English came in again, first Lord Selkirk's colony, which died a bloody death. Then a group of private gentlemen under the patronage of Prince Rupert entered James Bay, incorporated by Charles II into a company under a charter which gave them the sole right to trade in the bay, alienate lands, erect forts, build ships, send home all English subjects trading without a license, and to declare war or make peace with any prince or people not Christian. This was the Northwest Company which, after years of warfare, transferred all its posts to John Jacob Astor.

The struggle for conquest continued. The French warred with the Spanish, the Spanish with the English, the English with the French and the Americans, the Americans with the Indians, until John Jacob Astor established his own company, drove the Hudson's Bay Company north, murdered traders and English territorial governors alike, and passed a law that nobody could deal in furs but an American.

Buffalo

Prepare for me a pasture for the buffalo bull, his wife and young, at some distance so that by means of them I and my people may keep alive. Among them I shall survive.—SIOUX SONG.

Animals live, are devoured by other animals, are destroyed by man and disappear forever. The buffalo was the great beast of the plains, roaming in great numbers down deep trails into the north country. One hundred thousand thundered the plains in herds that took five days to pass— twenty miles wide and fifty miles long. The Indians lived from this beast as we now live from the cow, using every part for food, clothing, shelter. Of buffalo skins they made robes, lodges, saddles, war bonnets, gloves—all their clothing. Out of the thick neck of the skin they made glue. From the tuft on the forehead ropes and lariats were made, and from the tendons, thread and bowstrings. From the shoulders, axes, knives, and arrows. From the hair, pillows. The trachea they used for a paint sack and the papillae of the tongue made brushes. The tail made knives, rattles; the dried udder, dishes; the ribs, small dog sleds. The gall became an intoxicating liquor. The paunch was a remedy for disease and the intestines were dried in the sun and eaten; buffalo chips were burned as fuel. After the extinction of the buffalo, the Indian was forced for lack of food to sign the treaties, sell his lands. Later, thousands of buffalo bones were picked up by Indians on the prairie and sold as fertilizer.

In 1883 the last herd, about seventy-five thousand, headed northward in migration, in a last instinct of escape, and were killed in the Red River Valley and the Black Hills, five thousand professional hunters shooting them down.

Creatures Lost, Mythical and Real

The wild pigeons once hid the sun. They went over a field like a great blue wave rolling forward and left not a grain behind them. The farmers caught them in nets; when the birds put their heads through the net, the farmers caught the head between thumb and finger and pinched the skulls. In their long migrations north it was said they flew a mile a minute for a distance of three hundred miles. They made fine pie and one bullet would bring down many. The last one died in an Eastern zoo many years ago.

The pioneer came into a strange land and the names he gave to animals, lakes, and rivers of the new country bore the mark of his nostalgia for the old. He saw birds with rusty breasts and called them robins, but they were not robins. They are stronger than the English robins, with better songs.

In the same way he saw a little animal on the prairie and called it a prairie dog; but it was not a dog. There were few dogs or cats—one miner brought over a boatload of cats and made a fortune selling them to pioneers who were hungry for domestic creatures from old firesides.

Did you ever shoot a prairie chicken in the early spring? An old man, who hates the hunting and trapping laws, tells this:

Snow has been off the ground for a week and you have built a blind and you get up early to get there before the cocks, who will be on the dancing ground early. Prairie chickens don't breed like quail pairing off together. The cocks meet on the dancing ground in the spring as soon as the snow is off the ground; they begin to crow. You hear them a long way. Bum—bum—booooooo. The hens hear them also and start coming. The cocks are calling them. Here at the dancing ground they will find a nesting-place for their young. They come and you stay still and watch because you'll only have one shot. They make a splendid dancing din with their wings lowered and their feathers antlered, neck puffing. Bum—bum—booooooo! You wait until you see when you can get the most for your shot. The gun goes off and they climb straight up into the sky. This is all you can get. They'll come back, but they'll keep out of sight now.

The early explorer Nicolet speaks of seeing snipe and plover flying in white thick swarms over the prairie. The flesh of larks was delicate, he said, and the only relief from salt meat. An early settler describes a time, in the swampland, when "some nights it was impossible to sleep owing to their clamor. The honking of the Canada goose, the mewing call of the canvasback, redhead and bluebill, mingled with the whistling call of the pintail and pigeon, mixed with the coarse quacking of the mallard and the more feeble call of the gadwall, made a strange medley of sounds. But the repeating shotgun and an influx of hunters from all over the United States made sad havoc."

Still along the river marshes stands the crane, and down from Alaska in the summer the whistling swan sometimes come, and the herring gull blows down from Superior, and it is strange to see them on the inland waters.

The rivers even now are full of rock bass, trout, crappie, smallmouth bass, in pool and gorge, cropper pike; mud cats, land-locked shad, muskellunge, sturgeon, perch, bullhead, channel cat, lake red horse, whitefish, and carp, the sauger of sand pike.

Paul Bunyan was a mighty fisherman and hunter. Once he shot some mallards so high in the air, they fell across another state line, and the game warden told him to quit firing at ducks so far away unless he was certain they would fall in the same state he shot them in.

Mosquitoes were mighty aggravating. Paul reports them

sixteen inches from tip to toe. He had bees brought in to eat the mosquitoes, but instead they mated and made mosquito bees which were a thousand times worse. He got some lumberjack whiskey and invited them to a jamboree in the washtub. They went in like a sawmill, got drunk, and were hauled out; then, their pinchers were cut off and most of them starved to death. They were so big, it was said, they could straddle a stream and pick the jacks off the log drive.

Bedbugs were the curse of the itinerant worker. They climbed into his bed roll when they heard he was off for other parts. They beat him to the Black Hills during the gold rush and were waiting for him. Paul found an abandoned camp once with owl and rabbit bones in the bunks. It turned out that the bedbugs, left alone, found first mice as hosts, then attacked wildcats, grew fur to keep themselves warm, ran in packs. The jacks had to catch them in wolf traps. Called them bedcats.

They used to tell a story that the boss came into the bunk house of a lumber camp once, and the bedbugs all tipped their hats to him, saying, "Hi, brother." The boss was a little angry at this familiarity. But the bedbugs said, "You are our blood brother; we both live off the jack, don't we?" And then they got enthusiastic and they said, "What's more, you owe us something, brother. If it wasn't for us you might have trouble. We bleed him all night so you can bleed him all day. How are you, brother?"

In April 1876 Governor Pillsbury issued a proclamation asking spiritual help against an enemy that was invading and ravishing the country. This was a small creature a little bigger than your fingernail called the grasshopper. They came in swarms, in a black cloud, with a noise like a roaring wind and the sound of hundreds of hogs eating. They blocked trains, swept the fields cleaner than a herd of hungry steers, closed the mills, riddled the corn, piled in mountains in the fields. They rode the wind like an eclipse, darkening the sun.

We are eaten up by speculators, politicians, now grass-hoppers, the people said. Hoppers eat everything but the mortgage.

A woman wrote:

I went out and looked at the crops in the fall, everything ripe, the field lay ready to thresh. While we were eating a cloud came over like night. We opened the door and the tomatoes were gone. My husband's coat hanging by the wash basin was gone except for the seams. The wheat fields were gone, the corn stood riddled. The rail fences were swollen bronze with hoppers and a hill stood behind the house of dead ones piled up.

There are animals seen only by a few. It was easy to see strange animals in the solitude of the woods. Many went crazy. It was said that only Finns could stand to work alone. These animals were variously seen but were never caught for museums, or their bones found for study:

The *ax-handle hound* prowled around lumber camps looking for ax or peavey handles to eat. The *argopelter* lived in hollow trunks and threw things at the jacks. A *hangdown* was found hanging like lichen from a limb and could be caught only by placing a tub over it. The stone-eating *gyascutus* was like a deer, with rabbit ears, teeth like a lion, and telescopic legs for hill grazing. It was never seen except after snake bite.

The *tote-road shagamaw* had hind legs like a moose and fore legs like a bear and walked on one or the other end making different kinds of tracks to add to the confusion. The *goofus bird* flew backward because he didn't care where he was going but he wanted to see where the hell he'd been. The *gillygaloo* was a hillside plover that laid square eggs so they wouldn't roll, used by the jacks, hard-boiled, as dice. The *pinnacle grouse* flew along a conical hill, and its plumage changed according to the condition of the observer.

Today there is one animal in the North Star Country as important to our economy as the buffalo and the beaver once were—the pure, high-bred dairy cow, holding the world's record for butterfat, hardly recognizable as any relation to her scrawny small-uddered sisters of the Civil War. She stands opulent at the Fair, curried and curled, with roses woven in her tail and garlands on her horns. It is from this invented animal that we now live.

Freedom Roads in the Wilderness

Listen for the Summons Far Away!

THE RIVERS OF THE NORTH MARKED BROAD
highways of communication and progress for supplies, trade,
news. Frozen in winter, they made glassy roads for explorers,
voyageurs, *coureurs-de-bois,* traders, priests, and later the
men with the plows and women and children. Down the
rivers they came in canoes, piroques, mackinaw boats, rafts,
flatboats, keelboats, and then steamboats, carrying the new
rich life—opening into vistas of new thought, and space, into
wider horizons, creating a river folk, sagas of the waterways.

The voyageurs—"half Indian, half French, half prairie-
wolf"—made a light craft. There were many portages. The
boats were about twenty-five feet long, paddled by six to ten
men, the bowman in the prow wielding a long thin blade,
the steersman in the stern, while the most expert, the *milieu,*
sat between, leading the paddling and singing.

They came down in the spring race of water, their narrow
piroques laden with furs. They were for the most part the

ragtag and bobtail of the wilderness; rascally, hiring themselves out—men who could bear the pinch of hunger like
stoics and eat like hungry wolves, grumble when there was
nothing to complain of, and endure the hardships of the
wilderness without a murmur. They could cheat, drink,
work like slaves, swim like otters, sing profane songs in the
evenings that sounded like a hundred foxes with their tails
in a trap.

They came before the law did—the statute and the common court—of attorneys they knew nothing. They baptized
the inexperienced, called "pork-eaters," by sprinkling their
nor'westers with a cedar bough dipped in water, and this
entitled them to wear a plume in their cap. They had also
the ceremony of the lob pine—a maypole of the north woods.
A pine of great size and prominence was selected, a man
climbed it and "lobbed" off the central branches; the tree
was then named and became a landmark.

The work of paddling was relieved every hour by rest
periods when the men smoked their pipes. Thus a journey
might be four pipes long.

> Fifty miles to water.
> Twenty miles to wood.
> Ten miles to hell
> And I've gone there good!

The roads were silent and lonely. From Green Bay to
Prairie du Chien was like going from London to Bombay
and as dangerous. But man had far places to go and many
things to take with him, and what he takes with him has the
say-so about what he can do.

So he made vehicles and improved upon them, and he
made roads and made them better, so that two-legged men
could get around. The prairie was an open road, frozen solid
in winter. A network of Indian trails, warpaths, connected
the territories occupied by the Sioux and the Ojibways. Buf-

falo trails paralleled the Mississippi, and when the buffalo were gone man used them. The long haul on the prairies called for a new kind of wagon. The Norwegians made one of solid wheels carved from a tree-trunk, with planks laid across, called the "kubberulle," and used to haul crops, grain, families, and, finally, their coffins to the last hill.

Concord coaches, horse-drawn, gilded and painted like circus wagons and named "Prairie Queen," "Star of the North," "Western Monarch," went swaying over the prairie ruts.

The frozen prairie and the glassy rivers created new kinds of sledges for horse and dog teams, and trial inventions of ice ships, and steam-run prairie boats to cross the broad spaces. Ahead of the ice express rode a riverman, most likely a Norseman, testing the ice by the ring of the horses' hooves.

Down the long plains came the high-slung Red River carts, duplicate of the carts of the Trojan column, made of two solid disk wheels from the round of a tree with the marks of an ax on them, six feet high with three-foot rims. They were the Model T of the prairie, fording the rivers; you could pick them up and lift them out of sand or spring freshets, and you could repair them easily. They could cross water, marshes, and the high-grassed land.

You could hear them for miles, the shrieking of the ungreased wooden wheels, pulled by oxen, pony, sometimes a buffalo, filled with furs and pemmican and the families of the *coureurs-de-bois,* all dressed like gypsies, spangled brass and clinking beads and buttons, red sashes and jaunty caps— wilderness mixtures, half-breeds of every kind, blonde and dark, lashing their oxen with bursts of profanity, singing a motley song.

A minister at St. Anthony heard them coming and just had time to shout that the services would be resumed the following Sunday. They would bring down the wealth of the forest and take back supplies, following the sandy ridges and the ancient bed of Lake Agassiz through the Red River Valley, usually on the Dakota side, crossing between Lake Traverse and Big Stone, heading for Traverse des Sioux.

Pierre Pauquette was a man of endurance, a prodigious worker, a half-breed and French trader—kept twenty yoke of oxen to haul goods across the portage. He was six feet two, with flesh as hard as nails and a thigh as large as your waist. He could pick up a pork barrel as easy as a ten-gallon keg and once lifted off the ground a cask with eight hundred pounds of lead in it. When one of his oxen gave out, he pushed it aside and stepped into the yoke himself. In the game of lifting heavy sledges he could lift the heaviest, and sling it a hundred yards into the river. He could keep accounts in his head and could lick anyone in the country with one hand tied behind him.

Fred Evans and Duck Leg Shorty were famous and expert bullwhackers. The high prairie schooners, the ships of the wilderness with canvas covers and rimmed wheels, carried freight up to the building of the railroads and hauled some of the ties. A typical prairie bull-team was usually twenty head of oxen yoked into ten teams, pulling three wagons one behind the other. Twenty such units could follow each other, each with its bullwhacker walking his team with a great wood-handled, twenty-foot braided leather whip, by which he expertly guided the oxen, with the aid of loud and choice profanity. The flat buckskin popper cracked like a rifleshot as the whip flicked the ox's broad back. There was no line or harness. They didn't need the care that mules did.

It was said that oxen could never be driven by New Englanders, whose Christianity made them nervous.

Many tough hombres were bred in the thirty-day trip from Fort Pierre to Deadwood, and thousands of pounds of goods were carried overland in this way. It took a tough breed to get through the mud, gumbo, the swollen streams, on beans, bacon, coffee, blackstrap; fighting bandits, Indians, rattlesnakes, and death.

Duck Leg Shorty had one leg smaller than the other from walking in ruts. They said that when an ox died the bull-whackers lassoed a buffalo, broke it, and drove on.

Pike, first great American explorer, set out from St. Louis toward the headwaters of the Mississippi with twenty soldiers, in a keelboat propelled by oars and poles; he took down the British or French flag in Indian village and fort, and hoisted the American colors.

Possessing a country is not as simple a thing as flying a flag over it. The old modes of life went on: hunting, fishing, trading, wars. In the War of 1812 some of the traders sided with the English, some with the Americans. But when Pike planted the American flag everyone was in a hurry. The glut of people pushed at the gates, clamoring for ways to get to the northland quick.

Within five years the great cry for roads and means of travel had shovels busy in Ohio, Indiana, Illinois, building broad roads from Indian and buffalo trails. Men with pick and shovel worked day and night in the pits of the canals at Erie and Sault Ste. Marie. At last, with the opening of the canals, the steamboat made mass migration into the North Star Country possible. A man in a canoe cannot bring his wife and his plow and his anvil.

And the steamboat started coming up the Mississippi, then ran up the Fox and the Wisconsin. When the first steamboat came to Fort Snelling, everyone knew something great was about to happen—a new era was coming. It was a bright summer morning, the people on the high cliffs waiting, shading their eyes to see down the river. Smoke was sighted and the cry broke, "The steamboat is coming!"

Now she rounded the point, coming in with pride and beauty. And the terrified Indians looked on in amazement, cried, "Bad spirit!" and "Fire canoe!" and ran into the woods.

Many stories are told about the Mississippi steamboats and the miraculous pilots who found the shifting channel without charts, in the fog, in the sudden storms of Lake Pepin and Coon Slough—set the little stern-wheelers that would hold on a star all night and then let them go. There were exploding boilers, races, fire, and the continual journey out of the mystery of above-river to the mystery below, over the soft alluvial bed of the Father of Waters, who shifted and twisted, so that tales were told of running the light-draft boats over meadows in the heavy dews. When the *Monitor* went around broadside, the pilot said he didn't do a thing to upset her but shift his quid of 'baccy.

Strange notions were conceived. The Minnesota flows out of one end of Big Stone Lake and the Red River of the north from the other, one making for the Gulf and the other for the North Pole; so one John Davis, a daffy pilot, conceived the notion of taking a boat up the Minnesota, across the Big Stone and into the Red River. The boat was wrecked and abandoned on the prairie, and the Indians took everything but the boiler.

As if life wasn't dangerous enough, the pilots raced each other, exploding their boilers, hanging themselves on snags, crashing into sandspits and bridges. When word of the first Atlantic cable came with greetings from Queen Victoria, two boats raced to St. Paul with the news, dug up the river-bottom, boomed into the town almost neck and neck, and one of the captains tied the message to a lump of coal and threw it from the upper deck to the levee.

The pilots and roustabouts had to be rough and ready men. Besides the difficult job of navigation, the pilot com-manded from twenty to thirty roistering savages who loved nothing better than to shoot him. . . . Where the raft ran in safety one season, grass grew the next. The river shifted under the surface, the whole conformation changing every hour.

Wooding up at night along the banks, the peculiar ruffians who risked their lives every season to bring the rafts down, the rapscallions of the river, the Black Gangs, the wild yarn-spinners, singers, dancers on the knife-edge of disaster, would sing:

> O corn-fed girl, see the moon shine bright,
> Ain't you comin' out tonight?
> Ain't you comin' out tonight?
> O, corn-fed girl, ain't you walkin' out tonight—
> With your hand laid in mine?

At one time Red Wing was the biggest wheat market in the world and the boats tied up at the levee in St. Paul carried a total tonnage larger than the shipping of Great Britain. The lumberjacks then became rivermen, riding the drive down to the booming yards. And in the summer they were raftsmen, riding the islands of pine raft, six brails, 1,500 by 300 feet of the best timber lashed together with no bond but the river and the skill of pilots like Lincoln's cousin Stephen Hanks, who could smell a change in the channel and guide the raft through solid darkness.

> Dandy Handy Raftsman Jim,
> There ain't no cub as cute as him.

> And stealing logs and shingle bolts, and telling awful lies,
> And playing cards and swearing is all their exercise.
> So if you want to marry for comfort or for joy
> I advise you to get married to an honest farmer's boy!

In 1852 there was talk in the village of another "road," the railroad. There was a scattered population yet, but the railroads would help to settle the wide country.

On these trains were to come the farmers, dairymen, wheat-growers. In the space of a few years the empire of the fur traders, whose solid wealth blocked the wilderness, was broken and its peculiar culture of noblemen, trappers, Indian chiefs, half-breeds, disappeared. Steam, then the railroad, made new empires, opened the way to migration of a new nation.

The days of the bonanza, the speculator, trader, quick fortunes and sudden death, were over.

Woe to My People!

Traverse des Sioux

Before these two great engines of civilization, the whiskey shop and the printing office, the poor Indians stand no more chance than so many Mexicans between two batteries of grape and canister.

—GOODHUE

My reason teaches me that land cannot be sold. The Great Spirit gave it to his children to live upon, and cultivate as far as is necessary for their subsistence; and so long as they occupy and cultivate it, they have the right to the soil—but if they voluntarily leave it, then any other people have a right to settle upon it. Nothing can be sold except such things as can be carried away.

—BLACK HAWK, OF THE SAC AND FOX TRIBES

WHERE THE GREAT FOREST OF THE EAST AND the vast plains of the west meet, where the Blue Earth and its tributaries are passable, where the headwaters of the Minnesota and Red Rivers could be reached by a short cut over land, was the capital of one of the great nations of the earth, the Nation of the Buffalo: the Sioux.

The treaty of the Traverse des Sioux, signed in June, 1851, released the Long Knives (Americans) who had been

83

bottled up in the narrow and not over-fertile land between the Mississippi and the St. Croix, and the stream of immigration began to flow over the vast prairies.

For settlement of the new country the rich land extending south of Shakopee and continuing hundreds of miles to the west and south was indispensable, and the Indian, loath to give it up, was nevertheless forced to it by the extinction of the buffalo, by the pressure of all the East against the barriers for admittance.

By the treaty, the articles of which were never fulfilled, the United States Government got possession—for a sum of money which was never paid—of nineteen million acres in Minnesota, nearly three million in Iowa, over one million, seven hundred and fifty thousand in South Dakota: in all, nearly twenty-four million acres of the choicest land existing on the globe.

This treaty and its betrayal led to one of the bloodiest days of American history, which was to make the prairies and the rivers run red and give the region the name of Golgotha, Land of Skulls. It led to the massacre of 1862, when guerrillas defended the country against Indians who had gone mad like the locusts, killing eight hundred whites. Refugees fled along the roads and the rivers. Starving Indian women with their children picked grain from the dung of the cavalry horses and marched two hundred miles in the dead of winter to the missions for help; three hundred of them died of bad meat, government issue, in one week at Sandy Lake, and the progressive debacle of this hunted group in a few years reduced a great nation of over twenty-eight thousand people, representing an old and noble culture, to a few hundred—mostly old men, women, and children—who were stoned as they were deported over the border.

Skulduggery

We left them without government. The Chiefs became the pliant tools of traders and agents, powerful for mischief but powerless for good. The penalty of theft was deducted from the annuity of the tribe. This system of trade was ruinous to honest traders and pernicious to the Indians, and was made a hundred-fold worse by making the office of an Indian agent one of reward for political services. The voice of the whole nation has declared that the Indian department is the most corrupt in the government.—BISHOP WHIPPLE.

He [Bishop Whipple] came to me the other day and talked to me about the rascality of the Indian business until I felt it down to my boots.—ABRAHAM LINCOLN.

Why did the Indian greet the white man as a long-lost father? Well, there was, as Radisson showed them so thoroughly, the gunpowder, and that was a powerful speech. There was also the horse of the white man. There was his fine way of making speeches. The Indian also liked to make speeches, liked oratory that lasted all night by the feast and the fire.

The Indian learned bitterly how words could stand as a shield to greed. Bishop Whipple of Minnesota tells a story about a legislator who came to him in 1864 for aid in influencing the Ojibways to release the land of their reservation and go on another of poorer land. Bishop Whipple refused, and the legislator said that he would do it himself; he guessed he had enough language to get around an Indian. He called the Indians together. "My friends," he said, "the Great Father has heard how you have been wronged. He looked in the north, the east, the west to find an honest man; I will send him to my red children. Now, my friends, look at me. The winds of fifty-five winters have blown over my head and have silvered it with gray, and in all that time

I have done no wrong to a single person. As your friend I ask you to sign this treaty at once."

Old Shabaskong, a Mille Lacs chief, sprang to his feet and with a wave of the hand said, "Look at me. The winds of fifty-five winters have blown over my head and have silvered it over with gray, but—they have not blown my brains away. I have done." The council was ended.

The destruction of this nation was tragic. The democratic forces of the frontier might have worked out peaceful relations with the Indians, but speculators, merchants, and various national interests made a bloody war inevitable. Britain incited the Indians of the northwestern forts, converting them into a police force. Spanish agents engendered hatreds, as did the French and American traders, using corruption, lies, and whiskey. There were also Indian spies, traitors, those who feathered their own nests, sold out, became lovers of the white man's vices.

The Indian had no comprehension of the new social system—of the concept of private property; the principle of democracy also was meaningless for they had never known any form of state oppression or the revolt against it. Americans never understood the Indian forms of social organization. They considered the petty chief a monarch with the right to alienate lands, which was not the case; thus contracts were broken, hatreds intensified. Both sides were fighting for land, freedom, home. Tragically it was the most democratic forces which came into bloody and violent conflict with the Indians.

Chiefs

Forsyth, Indian agent at Fort Snelling, as early as 1819 could write sadly, "Everything that one could say of another, Father Hennepin said of the Sioux; but I am sorry to say that they are at present much altered. How this alteration has taken place . . . can be attributed only to their too great intercourse with those whom we call civilized people."

Missionary Pond said of the great chiefs that if you saw them—tall hunters magnificently accoutered, dignified, reticent, with reserves of strength and feeling—"they were not likely to be soon forgotten."

Radisson describes them in their heyday, coming to sign the first treaties for furs:

Soon 30 young men of the nation of the Beefe arrived. The first were yong people with their bows and arrows and Bucklers on their shoulders uppon which weare represented all manner of figures as of the sun and moon, of terrestriall beasts. Their hair turned up like a Crowne, and weare cut very eaven, but rather burned for the fire which is their cicers. They leave a tuff of haire upon their Crowne of their heads, tye it, and putt att the end of it some small pearles or some Turkey stones and bind them. They grease themselves with very thick grease and mingle it in reddish earth. They cutt some downe of Swan or other fowle that hath a white feather and cover with it the Crowne of their heads. They are clothed with Orinach and Staggs' skins, but very light. Every one had the skin of a crow hanging att their guirdles. Their toekens all embroidered with pearles and with their own porke-pick worke. They have very handsome shoose laced very thick all over with a peece sowen att the side of the hele, which was of a haire of Buff. After all, they have a white robe of Castor's skin painted. The Elders came with great gravities and modestie, covered with Buff coats which hung downe to the grounde.

Chief Red Wing was of those not soon to be forgotten.

He was of the dynasty which wore a swan feather dyed scarlet, and ruled the rich countryside along the Mississippi before it is joined by the Wisconsin, where the town of Red Wing is today. He was one of fine speech, who visited Canada during the War of 1812 and made an alliance with the English against the Long Knives.

He opposed the Indian outbreaks, but led his tribe to

death when death was their will. "I must go with my band
and my nations. I said to my men that I would lead them
into the war and we would all act like brave Dakotas and
do the best we could."

He is˜said to have been buried astride his horse on the
high mound of his village on the shores of Lake Pepin.
Actually he was taken to Nebraska, where he died.

Little Six, or Chief Shakopee, was a man of marked ability
in the council and one of the best orators of the Dakota
nation, with a wonderful voice; his speeches in the evening
could be heard clearly throughout his village.

He was fond of the epigram: "No man absent from battle
but would have been brave had he been there; no man
absent from council but would have been wise had he been
there."

Not bad for a live Indian, the sheriff said.

Before the 1862 massacre Shakopee said to his tribe:

You are like dogs in the hot moon, when they go mad and
snap and bite. We are only a little herd of buffalo left scattered.
The great herds that once covered the prairies are no more. The
white men are like locusts when they fly so thick that the whole
sky is like a snowstorm. You may kill one, two, ten; yes, as many
as the leaves in the forest yonder, and their brothers will not
miss them. Count your fingers all day long and white men with
guns in their hands will come faster than you can count. You
are fools, you die like rabbits when the hungry wolves hunt
them in the hard moon. I am no coward. I shall die with you.

After the last defeat at New Ulm he led the retreat to his
village, where there were about a thousand lodges, sur-
mounted by a big American flag they had captured, flying
on a tall pole. They moved west in a train three miles long,
into the last sun.

Little Six, along with Little Crow and Chief Medicine
Bottle, escaped to Canada when the hunt began. According

to a recently discovered order of General Sibley, with the
aid of three gallons of firewater—historically recorded as
"toddies," with laudanam added—they were kidnapped il-
legally by two men commissioned by Major Hatch of Fort
Snelling; with the aid of the Canadian government they
were brought unconscious in a dog sled and delivered to
the fort.

"What will they do with me tomorrow?" Shakopee asked
the minister.

"They will hang you."

"I am not afraid. When I go into the spirit world I will
look the Great Spirit in the face and I will tell him what
the whites did to my people before we went to war. He will
do right. I am not afraid."

He was given what the jailer called the "hemp cure,"
hanged by the neck until dead.

"I want to live like the white man. I am a farmer. What
can I do now? I am watched. If I move they will kill me.
But I will sign my name. I will do what I can."

Chief Wabasha said this after the massacre had begun, in
a letter sent to Fort Snelling, pledging the aid of the Christian Indians to the refugees.

But he too went with his tribe to death, in the last great
gesture of courage, in the fatal terror of annihilation. Seated
on a white horse, dressed in the full costume of the chief, his
bright headdress showing on the prairie so that in the battle
of New Ulm he was remarked by many—he wore wings over
his shoulders, strings of beads and a belt of wampum; he
carried a rifle and two pistols that caught the sun. He was
seen at the battle of Mankato; he was seen at New Ulm on
August 23, in the last days of the fighting, advancing up the
Mankato road in full view, directing fire with a lacrosse
stick. His horse became fractious from the firing, screaming,
the smoke and shambles of battle; it reared, and he dropped

the stick, which was picked up by a white fighter who saved it.

He wept with Little Crow after the battle of Wood Lake, when a Christian Indian had thwarted their attack on Sibley's camp and it became clear that they were being betrayed by their own people—the "friendlies"—and they looked at annihilation straight. "It is too late for us to keep aloof from this trouble. The whites will not discriminate. Those who have killed are our relatives, our countrymen. They have now involved us in their ruin."

Sun Dance

A DOCTOR ADVERTISED IN THE ST. PAUL PAPER for Indian scalps, offering five bucks apiece for them. A merchant said he had had the pleasure of taking many scalps with his own hand and did a very good job, taking not only the scalp but the ears as well.

"We have spent more money on Indian wars than all the Christian churches of America have on missions," said Bishop Whipple during the Indian wars.

The only Christian in an Indian village died, urging his friends to follow him to the great spirit's home. Worried, the medicine men left the next day for fast and meditation to try and influence their people.

They returned in rags, the sign of mourning, their faces blackened, and said they had seen the dead and that he was in great trouble, wandering alone in the nether world. He said he had been to the white man's heaven and the angel who guarded the gate asked him who he was. He said he was a Christian Indian, and the angel shut the gate, saying, "This is a white man's heaven. There are happy hunting grounds to the west!" He went there and asked for admission and the medicine man said, "We are medicine men. If you are a Christian you must go to the other heaven."

Red Bird, speaking to Frances Densmore, giving her the records of the great Sun Dance, said:

There is a great deal in what a man believes, and if a man's religion is changed for the better or for the worse, he will know it. The Sun Dance was our first and only religion. We believe that there is a mysterious power, greater than all others, which is represented in nature, one form being the sun. Thus we made sacrifices to the sun and our petitions were granted. I believe we had true faith in that time. But there came a year when the sun "died." There was a period of darkness and from that day a new religion came to the Indians. It is the white man's religion. We are timid about it. In the old days our faith was strong and our lives were cared for. Now our faith is weaker, and we die.

Mr. V. T. McGillicuddy, agent at Pine Ridge, South Dakota, said in a report in 1882: "The heathenish annual ceremony termed the Sun Dance will, I trust, soon be a thing of the past."

> May the sun rise well,
> May the earth appear
> Brightly shone upon.
> May the moon rise well,
> May the earth appear
> Brightly shone upon.

The prayer for fair weather, sweet grass, and sage went up over the prairie in the midsummer solstice to the four cardinal points of the earth, through the Sun Dance, which strangely resembles Hebraic ritual, its symbolic ceremony like our own of repentance and the remission of sins.

From every direction the tribes came at an appointed time to the unmarked circle of that round and swinging prairie horizon, to erect a cross. Here greetings are made, new babies shown, tales of war and love related, and the young braves come to fulfill the vows they have made before the wise men, for the redemption of themselves and their people.

Election of dancers and "intercessors," challenged by all the tribes, is made. Gifts are exchanged. An Announcer on horseback, gaily accoutered, wearing an eagle feather, rides through the camp, which is arranged in a circle, announcing the decisions of the council and the commands of the Intercessor.

Amidst the many preparations—the painting of the dancers' bodies according to the color of their dreams, the rehearsing of the drummers and the singers, the vapor baths of the supplicants—the young men elected, singing, go out to cut the tree that will be transformed into the cross upon which they will hang their flesh. They return singing, and the people wait. They sing jubilantly to the tree, the sacred pole:

> I am only a man,
> You falsely implied.
> Now you cry.

They raise it in silence against the flat horizon, but when it stands there a cry goes up from the Intercessor, answered by the people, a high note descending in a wail; the ponies trailing vines and wreaths race around the pole, and the people surge forward with their gifts.

The Intercessor prepares the cross, stripping, painting the trunk, and attaching a crossbar north and south, the length of a man, while the song then is:

> Father, all these he has made me own—
> The trees and the forests
> Standing in their places.

Two effigies in rawhide hang from the crossbar, one a man, the other a buffalo, to show they have both been conquered by supernatural help; also depending from the bar are the thongs upon which the supplicants will hang. From the top of the pole swings a tanned and colored buffalo-calf skin.

They all face the sacred pole, the supplicants toward the sun which will rise in a few moments and the people behind, raising a cry of suffering to come, all amid the four winds in the center of a wide, voiceless wilderness, singing:

> Sacred I stand
> Within the four winds.
> Behold me
> At the center of the earth,
> At the wind center,
> At the place of the four winds.
> May you be reverenced—
> The tribes sit,
> They wish to live.

The Announcer then cries to the dancers: "It is finished. Come!"

They move around the buffalo skull and the ceremonial pipe. The sun rises. The young men raise their arms. The Intercessor cried out, "Repent! Repent!" and a cry of lamentation rises from the people.

The drumming and the singing move out on the winds and the dancers move upon the earth. The flesh-cutters come to the young men, lift a portion of the flesh of the chest with an awl, cut it with a quick knife-stroke, lift it to the sun:

> This man promised to give you his flesh;
> He now fulfills his vow.

Through the flesh he passes a blue stick, and to this the thongs of the cross are tied until the young man is suspended by his own flesh, his toes touching the earth upon which he continues to dance, blowing the eagle-bone whistle in his mouth, while the people cry out in lamentation for his suffering.

All day the dancing upon the rack continues, and men sing of their suffering; all night it continues and those who faint are laid on the earth. The young men dance until the tearing flesh releases them, in the hot prairie sun without food or water, and then in the dark.

When the sun rises the following morning, it is done. Camp is broken by evening and the tribes move away to the circumference of the wheel of prairie, and looking back they see the cross, the red-painted buffalo skull, and the bits of white eagle down. The young men's wounds are dressed by the women, and Wakantanka, the spirit, is left on the silent prairie.

Soon the plows dug deep into the hunting grounds, the children died, and their fires went out from shore to shore.

Treaty

Barrel of 32 gal., bushel of rank black twist chewing tobacco, 3 or 4 of bad whiskey or quantity of raw alcohol—fill in with river water. Let stand awhile and serve to Dakotas. Inflamed corrosion. Bit off each other's noses, gouged out eyes, broke heads, disembowelled each other, drowned themselves in the river, froze on the prairie, and signed anything.

—OLD RECIPE FOR DEALING WITH INDIANS

IT WAS RAINING HARD, THE RIVERS WERE swollen, and Governor Ramsey and Colonel Luke Lee, Commissioner of Indian Affairs, were nervous, starting by boat down the Minnesota toward the rendezvous at Traverse des Sioux, the treaty neatly folded in the governor's portmanteau. Mr. James Goodhue, editor of the *St. Paul Pioneer Press*, was aboard, and artist Frank Blackwell Mayer, to record for posterity the signing of the document which nobody doubted would be signed.

Just the same, the governor was nervous. Would the chiefs get there?

Colonel Lee reminded the governor that the traders had promised to deliver the Indians, and as they had so much at stake they would get them there, come hell or high water. Besides, the colonel said, the Indians were hungry and would want to sink their teeth in the drove of cattle that lowed on the forward deck of the *Excelsior,* ready for the feast that would follow the treaty.

The Indians always came to a powwow anyway, and the winter had been a hungry one with little game, while the traders had helped to make it leaner, just for good measure, to prepare for this event.

The painter Mayer went with Colonel Lee to look at the huge pile of colored blankets, cheap cloths, and thousands of looking glasses that would be passed out after the twenty-four million acres had been sealed, signed, and delivered.

Mr. Mayer wanted to know what power the traders had over the Indians and it was explained to him that they were always kept greatly in debt to the traders, who were mostly of Scotch and French descent, many married to Indian women, and that the first annuity of the sum paid in the treaty would go to the traders, and, as they kept the books, this could be a tidy amount, the basis for large fortunes in the northwest.

Take Joe Brown, for instance, "the best lied-about man in the country," a man who already had his weather eye on the choice land all up and down the St. Croix; he would get every chief there if he had to shanghai him.

But the governor was still worried about how, after the Indians had signed the treaty, they would also sign the paper authorizing payment of the annuities to the traders. They would be sure to balk at that.

"Leave that to Joe Brown," they all said, laughing. "He's an old drummer from the army, been here since 1819, selling them whiskey from Gray Cloud Island. He'll cook up something."

At sunrise on June 30, the *Excelsior* reached its destination at the great junction of the rivers, and they pitched their white tents in an old French cemetery, erected council chambers of poles covered with leafy branches, and ceremonial platforms.

"In a treaty with the whites," one recorder said, "the part played by the Indians is always more in appearance than in fact." Colonel Luke Lee knew that the pomp and circumstance must be suited to the occasion.

But the chiefs were not there. They waited.

They waited three weeks.

The governor got very nervous.

The traders were a little worried, but Joe Brown said they would come. It was the rains, they could not get across the rivers, and of course they would bring their families. If the young men were against the treaty, Brown said, they were to be turned back. You could tell them the thing had been called off on account of the floods.

"Will they sign?" Some of them were nervous. "They've kept even squatters off the land."

"You have to know how to handle 'em," Brown said. "You can get around even a dead Indian."

"But the signing of the treaty with the traders, giving them the first annuities, that's something else again. And have I got wonderful books, watered to the hilt!"

"Look," Brown said (he later became a legislator, a newspaper editor), "we have a barrel next to the table the treaty is signed on—they just pass on, sign their names again; they'll think it's just for good measure—besides they'll be making speeches and won't know what they're doing.

"Now, boys, round 'em up!"

To Bishop Whipple from a converted Indian:

The first treaty my people made was the most imposing gathering I have ever witnessed. The chief of each band wore the colors of his rank. His suit of clothing was made of the best dressed skins and furs, gorgeously decorated. His firm and independent step and his demeanor indicated his strength and purity. Did I say strength and purity? I say it knowingly. His growth was from the purest seed; an offspring which had not been contaminated by the white man's drug. He drank the purest water, breathed the purest air, as when the first man breathed it in the new-created world. He drank no devil's spittle to burn away his brains. There was a great crowd of warriors at that treaty, each wearing his eagle plumes which told of his bravery in battle, and of the enemies he had slain.

It was three weeks before the traders rounded them up, during which time the Indians who came entertained the bored white men with ball games, wedding feasts, and dramas showing hunting scenes, ending with a big dance to appease the storm god by breaking the thunderbird's wing.

On a Friday morning in July the bugle blew; they gathered in full regalia under the embowered council room. The commissioner informed the Indian chiefs of the wishes of the government, then adjourned to let the chiefs talk it over. The commissioner hoped they would get back to St. Paul for the week end.

Saturday morning, guns were fired; the reassembled Indians sat silent, in full regalia, knowing talk to be useless now, looking out from Traverse to the broad lands where their forefathers lay buried and which would be theirs no more.

The governor got nervous.

Finally, Wee-chan-hpee-ee-tay-toan ("Having-the-Face-of-a-Star"), Chief of the Sissetons from Lake Traverse, rose and complained that many of the young men of his tribe had been turned back by the whites, and at this Governor Ramsey spoke sharply of how they had waited three weeks and could wait no longer.

Nobody was satisfied with the explanation. There was another silence out of which Sleepy Eye of the Swan Lake band, who had been watching the young boys playing ball in the field that led into the prairie, rose, and the traders looked at each other knowing he was bitterly opposed to the treaty.

"Fathers," he said, "your coming and asking me for my country makes me sad, and your saying that I am not able to do anything with my country makes me still more sad." He said that the young men turned back were his near relatives, and as far as he was concerned it was over and he was going out and play ball with the young men.

Tumult followed. The governor was angry. The commissioners said that the treaty was immaterial to them and they would be glad to drop the matter. Orders were issued to give no more rations to the Indians and to strike the tents for morning departure.

But the young men wanted to live, even poorly, and all through the night council fires burned and messengers hurried back and forth between the tribes and the commissioners; traders whispered in corners to the young men, and that night a delegation waited on the commissioners begging them to remain—which, needless to say, they agreed to do. Mr. Goodhue describes the Monday morning gathering:

Indians are gathering all in high paint and feather. The corner in which the ceremony is to take place is piled with goods and presents, looking glasses, ribbons, powder and lead, and hundreds of items of utility and fancy. At twelve o'clock, the weather having cleared, the sun shining brightly, the commissioners took their seats and, after a grand smoke from Colonel Lee's magnificent Eyanshah pipe, the council was opened.

Sleepy Eye apologized! Addresses were made by the white men. But Sleepy Eye had something on his mind again, and to the unease of everyone, especially the traders who had the barrel prepared beside the treaty table, he rose and said that some provision should be made to give his people help before the year got white, as they would be very hungry then. He went into a wandering speech, claiming the sums to be insufficient, and was called to order by the commission and told that the treaty had been agreed to and he was out of order.

After a short pause, Colonel Lee stepped up and signed the treaty. He was followed by Governor Ramsey, who felt better. Then the chiefs began to sign. Having-the-Face-of-a-Star said as he signed, "Father, now when I sign this paper and you go to Washington with it, I want you to see all that is written here fulfilled. I have grown old without whiskey, and I want you to take care that it does not come among us."

Juggler Joe Brown said, "Sign right here, chief; we'll take care of everything." He indicated the second paper on the barrelhead. The chief signed the paper, saying afterward he thought it was part of the treaty.

Extending Tail said, "Fathers, you think it a great deal you are giving for this country. I don't think so, for both our lands and all we get for them will at last belong to the white man. The money goes to us, but will all go to the white men who trade with us." And he looked at Juggler Joe Brown who held out the pen to him.

They were all given a fifty-cent medal and there was distribution of tawdries, and the next morning the flag of the United States was lowered and the commission, jubilant, returned to Mendota and Juggler Joe set them up for all aboard.

The Indians would now have ten miles on each side of the river, until that would be taken from them. They went home slowly through the late spring heat.

> A fatal treaty—
> Huh quah ne sah ga nig!
> Huh quah ne sah ga nig!
> Woe, woe be to my people!
> Woe, woe be to my people!
> —HOLE-IN-THE-DAY

Massacre

———

TWO MEN WERE SILENTLY DRIVING OVER THE prairie from Fort Snelling toward St. Anthony Falls. It was a dark, cold December night and they were in a hurry, fearful that Major Plympton and Captain Scott might reach the falls ahead of them to put up a shack, so that the following morning, when the ban on settlement was lifted, they could file a claim on a hundred and sixty acres of the river front which is the present loop district of Minneapolis.

The two men, Franklin Steele and Commodore Norman Kittson—called "Commodore" because of his then visionary scheme to run a fleet of freight boats up and down the Red River of the north—had in the cart some odds and ends of boards and a sack of potatoes. It was pitch-dark when they arrived at the falls, and no sign of their rivals. They hurriedly built a jerrymander shelter, grabbed spade and pickax, dug holes in the ice, and planted potatoes in the snow.

At dawn they watched the others arrive, who swore mightily at having lost their chance of becoming owners of a future metropolis, which they all saw in their feverish land dreams that cold December dawn.

Mr. Steele often remarked much later—after he had

brought Caleb Dorr and Ard Godfrey from Maine to put up sawmills, and sold the land at a giant price to settlers—that though not a potato sprouted from that night's planting, the crop, nevertheless, paid well.

Juggler Brown was not sleeping. He had pre-empted a large tract of the Sioux land and had his eye upon the reservation itself, ten miles on either side of the river, which he often said was too good for the Indians.

The panics of 1857 sent thousands to the newly opened lands freed by the treaty, and by the time they got west the speculators were waiting for them, before the Indians had been removed or the land surveyed.

The lament of the Indian Chiefs could be heard:

LET THEM EAT GRASS!

The snow is on the ground, we are poor.
Your fires are warm—
Ours do not keep out the cold.

We have sold our hunting ground.
We have no place to bury our dead, yet you do not pay us.
If I look to the east, if I look to the west, a precipice awaits me.
My warriors look into their own graves,
Day and night my shadow falls against the graves of my people.
Woe, woe be to my people.

The Indians came for the first payment. The traders and agents showed them the second piece of paper, which many did not remember signing, and told them that the entire payment had been absorbed in the claims, except for $880, which would be their credit on the books at Washington. Of the $96,000 due to the lower Sioux not one cent was received.

The Indians were silent.

All but Red Iron, who organized a band of braves. Troops were sent from Fort Snelling under Captain James Monroe, forty infantry and five dragoons. Red Iron was arrested, jailed, and the band broken.

For two years unrest continued.

Joe Brown got the land along the river; the Indians were moved, settlers moved in. An Indian said, "Why doesn't our Great White Father put us on wheels!" Brown became a nabob of embryo cities: lumberman, legislator, politician, and inventor of a wagon propelled over the prairie by steam.

At Sandy Lake all the upper Mississippi Indians gathered to receive the colored flour and heavily perfumed pork, government issue. The old chief said, "Is that fit to eat?" But the Indians were starving and they ate it. About two o'clock in the morning the first gun, signal of death, was fired. An hour later another gun was fired, and then another, and another, until death seemed to be in every home. That night twenty children died, and the next day as many more, and so for five days and five nights the deaths went on. Weeping and wailing filled the encampment, wigwams were deserted as the people fled to the forest. They buried their dead in haste, without clothing.

There were three hundred dead.

At the next payment the Indians gathered, waited at the agencies for months, were refused credit. In August, Bishop Whipple asked a clerk what was due. The discontent was mounting, several Indians had refused to shake his hand. The agent said, "There will be no payments. The appropriation has been entirely used up to pay traders' claims."

A letter came to the mission for Hole-in-the-Day and the bishop asked one of his soldiers to read it. It was from Little Crow, "Your young men have killed one of my people, a farmer Indian. I have tried to keep my soldiers at home. They have gone for scalps. Look out!"

The Indians saw the papers with the pictures of the Civil War on the counters at the trading posts. The white man was losing a war, the men had gone to it; now was the time, and the last, to get their great lands back.

Trader Myrick had come to the front of his store and refused admittance to a committee of Indians who had come to ask for food or credit. "What shall my people eat?" the chief asked. Trader Myrick said, "Let them eat grass."

On Saturday, Bishop Whipple saw Sioux moccasin prints near St. Cloud, and he heard of a party back of Little Falls.

That Sunday, near Acton, four young Indians—Brown Wing, Breaking Up, Killing Ghost, and Runs-Against-Something-When-Crawling—were foraging for something to eat. They went near the Big Woods, found a hen's nest near a settler's fence, and they were afraid to eat the eggs because they belonged to the white man. They were very hungry. Then one of them became angry and dashed the eggs to the ground. "You are a coward," he said, half to himself. "We are afraid to take even an egg, though we are starving."

"I am not afraid of the white man," Killing Ghost said, "and to show you, I will go to the house and shoot him. Are you brave enough to go with me?"

"Yes, I will go with you," the others said. "We will go with you and we will be brave, too."

They killed three men and two women; then they went to Shakopee's camp and told him what they had done. Shakopee took them to Little Crow, who sat up in bed to listen.

Blood had been shed. The tiny spark lighted the countryside and would sweep over the borders, depopulating twenty counties. Wabasha and the chiefs cried for peace. But bands began to form and the cry rose, "Kill the whites! Kill the friendlies!" Small bands of hungry Indians rode in the darkness, the Indian women began to run bullets, and Little Crow at last gave the order to attack the agency next morning and kill the traders.

On the morning of August 18, 1862, Little Crow and the band of Little Six gathered, painted, at the trading post, saying they were going to attack the Chippewas. They stood in front of Trader Myrick's store. Mr. Divol, Myrick's clerk, was coming toward the house from the stable. Mr. Lynd was standing in the end door of the store looking at him. Two Indians with double-barreled guns stood in the front door and shot Mr. Lynd, who fell out the doorway and died instantly.

Mr. Hinman, sitting on the steps with a workman who was busy at building a church, heard firing from the direction of the trading post. Then White Dog appeared on the run, shouting, "The Indians have bad hearts and are killing the whites. I am going to Wabasha to stop it." In a few moments, running at full speed, Little Crow appeared and ran without speaking to the government barns for horses, shot the keeper, and rode off.

Taopi, a farmer Indian, also heard the report of the guns, went to the top of the house, and from there saw the store plundered. A messenger ran down the road shouting, "All the upper bands are coming down armed. They are killing the traders!"

Trader Myrick lay in front of his store, dead, with grass stuffed in his mouth.

Bishop Whipple rode all night through the terrorized countryside to Faribault to get aid for General Sibley at St. Peter. At sunrise he sent a boy ringing a bell through the streets, calling the citizens to meet him in front of the hotel. There he asked for volunteers to proceed immediately to join Sibley. He dashed on to St. Peter, where he found the wounded and dying coming in, beating their horses in out of the prairie. Families had been separated, children murdered before their mothers' eyes; a hospital had been organized and the bishop stayed to aid in the amputation of limbs and the sewing of dreadful wounds.

For the Indians had gone berserk. It was not only traders now, but every white skin on the prairie. General Sibley left them a note at Birch Coulee and they tore it up, laughing, because they believed now that no white man had his "tongue hung in the middle"; moreover, they did not believe their lives would be spared now. They sent back a saucy answer.

Little Crow said, "We do not war on women and children," but when they saw a white skin they could not remember that. They had gone mad with hunger and vengeance.

Two women sat in a wigwam holding on their laps the severed arms of two white victims, which they wrapped in linen and buried. They were Christian Indians.

Dark days deepened. The settlers fled toward a point in the valley where they could converge and make a stand against the attack. They left their dead and mutilated children in the fields, crawled through the swamp with their babies. They had bought their land in good faith and considered the Indians marauders. Later a woman, Sarah Purnell, remembered what she had seen when she was fifteen:

As a means of defense we filled every available tub and vessel with water and laboriously carried them up an outside stairway. Fires were kept burning all that terrible night, and had the Indians attacked us, they would have received showers of boiling water from our windows.

A family had been found murdered near our home, the children hanging by their feet from trees. We hid near our house in the tall bushes, and under cover of night the women and children left; the men stayed behind to fight.

The attack became general, spreading over the whole western frontier, down the Minnesota valley. The Indians, once committed to violence, now had nothing to lose. The settlers formed a line at last in New Ulm, organizing their defense under the leadership of the officers of the Turnvereins, with the aid of Charles Flandreau, lawyer and Indian agent, and the men he recruited from the outside.

The town was afire when Flandreau brought his volunteers across the lower ferry, but he found it organized by the Germans, one Jacob Nix elected *Platzkommandant,* picket guards stationed, houses fortified, signal fires lighted, refugees organized, and barricades built in the main street. Rudolph Leonhart, the German schoolmaster, brought his children in, one little girl died. The town was armed with only eighteen shotguns, fourteen rifles, stable forks, axes and bludgeons, and a few revolvers.

From the tallest buildings commanding the surrounding prairie, the settlers cou¹d see the Indians forming on the rise at the upper end of the town, could also see, painfully, the refugees lashing their horses trying to reach safety. Many of them lay crying outside the town all night until they died.

Houses were appropriated, medical aid organized; in three days the people had, themselves, organized the defense of the town and the counties in the rear, with only about three hundred and twenty-five poorly armed defenders and fifteen hundred women and children.

Saturday was so clear they could see the upland stacks burning and the smoke of razed towns. It was rumored that Fort Ridgely had fallen. Flandreau sent out seventy-five men to carry on an aggressive attack; they were cut off away from the river and could not get back. This left two hundred and fifty men.

The Indians appeared at the rear of the town, emboldened, swarming towards the slough which lay at the foot of the wooded rise. Flandreau could see them through his field glasses from the top of the general store, a party turning to the right and one to the left, and another coming down over the prairie bluff. He said later that the attack on New Ulm was a masterly piece of strategy.

He threw out skirmishers toward the slough and an exchange of shots followed which allowed him to bring up a main line of mounded defenders unseen by the Indians. He estimated that there were at least eight hundred Indians in this attack. At ten o'clock on Sunday morning the Indians formed a strong line along the slough with their flanks covered, as if to envelop the town, and began to advance across the prairie slope, then rushed with a yell from all sides into the barricaded street. The small band of whites held the first attack and retreated to another building, breaking its effect, and they fought in ambush from door to door, firing the buildings between them, disappearing in the covering smoke.

As the Indians came into the smoke Flandreau formed his defense at right angles, organized a feint—some of the defenders coming out the front of the building and drawing fire while he and his men came from the rear, rushing through the smoke and routing the enemy. After sundown the battle slackened, but the settlers lay on their arms on the barricade, every third man alternating for sleep.

Reinforcements arrived, the rebellion was broken, and the people of New Ulm went out on the prairie to bury their dead without coffin, book, or bell, while Flandreau organized a caravan of the sick and wounded toward Mankato, his men guarding the long sad column, on the lookout for wandering bands of Indians. "A more heart-rending procession was never witnessed in America," Flandreau said.

The money for the Indian payments had reached Fort Ripley the day after the outbreak.

Bishop Whipple made a report to Abraham Lincoln:

Our border stained with blood, our people cry for vengeance. We have persistently carried out the idea that we are a sovereign people. If it is true that a nation cannot exist within a nation, that these heathen were to send no ambassadors to us and we none to them, that they had no power to observe a treaty and that we did not look to them for power to observe it for themselves, then our first step was a fatal one. They did not possess a single element of sovereignty; and had they possessed it, we could not, in justice to ourselves, have permitted them to use it in the duties necessary to a nation's self-existence.

Who is guilty of the causes which desolate our border?
At whose door is the blood of these innocent victims?
I believe that God will hold the nation guilty.

Three hundred Indians were condemned to death by military court and taken to judgment through the villages in forty wagons drawn by horses, the Indians seated on the floor facing each other, chained together. Many wore bright shawls which they had taken from murdered settlers. Nearly all covered their heads, as the bitter feeling of the towns made it necessary for a detachment of infantry to accompany them, with General Sibley (called "Baron of the Border") and his staff, all in full uniform and mounted, at its head.

Reverend Riggs, missionary, present at the trials, said they were conducted with hate, forty men tried in one day. One, he said, was hanged for lying. He had boasted that he had killed a certain trader with an arrow. "We knew," said an officer, "that the trader had been killed by a bullet, so we hung the rascal."

One was hanged by mistake. The day after the execution the sheriff went to release one who had been acquitted for saving many lives, and when he asked for him he was told, "You hung him yesterday."

The angry mob wanted to kill Taopi, who had saved hundreds. He said, "I hear the white men want to kill me. If it is because the white man has the same law as the Indian, that when one of his people is killed another must die in his place, then tell them not to shoot me like a dog, but to send for me to go to the public square and I will show them how a man can die."

President Lincoln commuted the sentences of all but thirty-eight. On December 26, 1862, the condemned men in their cell in Mankato began singing their death song, a weird chant which they accented by the rattling of their arm-chains. They drew their blankets around them and chanting, marched out, crossed the street, mounted the steps of the scaffold before thousands of people who had gathered from the countryside. To the sound of taps from the drum they moved up the steps, formed in a line around the platform, and accepted the black cap that fitted over the eyes and the noose around the neck, each holding the hand of his brother next him, chanting their tribal dirge until the rope was cut and thirty-eight of the once great Sioux and Chippewa tribes hung dangling from the wooden beam above.

What was left of the tribes, a small band of old men, squaws, and children, were taken in freight cars out of the state.

On February 16, 1863, an act was passed whereby all rights and claims of the Sioux nation under the treaties not consummated were abrogated and annulled, their reservations decreed sold and themselves to be deported forever beyond the confines of their ancient homes.

Thunder On, Democracy

Bred in a Cabin

Thunder on, stride on, Democracy.

—WALT WHITMAN

Yes, sir, the town looks as if the seed for a multitude of tenements had been scattered yesterday upon a bed of guano and had sprouted up into cabins, stores, sheds, and warehouses, fresh from the sawmill since the last sun shone.

—ST. PAUL PIONEER PRESS

All I can hear is the din of land, land, land—land to divide, for a sawmill, to raise crops, cattle, chickens, pigs, children, and hell. It shakes the reason out of men.

—A PIONEER

Over there they got the real-estate offices on the sidewalk. They roll out the map, you fill in the deed, and they yell, "Sold!"

—ANOTHER PIONEER

Gee and Haw

AFTER THE TREATY, TO THE TIME OF THE Civil War, the pioneers kept coming on. The sound of the groaning axles and creaking cleats could be heard morning, noon, and night in the streets of St. Paul. Wagons coming in, made of solid blocks of wood, hickory withes, pegs, cleats, rough-planed boards, with the marks of the broadaxes on them and the cutting of the drawknives marking the spokes. The caravan would be pulled by a yoke of oxen, maybe four, with their heads in a wooden yoke, responding to the crack of the lash; bawling menfolk shouting "Gee!" and "Haw!" along the muddy river-town streets.

The wagon would be piled with what the wife could get into it: wooden churns, spinning wheels, flower seeds to plant in the new country. From the rear protruded the long beam of the breaking plow. Inside were the wooden dishes, the family Bible, the mementos of a life they would never see again.

The horses and their colts trotted behind, and the chickens made a racket from the coops. It was said in the grogshops that people moved westward so often that the chickens, knowing when moving day had come, lay down and thrust up their legs to be tied.

Often there came walkers, without horse or oxen, the man carrying his possessions on his back and his wife following barefooted, "bending under the hopes of the family."

Mr. Goodhue, from his printing office in St. Paul, where hard backs of pigs under the loose floor jostled his editorial chair, said, "We'll bet on that crowd. They're the right kind."

The Indian lands were open and the European flood tide driven from the old country; their tools taken from them, the people waited at the ports of Europe begging to be loaded like cattle on the sleazy merchant boats. The fabulous advertisements fed their "nostalgia in reverse" for land, higher wages, freedom from taxes and tithes; they braved even the terrors of the ocean and the horrors of immigrant ships where thousands died and were shoveled into the sea. They came as bonded slaves, selling their labor to shysters or loan sharks and lashing their oxen out to the wide horizon. They looked out through the cutting wind of the Great Lakes, prayed on the crowded decks, sank in storms and flaming ships in sight of free land, or died of cholera and malaria in the swamps of Illinois before the first cabin was built against the winter.

They came from the industrial cities of the East, also, where already the spindles of New England were taking the lives of girls at $1.70 a week for fourteen and sixteen hours a day; they waited at the gates of the new dynasty of the north, the future shining for them around the bends of the rivers, over the shining mountains, farther on, farther west, into Dakota, following the sun that went down before them.

One man said in western Minnesota, "I have got to go farther west. I am too far east now." He was a walker in a beckoning horizon which swung like a frail bridge in the tall walking wind; a traveler on an inland sea with many storms and wide rivers, the ground still bearing the scar and havoc of a glacier.

He was the inheritor of hunger and a believer in long chance, bred in a cabin, hunting the red sundown, pouring out his dreams on a soil that would blow away from him. Although he looked for no conquerors, he slept with a carbine by his side and moved when his neighbor's shot was in hearing distance.

But the evening sun swung always before him, a scythe cutting tomorrow; walking with his family behind the oxen into a new country, memory made him lash them hard, thoughts flicking at his brain like the rawhide whip in his hand. All the nameless ones not listed in old newspapers, coming day and night with the plows and the pestles, the blades of wood, the spokes of turning wheels. And the deep-breasted women who believed in hope and had pools of wishing in their eyes to match the blue water of the buffalo wallows, and the root of survival to hand down to sons in the evening—those with the habit of survival in them so deep they didn't know they had it, and never thought to speak about it.

Treading the long ruts and smooth distances of the wilderness, the prairie monologues went on:

If we can winter good—if you get through the first winter and the first child—

If we would only light somewheres is what I say.

As for me, I love the way the light changes, the land swelling at the coulee slopes, the morning light, the blazing moons, and the slow, long sunset of evening. It's open, clean, big, and a long, wind-spaced air. I lived in the London slums owned by the Crown.

We always movin'. I saw a wagon goin' back had a picture of a grasshopper fightin' with a man, with his forelegs around the man's throat, and it said on it: *He wins*.

These prairies are man-hungry. I buried four babies now, my man breaking the ground with an ax to make a place for the little bones.

First, as a squatter or landowner, you cleared a space in the wilderness, if you lived in the timber country. You got the ax out of the wagon and began to let in daylight in a little circle of forest. The neighbors, if there were any, came in to give advice and to help, knowing you would return it at harvest. You provided food, whiskey, and a fiddler, and they all came to the "raising."

With the aid of the jugs with the corncob stoppers, called "bug juice," "firewater," "blue ruin," "fool water," "moral suasion," and other names according to where you headed from and what church you went to, the talk grew tall, and it only took a few makings to roll up a good story.

Then the dancing began in the clearing or on the puncheon floor of the green-smelling cabin, the children slept on pallets, and there would be talk of how to get along.

I'll loan you my breaking plow. This is tough earth never laid to the plow before.

All you gotta do is gash the sod with yer ax an' drop the kernel in.

The best way, friend, is girdle the trees, cut a ring round the bark, keeps the sap from risin'—You kin plant yer fust crop between the stumps.

We'll all thresh together. You have to go ahead of all creation in this here country.

Ole here kin make you a scythe and a cradle. A man comes after and binds the sheaves which you put on a level ground, heads to the center and walk your ox around. The wind will blow the chaff away.

And the women heard the loneliness in the wind and saw ahead how they would be left alone in the dark shanty with the wolves at the door and prairie fires walking tall as skyscrapers on the horizon, and babies born with no hand to help in the one-legged bed that stood waiting in the corner. The low woman talk went on, alone, separate, a question in the look of the eyes over the cutting of fresh bread, the lifted head over the nursing child:

If yer potatoes is dried out, soak 'em in water.

In the spring the cowslips are good caught early before the bitter comes. In the prairie there is horseradish, dock, sorrel, and pigweed.

Wild strawberries come early. I'll show you the huckleberry swamp and the chokecherry trees.

Underground things plant in the dark of the moon, aboveground things in the light of the moon. Even rail fences I heard got to be set in the dark moon or they'll sink sure as rain.

Don't skip a row in planting or surely someone close to you will die.

Kill a snake in the spring and the Indians won't bother you.

If the sun shines while it is raining, it will rain the next day.

There were odd pieces of wisdom to put together, each coming from a far and different country. But mostly the talk reflected the life of the prairie and the endless transition from old homes to new:

My Sunday best is a linsey-woolsey, and when we get a church I'm goin' to wear it.

You been used to the woods; the prairies make you weep.

We got tired of old hillsides in New England. I like it here.

Hard for a woman, mighty troublesome for a woman. I had a little white frame house in Pennsylvania, with geraniums in the windowsills.

I tell you I saw that black smoke coming from the Northwest. My man had driven twenty miles with the wheat. I strapped the baby on my back, locked my two others in the house, and went to the firebreak and backfired, beating out the flames as they come on.

Wait till the blizzards come. I was alone. I had to stick the broom up the chimney so the fire would draw and we took the bread with us to bed to thaw it out.

So the talk went on and had to be improvised. New words, like tools, had to be invented. Old forms were of no use in a new country. A pioneer writing back to his New England friend said, "If you can't stand seeing your old New England ideas, ways of doing and living, and in fact all of the good old Yankee fashions knocked out of shape or thrown by as unsuited to the climate, don't be caught out here."

Marriage

You were married by the justice of the peace, who also ran the general store, filed deeds, was circuit lawyer, sometimes preacher. Sweating like a horse he improvised the marriage ceremony the best he could:

Faller citizens, this here man and this here woman want to get hitched in the legal bond of wedlock. If any galoot knows anything to block the game let him toot his bazoo or else keep his jaw shet now and forevermore. Grab yer fins. You, John, do you solemnly swear to the best of yer knowledge that you take this woman to have and to hold for yourself, your heirs, executors, and assignees for your and their use and benefit forever?

That fixes yer end. You, Maudy, will ye swear ye'll hang onto John for all comin' time and make him a good, true, honest, up-an'-up wife under the penalties prescribed by law fer sech cases in an' for this territory? That you are lawfully seized in fee simple and free from all incumbrances and have good right to so bargain and convey to said grantee, yourself, your heirs? Then by the power invested in me I announce ye man and wife, and legalize ye to remain as sech for ever, and ye stand committed till the fees and costs in the case be paid in full and may God have mercy on yer souls.

That'll be worth about a dollar and fifty cents!

Sunday Meeting

On Sundays at church meeting, when you got a church built, there would be a motley crew, women dressed in deerskins, traders, half-breeds, Christian Indians, women in neat homespun, starched and washed, for the pioneer also brought the Saturday night bath to the wilderness. A minister reports that from the altar one Sunday he could see through the window Indians covered with blood dancing around long poles from which hung fifty bloody scalps. He could do nothing but recommend the prayers of the congregation for these unfortunate beings.

Swap

There was little cash. When you wanted something you had to swap. Trading became a business with many ramifications, dexterous turns, and sinister risks, and a man had to know how to do it. A man wanted to buy a fifty-dollar horse, and he had no money. He found that Martin Sly owed him nine dollars, Jessie six, Hoyt ten, Ishmael seven, Philip twelve, Harper fourteen, and Righteous Mean eight—sixty-six dollars in all, but none of them had cash.

So I squared myself for a regular up-and-down trade. I found
the squire superintending repairs on the milldam. "Well, Squire,
how do you flourish?" "Pretty smart," says he. "You're early out
this morning—what's to pay?" "I must have a horse. Have you
any on hand?" "Wal, hitch yer beast and we'll take a look
around." He took me to the herd and asked me if there was any
I fancied. "I don't want a fancy animal so much as a sound,
steady, serviceable thing." "There's a beast'll suit you exactly,"
he said, pointing to a sedate roan mare. "What's her price?"
"Wal, I ought to get fifty dollars, but I might take less. How
are you goin' to pay me?" "I can't give you cash—will you
trade?" "Oh, I reckon, but you'll hev to allow me fifty dollars
in trade." "What sort of pay do you want? I might perhaps give
you a little cash." "Wal, I don't know what I want most. If you
could get me a wagon I guess we could trade. I'd like a new
one." "But a new one costs seventy dollars, not fifty." "I know
it. But if you get Charles Cain to make me a right good one, I'll
pay the difference." "Agreed—I'll see what I can do. Good morning." "Stop! Ain't you goin' to take the mare along? You may
hev her now if you're a mind to." "But suppose I can't get the
wagon, what then?" "Oh, we'll fix it somehow!"

A halter was put on her head and away I went to the town
and rode up to the carpenter's door. "Good morning, Mr. Cain."
"Good morning, sir. How do you rise?" "Have you got any
wagons on hand?" "No, sir." Then after a pause, "Do you want
one?" "Yes, how will you trade for a good wagon?" "Sorry to
say, I can't do it. I'm mighty badly off for the specie right now.
Couldn't make a man an ax helve without cash down. Been
making a gross of plows and I owe for iron."

This would be kind of discouraging to the beginner. There
was another carpenter, but when I started off Cain yelled, "The
day's young enough for you to wait a leetle. What trade could
you turn out?" "What do you want most?" "Wal, let me see, a
wagon will cost, wal, I guess we can make you a right good one
for sixty-eight dollars. Wal, I want a good awl badly, and a thousand shingles, a half-dozen sheep, some winder glass, and some
smith work and some teamin' and a ton of timothy, and some
things at the store: leather, nails, and a whole lot of notions.
And see hyar, couldn't you scare me up a dozen pork barrels? If
you can turn me out sech things as these I don't know but we
may make a trade on't yet."

I took down the wagon-maker's wants and set forth. Well, Harper's due bill would supply the store goods. Dr. Gorham had a shingle machine and I could take a day's teaming on behalf of Ishmael. So here was thirty-three dollars' worth certain.

I now made my way to Jessie's, which lay northwest. "Have you any sheep to spare?" "No, I would rather buy than sell. What else?" "Could you let me have some pork barrels?" "Wal. I think I can make a turn on that." By "making a turn" he meant that by trading with someone else he could get what was wanted.

Off I set then in the direction of home. I stopped at Martin Sly's, an offhand Yankee, one of those hardheaded men who will speak out their mind if the sky should fall. He was helping his old woman make soap. "How do you do?" I said. "Never better in my life, rugged as a bar, the Maker be praised. Now you're out on some express, I'll warrant." "Settling up some small accounts, Mr. Sly." "Then you'll be comin' on me, too. Do you want cash? If you do, I can't let you have it nohow. That's a hardy-lookin' mare. How will you trade against two colts?" "If you can't give me cash, Mr. Sly, I'm willing to take such trade as I need. Could you give me a good cow?" "By God, I could give you the smartest critter along in these prairies." "Is she a good milker?" "Wal, now, she gives a right smart chance of milk, don't she, wife? Take him down the crick-bottom and let him see Stubtail." "Does she want a tail?" "Wal, she wants it but she don't want it; there ain't mor'n a foot of it, but she's sech a spry thing she don't want a tail. Go 'long, gal, and show him the critter." I stood and looked at the man, who maintained the utmost gravity of countenance. At last he broke out in a loud laugh. "Wal, I'm only jokin'. Come along and I'll show you a *good* cow." I picked out a good-looking milk animal for which the charge was nine dollars, the amount of my claim.

The next man was Hoyt, on the prairie. He said, "I can't give you nothing. I hain't got a red cent worth more than the law allows me—now you cain't help yourself, can you?"

I still wanted twelve dollars of the price of the wagon. After dinner I went to see Righteous Mean, who paid me down in ready cash for what he owed me. I still lacked four dollars.

Going home I met Farmer Williams. "Well, how're things going? Hev ye got yer horse?" "Yes, but I haven't enough money yet." He pulled out his purse and gave me the money. "Pay me when you can."

I now rode off to town, told the squire his wagon would be forthcoming, communicated my success to Cain, and after some further troubles squared up matters, got the wagon to its destination, was paid the difference in cash, and found my mare a good and serviceable animal.

Refugee Seed

It is now not a barbarous multitude pouncing upon old and decrepit empires; not a violent destruction of tribes accompanied by all the horrors of general destruction; but we see the vigorous elements of all nations, peaceably congregating and mingling together on virgin soil . . . led together by the irresistible attraction of free and broad principles; undertaking to commence a new era in the history of the world, without first destroying the results of progress of past periods; undertaking to found a new cosmopolitan nation without marching over the dead bodies of slain millions.

Thus was founded the great colony of free humanity, which has not old England alone, but the world for its mother country. And in the colony of free humanity, whose mother is the world, they establish the republic of equal rights, where the title of manhood is the title of citizenship. My friends, if I had a thousand tongues, and a voice strong as the thunder of heaven, they would not be sufficient to impress upon your minds forcibly enough the greatness of this idea, the overshadowing glory of this result. This was the dream of the truest friends of man from the beginning; for this the noblest blood of martyrs has been shed; for this has man waded through seas of blood and tears. There it is now; there it stands, the fabric in all the splendor of reality.

—CARL SCHURZ

COCKLEBURS MIGRATED TO THE NORTH COUN-
try in the wool of sheep. Dandelion seed was brought in

women's aprons. Wheat came in the lining of a hat or the seam of a coat. Ideas also migrated in the hearts, gnarled and saddened by the growing brutality of the rising industrial cities.

America has not known how to evaluate the folk cultures that came from Europe; they are an underground stream, enriching, revitalizing, strengthening the fiber of the human spirit in a way that has never been measured.

Those of all nationalities who came to the North Star Country brought with them strains and tensions which would persist; but the long trek and tragedy of their migration indelibly impressed in the culture the dream of freedom which led them on, and still does. They brought it along with Baltic wheat and Croatian folk songs, Finnish forest lore and Scandinavian thrift, and it is still here, embittered, strengthened by the long winters and the incessant struggle— persisting, inextinguishable.

I see no class distinction here, not as in Sweden, where the working people are rabble and the lazy gentlemen are called better folk.

Neither is my cap worn out from lifting it in the presence of "gentlemen."

The hired man and maid eat at the husbandman's table. "Yes sir," says the master to the hand. "Yes, sir," says the hand to the master. Porters and coachmen are dressed like gentlemen. Pastor, judge, and banker carry market baskets.

Servants are not bound for a fixed time.

Nobody needs to hold his hat in his hand for anyone else.

We are free to move without certificate from the employer or pastor. A man can leave his job any time he wants!

A little boy said to his mother when she reproved him for eating forbidden cake, "Why, Mother, aren't we in a free country now?"

You can say "du" to anyone here. You can walk into a store and take off your hat. You can say "Hello, Pete," instead of "Good morning, Mr. Banker Gyllenvans."

Sometimes I am even called master here.

There is a higher value here on an intelligent workman than on all titles, bands, and stars that fall from Stockholm during an entire year. It will not do here to be haughty and idle, for that is not the fashion in this country; for it is to use the ax, the spade, and the saw, and not to be a lazy body. We believe that all the workers had better depart and leave the lords and parasites to their fate. There is room here for all of Sweden's inhabitants.

Blizzard, cataclysm, wind and fire, make cultural patterns and festivals, songs and mores of future action. So does exhaustion of soil and forests in a single generation—diminishing resources in the environment, and the swift pattern of shift between groups, nationalities, and habits of interaction and human impact; so does the rapid rise and fall of cities, of one industry and another, of new tools—a man's hand curving around a new lever and forgetting field craft and handcraft and woodcraft for metal, speed, and dynamos. And the swift throttling of absentee ownership, the shift back to the East, so that today the major part of the land is owned by Eastern capital—this also makes a change in the person and the community.

But in the swift, incredible panorama of the last hundred years still the "idea" of which Carl Shurz speaks persists. The West became the center of democratic ideas both before and after the Civil War; land ownership, Jeffersonian democracy, people thought, was the basis for economic democracy, and the Homestead Act is evidence of their demand for a direct relationship to the government.

Puck Moses

He was a card, they all said, came from Stavanger in Norway, a sailor, tradesman, friend of Quakers, dissenter from state and church, pathfinder, colonizer, frontiersman, legend.

A pixy Pied Piper, piping them across the dangerous ocean, in burning ships, over terror and loneliness. With never a home of his own, piping thousands into the wilderness, into the land of Canaan.

People who never saw him had tales to tell. Never worked for anybody, they said, never laid a shingle for himself or turned a wheel. Worked only for others, he did, with a silver shilling in his pocket which he never had to spend all his life.

You were apt to see him anywhere at the docks, along strange roads; a knock at the door and he would be there, hat in hand, peering sideways as if it were painful for him to focus on anything less than fifty miles away. It's Cleng Peerson—they'd say—come in and welcome. He was a letter from home. He was a drink of water. He would lie on the bed, his heels in the air, knitting, and his mouth full of tales to make your ears grow longer.

Why, once, he said, he was sitting under a tree and an Indian half-breed offered to exchange the land he sat on for his clothes and the pipe he was smoking. Cleng refused, saying he liked his pipe and the other man's clothes might have lodgers. That spot he didn't trade for turned out to be Chicago, today worth more than the whole of Norway!

He led them on and kept on walking. He went back to Norway talking at meetings of the crofters, and returned in the sloop *Restaurationen* with fifty-two persons, sailing from Stavanger on July 4, 1825, thus beginning the great wave of Scandinavian immigration. The Sloopers came. The Quakers came, following the first Norsky on the prairies piping a new land, his skin burnt, the sun squint in his eyes, distance in his face, the treadmill swing to his horizon walk. He thought nothing of walking fifteen hundred miles, his sack on his shoulder, liking the sun slanting on a man bound off alone.

Yes, sir, he was a card, begged from the rich to give to the poor, never owned a rod of land—a troll, an imp, a tiny speck on the horizon getting bigger, the sun in his hair, the smell of woodsmoke on him, berries and prairie flowers in his hands.

He pied them in.

He walked on.

Most likely he just kept on walking until he disappeared over the thin horizon, the wind blowing him into the West.

Ole, Spokesman of the Poor

Ole Rynning brought another group farther west to La Salle County, Illinois, coming by steamer on the Hudson, by canalboat to Detroit, and thence to Chicago where land speculators talked them into buying a malarial swamp south of the city.

That winter amid the dying Ole wrote his *True Account of America* . . . , advising who should come to this country where "everything is designed to maintain the natural freedom and equality of man." He also was dying, but his book was believed, read by peasant and commoner all over Norway.

Hans Ole, as they called him, was known in the old country as "the friend of the people, the spokesman of the poor and one whose mouth never knew deceit." Writing from a log-hewn cot in the forsaken colony, he described before his own death the prairies, the wild game, the bees, fruit, rivers, and said, "Bring some seed with you of the Norwegian birch and fir." He did not tell how the entire colony had died that year or fled the swamp sickness. He saw the future and he knew it would work. He told them how to get free land, and that a section of each town was always school land and common property of the township.

He made a list of what to bring. Four or five dollars if possible, fur and clothing of *radmel,* a *bakstehelle,* a round iron plate for baking *flatbrød,* a spinning wheel and hand mill, and some tobacco to sell. Tools of every kind and good rifles. A little brandy vinegar and a couple of bottles of wine, and a cathartic, and sulphur powder for the itch. Hoffman's drops, spirit of camphor, linen for a change, salt-water soap, and a good fine comb.

Those who should not come, he wrote, were: "1. Drunkards, who will be detested and will perish miserabiy. 2. Those who neither can work nor have sufficient money to carry on a business. I don't advise any persons to go un-less they understand at least how to use oxen, or have learned a trade."

Hans Ole died that spring at the thaw and was buried in a coffin carved from a whole tree, in an unmarked grave in the swamp. But the book passed along the streets of Norway and was read by his people, and they came to the land of Canaan.

Feudal Lord

Nils Otto Tank was the son of an aristocrat, a friend of kings. In a Saxony hut he became a convert to a Moravian pastor. He came walking through America, six feet four, a blue-eyed Norseman, talking and teaching the doctrine of John Huss, speaking to the Negroes, founding schools and workshops.

In 1850 he showed up in Milwaukee. It was said he brought a billion in gold. In the pineries at the mouth of the Fox River, he founded the colony of Ephraim, the "very fruitful."

He sent for his library of five thousand volumes. He estab-lished the first Norwegian academy in America. Communes and halls of learning flourished beside the wilderness rivers.

Long Prayer

Eric Janson burned Luther in effigy in the old country. Hunted like a wolf, he fled over the mountains, across the black ocean to the buffalo grass of the north country, the long column of devotees winding through the dusk after him to build a church where the oxen lingered.

There the colony was built, where there would be "no poor, and no oppressed, a true division of labor and sharing of products." When the harvest ended they walked through the yellow fields, hands joined, faces lifted, singing. A harvest feast was held in the Long Hall.

Eric could pray two hours hand-running.

Black Forest Village

Led by Reverend Ambrose Oschwald, from the Black Forest of Germany in 1854 came a whole village—a parish of one hundred and thirteen souls migrating in search of freedom and "self expression and home life through the communistic idea of settlement."

To St. Nazianz they came, in the kettle ranges of the west shore of Lake Michigan, and there they built their church. Daily they labored. At night discussed the world. A new community arose in stone and wood; the married lived in the village and the unmarried in the Brother House and Sister House. After the death of Father Oschwald, private holdings of property were given to the children. The village still stands, with shrines and flowers, the housewives still remembering Father Oschwald's medicinal magic with herbs.

Without Rum

Arthur Brisbane, Senior, heard François Fourier in Paris. Horace Greeley became his disciple. As early as 1843 in Kenosha, Wisconsin, Fourier's social theories were discussed heatedly. During the depression of 1837 Warren Chase took the rolling land in the "Cerese" valley of Wisconsin, founded a colony in the wilderness after Fourier's concept, one of the few to prosper in the United States.

With nineteen men and a boy, they went out to tame what they romantically called "Ceres, the Goddess of Grain." They worked under a foreman who made weekly accounts, paid each member according to his skill and industry. In the evenings in the Long House they met for music, lectures, cotillions, "without rum, vulgarity, or profanity." Also lectures, classes, and discussions. There was much talk of collective living, the economic ills that created poverty; and what, where, and whither was the Manifest Destiny of our country?

Surrounded by the inflowing tide of farm settlement and one of the growing industrial empires of the world, they disbanded after six years, all wealthy, to wend their individualistic ways alone. Forty thousand dollars were divided among the members, besides the land they had successfully cultivated and the Long House and the living quarters.

During the recent depression, ironically, the old Long House was used for families on relief, the ills they had discussed recurring after a hundred years.

That Tremendous Dutchman

"You are an awful fellow, I understand your power now," **Lincoln** said to **Carl Schurz** after a speech in Springfield during his first campaign for the presidency. "You are a tremendous Dutchman."

A Negro preacher was so accustomed to hearing the copperheads inveigh against the "damn Dutch" because of their passionate partisanship for the Abolitionist cause, that he prayed, "And may the good Lord bless the damn Dutch!"

The German forty-eighters contributed to the struggle of the Civil War. They raised the ideological level of the Middle West, giving it voice, met with the Republican committee in Chicago, nipped in the bud the secessionist plot against the border states of the Northwest.

Carl Schurz, whose eloquence contributed to Lincoln's election in '61 and in '64, was born in the atmosphere of the eighteenth- and nineteenth-century revolutions, two months after Waterloo, a dozen miles above Cologne on the banks of the Rhine—a true child of the War of Liberation.

He was a student at the University of Bonn when the Frankfurt Assembly of '48 tried to organize a constitutional federal monarchy. With his master, Friedrich Hecker, he joined the insurgent students and radicals who had taken up arms in South Germany. Defeated by the preponderance of Prussian bayonets, Schurz fled safely to Switzerland, went back to rescue Hecker, and finally both came to America where "these new ideas will find their soil, and many have already taken root."

Schurz and his family settled in Wisconsin, but he was impatient of buying and selling land while he waited for revolution in Germany. When the Civil War broke in America, he became active in the formation of the Radical Republican party, fought the Know-Nothing and Nativist movements, became an American, and supported the "good, good Lincoln," as he called him.

Lincoln sent him to Spain as American Ambassador, but after the Battle of Bull Run Schurz could not see a Spaniard smile without suspecting ridicule of the Union cause, and asked to be recalled. He joined his fellow-revolutionists and became a brigadier general in the Army. In '64 he toured the country for the Union Party and Lincoln, and now he became an American legend, an orator:

> I am an American by choice, not by chance. . . . Ideals are like stars. You will not succeed to touch them with your hands but like the seafaring man on the desert of water, you choose them as your guide and follow where they may lead you. . . . This faith lives not only in the heart of the man of thought, it hovers over the plough of the farmer, over the anvil of the mechanic, over the desk of the merchant; it is the very milk with which the American mother nourishes her baby. This faith has put our armies into the field and set our navy afloat.

In the darkest days of the war there was a story told of Carl Schurz playing Beethoven to a tired and sad Lincoln in a room of the White House—so that the tired leader slept.

Co-operative

The Danes and the Finns brought communities of co-operation to the North Star Country. The Danish community founded by Ludwig Mosbaek at Askov was for homes, not for speculation or to make money. They did not expect to move on, but to live and raise their children there; which they did, establishing successful co-operatives, raising rutabagas, founding Danish and Finnish societies and churches, and great singing societies. "We have dispossessed nobody. We took poor land and made it fertile by intensive farming," they say. There are bookcases in the rutabaga farmhouses with Marx and Lenin on the shelves.

Jim Hill brought the Finns to the Mesabi and the timber country, where and when he needed them; eager enough they were to leave the poverty of their homeland and the wave of oppression and terror that followed the Finnish revolution—defeated by anti-democratic forces aided by the German Junkers. Many of them, blacklisted in the range strikes of 1908 and 1916, squatted in tar-paper shacks, their meager farms marked by the pole-anchored birchbark or shake-shingle roofs, the gumdrop haystacks toothpicked to the ground, and beside each house the inevitable *sauna.* For the Finn starts building with the *sauna,* or bathhouse, where he may even live until his house is built. The steam in these Finnish baths comes from pouring water over hot stones, three steps at the side grading the heat. The bather beats his body with white cedar branches.

When the Finns first came, these were said to be houses of witchcraft. The Finn is silent in a strange environment and has a deep suspicion of government and exploitation. He brought with him his own culture and rapidly began to create plays, poems, novels, in Finnish but about his experience in the new world. Being the most completely dispossessed of his own culture, probably more than any other nationality, he produced—still untranslated, for the most part—a wealth of literature of the new life. He had his mining and lumberjack poets, his own newspaper in Superior. You will find circulating on the range worn-out, threadbare current Finnish literature.

Like the German Socialists in Milwaukee, the Finns created a socialist culture on the range, with its festivals, songs. You can go into a Finnish co-operative and see the picture of Marx or Lenin beside that of Governor Olson or Benson, or Franklin D. Roosevelt.

At one time, before the Pinkerton Detective Agency and United States Steel broke the range, there were May Day parades which drained the small range towns of men, women, and children, who walked for miles singing along the road, converging at Virginia where they met at the Socialist Opera House—now the Range Cooperative Creamery—from which a red flag and an American flag flew side by side.

Man Alive

The ideal of the West was its emphasis upon the worth and possibilities of the common man, its belief in the right of every man to rise to the full measure of his own nature, under conditions of social mobility. Western democracy was no theorist's dream. It came, stark and strong and full of life, from the American forest.

—FREDERICK TURNER

Others appeal to history; an American appeals to prophecy and with Malthus in one hand and a map of the back country in the other, he boldly defies us to a comparison with America as she is to be!

—LONDON PERIODICAL

EVERY MAN'S FORTRESS WAS HIS CABIN. HE didn't believe in too much government. The state didn't worry him; he believed in the future, in his own house and farm.

What did you talk about in the long winter nights?

Oh, we spoke about the future, said one. We planned it all out. We invented things. We saw how it could be.

A man came to the log-rollings, the house raisings, the husking bees, the apple-parings, the camp meetings, and

136

the association meetings of squatters to protect themselves against speculators. He got sallow and tall from forest living and hard as nails, with muscles of long hickory. He got beaten and his skin was pocked and pitted with wind and cold and heat and sand. He believed in backwoods democracy, in open meeting, in stump speaking, in everybody knowing everyone else and being equal, in going places all the time, in speaking out your mind no matter how humble. Men in those days didn't want a cabin too close, or a man to bother them in the morning, or a law to tether them, or a state to impeach its motives and stay their hand—to nip and bark at their heels. They were against monopoly and vested titles and doors closed to them.

They also took something from the wilderness: from the Indian the keen eye down the gunsight to the heart of bird, hare, and buffalo; the color of butternut tree; strength of woodland milk and the golden sweet milk of corn.

And what the weather did to Eastern man as he came West is a story. Gales, winds, cold, the high thunderheads, the heat siroccos, the Indian-summer winey air made a man with legs of oak, breast of birch, whetting skull and skin with wind and sun, the weathered farmer, half gargoyle and half seraph. It made him tremendous in size, tough as a gut string with as sweet music, wily as the west wind, alternating as sun and thunder.

Country Store

Opinion, deep conviction, the warp and woof of a nation was woven at the country store; after the harvest, in the nippy days, you could gather around the pot-bellied stove, mixing talk and the smell of the molasses barrels, the tang of vinegar. Farmers, lumbermen, rivermen, sat in winter shifting the cud with the talk about old Andy Jackson, and the agents and traders who went to Washington, shined up to the ladies, and came back with land grants.

You could talk long and slow, accurately hitting your favorite crack, smelling the grinding coffee, or if you were a regular customer you could take a herring or a cracker or a sliver of Eastern cheese. Each man had his own seat fitted to his foundations. Each one had his opinion stubborn and strong:

Maybe we'll join the United States back east, maybe we won't.

The people got to expect, calculate, reckon, and guess—and be a jump ahead of speculators, grasshoppers, tornado, and the mortgage.

In a new country there has got to be new ways. The one who can git along and not be got has got to figure out new ways.

Did ya hear the one about the old couple wanting to go down river with a captain who was a religious man? They went to a old hell-raisin' cap in St. Paul and said they heard he was a religious man. "The hell you have," the Cap said, and when he wrote home his letters burned up the mail bags. "Get out, you blankety-blank so-and-so's! More lunatics come to me than any dash-dash captain on the river."

The old lady whispered to her old man, "He's not very religious, do you think?" The old man said, "Well, I dunno. This is out west, Mama. He swears, but he looks like a man to depend on in a storm. I guess religion out here has got to be kind of sketchy and useful. We'll go by his boat and if he don't swear any harder than he just done, mebbe Providence will let him squeeze through on the down trip and sink him when he comes up!"

Measuring two ax handles in his stocking feet he built a town in an hour.

Nerves like an ox, sinews like a whale, it was little he feared on earth or beneath it.

The People want men.

I can shoot a barrel going downhill straight into the bunghole.

That's nothing. I can shoot a bumblebee in a thistle at 300 feet!

We're full of jackass brandy, scamper juice, and mare's milk. We're fox fire and lightning. We're man alive, ready to green up, sure to make a die of it.

It is glorious to see a people stirred at heart and brain; when they are moved nature has no power like it. Their power is greater than the sweep of the wind, stronger than the roar of the tempest. Their voice is the voice of God on earth. Spread out the tones of their thunder and it becomes a lullaby for children.

To a crowd that pressed too closely on a political procession the leader cried, "Make way for the representatives of the people."

"Make way yourself," a voice thundered back. "We *are* the People."

Camp Meeting

To a gently sloping cleared ground, with the trees meeting overhead, the people came from all directions in the wilderness morning for the opening of the camp meeting. An immense congregation of wagons was drawn up alongside and others arrived every minute through the timber; the women moved amongst the green in their gowns and shawls and sunbonnets and the hum of voices; dogs barked and children shouted, with the sound of hammers making the rough pulpit of wood and the wooden tents for the use of the preachers—who might be as many as twelve in number, coming from all over. In front of the pulpit was the mourners' bench, a square space enclosed with a stout railing and strewn with straw. Behind were rough planks for the audience, and still behind these, the hickory poles covered with blankets and bedquilts where they would camp out. For the night fires, a dozen raised platforms of forked sticks with earth and ashes on top.

The first preacher would rise and speak to the people, who had brought with them their loneliness, the long defeat, the silence, the terrors of storm and cataclysm. The rustic preacher called down upon them the blessings of the Immortal Father, deprecated the wrath due to sin, implored forgiveness and a new heart for all and a tractable spirit to bear the sufferings of this world, and promised a right judgment in the end, an earnest purpose. The tall oaks lifted their arms into the pure sky forming their own cathedral arch. The preacher spoke of death, and the women who had not been allowed to weep—without time in the duties of the day, without place in the confines of the cabin—with the eyes of the yet living on them, now wept for the bodies they had buried in the prairie—they could now weep and their men sat rigid, afraid to look at them, the words forming in the lonely breast and the break of despair gathering in the hard gnarled hearts like the boles of wounded trees.

"In the darkness, death is near, and, oh, to go to that happy shore, to cross the River Jordan (How many rivers have we crossed to get here?), to enter that Kingdom where all is peace, where you will meet your dear ones—over the darkness of the ocean, oh, where lost, torn, forgotten? Oh, remember, how is it with you, O sinner? Who is to be your guide and comforter through the dark valley? If there is any hungry, thirsty, lonely, longing soul who has this day resolved to turn his face heavenward, let him now come forward and witness before all men the good confession."

And then they sang: Come home! Come home! Jesus is tenderly, tenderly calling. Calling for you and for me— And for those who listened in the wilderness and heard no call but the bluejay and heard no voice, this was like a freshet of spring, a madness of breaking.

They begin to come shamedly or frenziedly to the altar amid the cries of "Glory, glory, remember your sins!" All the preachers call at once, exhorting, singing, loosing their silver tongues, "Renounce your sins!"

The thunder of song, the roaring of the preachers, the excitement and ejaculations of the people long suppressed rise as the dusk falls. The great congregation, the babel of voices, the body without voice through long winters, the cry without solace, the fear and the brutality of frontier life, released at last, purified of madness.

"I wouldn't give a straw for a camp meetin' without noise," one of the neighbors would say.

"Wait till night, then you'll hear somethin'—speakin' in tongues, strange jerks, and dancin'— The night's the best time."

Carpenter

There was Jacob from Hungary who came to North Dakota across the plains from St. Paul on the first railroad, after a journey of three months with his wife and three children. Jacob was a carpenter, a good cabinet-maker, and he saw the flat prairies with only a few ash trees; when they came to the end of the line they stepped off into snow to their knees, into the biting forty-mile wind, and the friend who was to meet them did not come. For the first time he became discouraged in a strange land, unable to speak the language, and his children and his wife looking at him, asking, "Where? What now, Jacob? We look to you."

A man came and asked in Hungarian, "Who are you? Are you an emigrant? Are you Jacob? Your friend cannot come, as he is snowed in. The roads are impassable. You stay with me."

When asked if he had room for them all the man said, "I will make room. I was glad when I came from the old country, when someone sheltered me."

Jacob became the village carpenter and there are people today who can tell anything that Jacob built. They can tell the barns—so solid they have grown like a living body and become part of the ground—and the houses that have to be torn down bit by bit.

"Look at the chisel handles," he used to say, "to see what

kind of a workman a man is." He could not write, but he wrote in wood, and you can read the scroll of a good workman, a craftsman.

He could sharpen a saw from heel to point in graduated perfection. He always worked wood well with the grain. "Don't brush a colt's fur the wrong way," he would say. "Plane a piece of wood with the grain, smooth, clean, and fine." He made fine staircases for the mansions that grew up swiftly and were deserted and are still standing—mitred moldings, handrails, banister bars. There is in the things he made the spirit of growth and aspiration. He always said, "Learn everything from a tree. You don't have to have any other book but a tree. It will tell you all you need to know. It grows from the bottom with the greatest pressure there, dignity and ease come between, and the tree diminishes toward the top, where there is to be decoration if you want it."

He handled all his life the lathe, the center and the spiral bit, the brace, the ax, saw, claw hammer, small augers, mallet gouges, gimlets, and the bradawl. He had in his toolbox the chisel, the iron square, the rule, and the chalk line.

In his early buildings you can see the wood pins, squared off neat as you please with an ax.

When he came to this country he had to get used to the woodcraft of the open fields: how to hang a gate, which is an art in itself; how to make roofs for the prairies, strong king posts to hold against the wind; roof trusses, slopes, and splays, balanced and low to let the wind draw off.

When building stopped, Jacob became a coffin-maker and a cooper, making the best barrels in the country, iron-hooped ones and also wood-hooped, without nails—wet and shrunk in such a way that the hoops never came off. Then tin and galvanized iron came in and barrel-making was not wanted, so there were only coffins.

"It matters not how proud or rich a person may be; he

will get four planed boards and five feet of earth on top,"
he said. But undertakers came in and he could no longer
make pine and oak coffins.

He did not like business, but he took to building a house
for the pleasure of building it; he and his wife would move
into it and then sell it for a small sum and build another.

It can be safely said that Jacob did more building and has
more monuments to his skill—to the beauty and the harbor
of a snug house and the great burgeoning of a full barn—
than any man in the north.

Other people made money, took it away.

Jacob was one of the builders. He just had two hands, a
level head, and his tools.

Times got bad and he raised bees but it was not in his
line; and he disappeared, but his work remains and neighbors point out to you the things he built which stand against
time.

Wagon-maker

This is the story of a good Norwegian wagon-maker. He
came to America from Norway, started with forty dollars
and an opinion about how a wagon should be made to be as
strong as an oak axle.

He gave his life to the wagon. His father had a blacksmith shop where he made plows, using horsepower for
grinding, the blindfolded horse moving around the huge
grindstone, the sparks flying. He was a very careful plowmaker, always studying to make a plow better so it would
run true, a balance between the point and the heel and the
beam handles. He wanted a perfect run of the plow, and it
was all handwork.

His son thought of nothing else but making a strong and
beautiful wagon; every triviality was beautiful to him, down

to the last little painted scrolls on the wagon body. Even his daughter became a wagon-maker. He had no art or religion but the making of a good wagon, strong, useful, and enduring.

At one time he heard wagon men trying to save money, saying they would make one first-class spoke and one second-class spoke, alternately, and save the difference.

None of that for the Norwegian workman.

He was a powerful, strong man, built like his father the blacksmith.

When you meet one of his wagons on the road, and you do to this day, you say, "What a good and fine-looking wagon—it does not roll and is well put up and solid on the ground." A man has, through all these years, saved a hub of one of the first wagons made by this pioneer, and the hub standing now in a museum seems to say, "See how strong I am put up! See how durable and how beautiful he made me!"

Live Yankee

"I calculate I couldn't drum up a trade with you today?"

"I calculate you're right, you can't."

"Wal, you needn't get huffy. Now here's a dozen real razor-strops worth two dollars and fifty cents. You can have 'em for two dollars."

"I tell you I don't want any of your trash, so you'd better get along."

"Wal, now I declare! I'll bet you five dollars if you can make me an offer for these here strops we'll have a trade yet."

"Done!" They both made a deposit of five dollars apiece with a spectator.

"Wal, what do I hear?"

"I'll give you two cents, peddler."

"They're your'n," and the peddler pockets the stakes. "I calculate a joke's a joke, and if you don't want them strops I'll trade back."

"You're not as bad a chap as you're cracked up to be after all. Here are the strops; give me the money."

"There it is," and the Yankee passed the two cents. "A trade's a trade and you're wide-awake and in good earnest. I guess the next time you trade you'll do a little better than to buy razor-strops." And away he went with his strops and the wager amid the shouts of the laughing crowd around the store.

The Yankee culture in the North Star Country is indelible. They were persistent, practical, and they kept coming. Merchants, peddlers, artisans, millwrights, lean, driven, "hell-bent for election," they started schools, built churches, swapped for whatever you had. These definitions of a Yankee are taken entirely from Northwest newspapers between 1850 and 1860 and most of them had Yankee editors:

A Yankee, green as a pine, sharp as a briar, polished his wits keener than a needle. This is a live Yankee.

A Yankee is self-relying, prying, with love of piety, prosperity, notoriety, and temperance societies. He is a bragging, striving, swapping, wrestling, musical, quizzical, astronomical, poetical, criminal sort of character whose manifest destiny is to spread civilization to the remotest corners of the earth.

Yankees are always labor-saving, haggard, nervous, of a dead-leaf color. They are always crying—screw up your courage and pitch in.

The Yankee can do almost any and everything. He's an animal made of hard knocks and of the stick out and up and dressed school. His hand can turn to this and that and mostly to his pocket. He can preach, keep store, shoe horses, peddle, go to war, teach school, doctor, love the girls, start saw mills and singing schools, make steamboats, railroads, gravestones, an eleven-pronged pitchfork, patent medicine, and churches; cultivate the earth, go on the billowing ocean, mount the air, make laws, cheat, swear, and lie a granite rock out of countenance; go to Congress and the uttermost parts of the earth, to be the hopeful father of huge families, edit newspapers, write books, recite the Bible from Genesee to December. A great inventor, the Yankee, well, he is. Trade with him and see, and the above isn't a priming to what he can do when he gets started.

Clocks, nutmegs, and whatnots are a Yankee crop. If you have
cash he's glad to sell; if not he'll always swap. For he was a born
merchant's son, a Yankee trader bold. He swapped his whistle
for a knife when he was two years old. No matter where his
home may be, what flag he may unfurl, he'll manage by some
cute device, to whittle through the world!

He was good mixings for the new man and has his part
in the makings of a middle-border culture, with its strong
speech of double negatives, its new face with the laconic
squint of horizon people: the foxy prairie folk god with a
new unraveling of melancholy; a sharper edge to the ax and
his mind; the myth that was expressed in the tall man walking the White House at night in his night shirt, who wore
a shawl and a tall hat and a tall joke with the sly double talk
of a new country; the understatement; all the Yankee mixtures which were a medicine bag, stirred with many "nar-
wiggin," dreams, Irish tales, refugee songs, making the backwoods parable, the ax handle and sharp-bit language; never
answering a question direct; a man slyly digging himself to
obscurity like the prairie dogs in a dust storm, scrambling
down a hole in the air.

Are there any noblemen in your country, Jonathon?
Nary a one and I am one of them!
What kind of country is there where you come from?
Mixed and extended, land and water.
What kind of weather do you have?
Long spells of weather. Frequently!
Is there water there?
There is water scattered about. You'll also find it in whiskey.
What kind of buildings do they have there?
Allegoric, Ionic, anti-bolero, log and slab. People live mostly
out of doors in houses so low the chimneys stick through the
roofs.
What do people do?
Some work. Some laze. Several are drunkards.
Is the living cheap there?
Five cents a glass, water thrown in.

What do people do for a living?
Work. Shave notes. Fish, hunt and steal. If hard pushed buy and sell town property, corner lots preferably.

Hello, traveler, you appear to be traveling.
Yes, I always am when on a journey.
I think I've seen you somewhere.
Very likely. I've often been there.
And pray what may your name be?
It might be but it ain't by a long shot.
Do you have something to sell?
Yes, a whitstone.
I thought so; you're the sharpest blade!

The Hutchinson family were also Yankees. A famous troupe of family singers from New Hampshire, they arrived in St. Paul in November, 1855, gave a concert, then left in two wagons drawn by four horses for what was then known as the Hassan River. The first number of their program always introduced them as:

David, Noah, Andrew, Zepha, Caleb, Joshua and Jesse,
Judson, Rhoda, John and Asa and Abby are our names.
We're the sons of Mary, of the tribe of Jesse,
And we now address ye, with our native mountain songs.

Liberty is our motto, and we'll sing as freedman ought to,
Till it rings o'er glen and grotto, from the old Granite state,
Men should love one another, nor let hatred smother;
Every man's a brother, and our country is the world.

Stopping at the town that is now called Hutchinson, they drew up a constitution, laid out ground for school houses, libraries, forbade liquor, bowling alleys, and gambling. The constitution also said that "women shall enjoy equal rights with men and shall have the privilege of voting."

In their tours of America and the world they began their program with a lecture on Minnesota, "of Hassan valley where we have raised more good sound plump wheat than our fathers and ten brothers have raised on the sterile hills of New England in a lifetime." The program following would include: "The Congressional Song of Ten Dollars a Day," "The Freeman's Song," "The Kingdom of King Alcohol," "My Nation Shall be all Mankind and Every Land My Own," and Abolitionists' songs like "The Slave's Appeal" and "The Little Topsy Song." During the Civil War General McClellan tried to have them thrown out of the Union lines because they were singing "The Battle Cry of Freedom," and the mighty freedom song:

Ho, the Emancipation, rides magnetic through the nation,
Bearing on the train its story, Liberty a nation's glory.
Roll it along! Roll it along! Roll it along through the nation,
Freedom's car—Emancipation!

"I never knew a man who loved to sing or who had such power to make others sing," a later inhabitant of Hutchinson said of Asa. "He was a minstrel of the world. It was a sight to see him with his long gray beard, his head and arms raised, singing away at the top of his voice. On a train or a boat he could set a crowd of perfect strangers singing away together as loud as they could." It was Asa who composed the music for "Tenting Tonight on the Old Camp Ground."

Han Skall Leva!

Cut and cut the golden oats,
Who shall do the binding?
I shall take my dearest dear
Wherever I shall find him.
I saw him by moonlight last on yester even.
Do thou take thine,
I'll take mine,
One alone we're leaving.
Ha, ha, ha! We will all forsake him!
Peter now must stand alone

Because we didn't take him.
(All point fingers at odd man in center.)
                    —FOLK ROUND DANCE

The Yankee culture in the North Star Country is indelible.
They were persistent, practical, and kept coming. They knew
what they wanted and they got it. But the peoples of the
European countries also influenced the fabric of our life.
They brought with them ancient cultures of shepherds, villages, hills, and plains of old countries; they brought the
poetry, the embroidered peasant village costume of fine
linen, the vivid group dances—Polish-Ukrainian ballet, and
Czechoslovakian and Serbian dances—the singing of the
hymn, ballad, and comic ditty.

It was remarked once by Judge Flandreau of St. Paul that
America had created religions and institutions of government but not one good sauce. The French founded towns
built on Limoges cheese, the Germans on Limburger; Fort
Atkinson, Wisconsin, was the home of the delicatessen introduced by the burghers of the new Rhineland: the pork wurst,
German sausages, roast goose stuffed with noodles, *Apfel-
küchle, Hasenpfeffer, Gefüllte,* and always *Suppen* and
Würstchen. The Scandinavians brought the delicious *smörgåsbord,* a rich varied buffet supper of *kjøttkaker* (Norwegian meat balls flavored with nutmeg, allspice, and
ginger), *rullepølse* (collared beef), *sursild* (pickled herring),
sildesalat, stekt lax, escalloped herring, potato and anchovy
salad, and the special *lefse,* a kind of flatbrød; and for des-
sert, *eplekaker* or *stikkelsbaer pylse* (gooseberry pudding).
The *lutfisk* at suppers of church and club is very delicious;
it is a cod soaked and boiled and served with white sauce
or butter. The special cakes of the Czechs, who raise poppies
for their sweet turnover kolacky rolls, have become part of
North Star Country tradition; the kolacky festival takes place
every year at Montgomery, Minnesota, on September 27. The
special dishes of every nationality for folk and religious cele-

bration have become part of the country, have incalculably enriched the Puritan tables.

The annual events listed each year record the rich gifts of festivity and culture, which the peoples celebrate from old memory and new habitation. There are the wonderful music festivals: that of the Norwegian *a capella* choir in the third week of May, at St. Olaf College in Northfield, Minnesota; the Bach Society Concert in Minneapolis; the Festival of Mennonite Choirs, held at Mountain Lake in May; and the Danish Male Chorus. Music has been a great gift and addition to the hymns of the New Englander and the square dance and the Indian powwow.

Then there are the harvest festivals: raspberry and melon, sweet corn, and lefse fêtes, kolacky and sauerkraut days; the Indian festivals, with the Indian Powwow and Carnival at White Earth in June and the Indian Rice Dance at Milaca in the first week of September, when the rice is knocked into canoes in the swamps. And the work festivals—Lumberjack Day at Stillwater on the St. Croix, where birling and beard-growing contests are held for two days of mighty celebration—the Paul Bunyan Parade at International Falls, and the Bunyan Carnival at Brainard in June, with its big statue along the lake of Paul himself and a paper mock of Babe, the Blue Ox.

But it is the winter festivals and carnivals that mark the region, with the meeting of old and new in the ancient rituals and the more modern ones of the Chamber of Commerce. All over the country the nationalities hold their winter celebrations, variously called fairs, carnivals with snow modeling, dog snow derbies, ski meets, and skating tournaments.

On the range, the day famous in Swedish folk culture as "Luciadagen" ("Lucia Day") has become an annual event. In Sweden this comes around December 13 and opens the winter season with snow sports and country-wide frolic. It is really a fire festival of the north country people, coming from the folk feeling of the preciousness of fire and light when the winter sun falls pale and the evenings strike the northern lights across the zenith, and snow begins to come down over the countryside.

The central ritual of Luciadagen is the crowning of a young girl as the Lucia bride with a crown of flaming candles. It is said that in early times a heifer was led a Swedish mile during the Lucia night to play the part of Lucia in some rich farmer's home, wearing a crown of candles between her horns, walking through the frosty darkness, and twinkling among the black thickets.

That night after midnight the women begin to cook roast and cut the *grissylta,* or headcheese. Animals are given a treat of cream or bone or hay; the sheep are brought leafy boughs to nibble. After a hearty breakfast the men go out shooting, and there is sleigh-riding and singing. It is said that the little people, the gnomes, are about at this time of year, in the winter solstice when the year's threshing and the winter's baking must be finished. The *lussikett* ceremonial bread—the sacrifice to the powers of the earth—is made of saffron dough in the shape of cats, with brushed tops of beaten eggs, sugar, cinnamon, and chopped nuts, and raisins for the eyes.

The children and the young people go to the country for the winter sports, sliding down hills, sleigh-riding, skating; and the *smörgåsbord* is laid out in the communal hall on lace cloths with red and white candelabra, Luciadagen in meringue, and the tables laden with salads of every kind, pickled fish, *pepparkakor, svensk fruktsoppa.*

Many rituals and superstitions are observed and spoken of:

If you do not fall off your sled you will have good luck for a year.

Wash your face in the evening and you will marry a widow or a widower.

If you are silent after eating the midday meal until the next morning, the mosquitoes will not bother you all summer.

If you go to sleep before dark the spirits will move about freely and bring you luck.

At night, measure the distance around your bedroom four times and you will dream of your sweetheart.

And before the evening is over the skaters will be moving in their bright costumes in the frost and the torchlight, and there will be singing from the hills—the famous *skall* song will be sung:

> Han skall leva, han skall leva, han skall leva,
> Hogt! Hurra, hurra, hurra!
>
> They shall live, they shall live, they shall live!
> High! Hurrah, hurrah, hurrah!

Corn and Wheat

The wind and the corn talk things over together.
—CARL SANDBURG

Dressed in garments green and yellow
Coming through the purple twilight,
Through the splendor of the sunset;
Plums of green bent o'er his forehead,
And his hair was soft and golden. . . .
—THE MAIZE GOD IN HIAWATHA

The corn! The corn! Within those yellow hearts there is
health and strength for all the nations. The corn trium-
phant!
—FROM GOVERNOR OGLESBY'S ADDRESS AT HARVEST
HOME FESTIVAL, 1892, QUOTED ON THE CURTAIN
OF THE OLD GARRICK THEATER IN CHICAGO

Corn Mother

WHEAT CAME TO THESE SHORES AS AN IMMI-
grant also. Seed goes with people, sewed up in the full
petticoat, hidden in the hide of a trunk, secreted in a sun-
bonnet, or shaken out of an old hat.

Corn was here. The Zea maize was divine; the Ojibways

called it Mon-da'-min, "spirit grain," and the stalk in tassel was represented as descending from the sky, under the guise of a handsome youth, in answer to the prayer of young men for virility.

They planted it in the forest, girdling the trees to let in the sun. The plains Indians planted it in mounds year after year—some still exist of those baked clay-hills. They fired the hills in the fall, making them loose and mellow for planting. They dug with ash digging-sticks and hoed with a bone hoe. When planting season came, the women and girls planted sunflowers around the edge of the field and beans and squash between the corn hills, and over the field they built a resting stage, where in corn season after the time of the "young bird's feather tail corn" the women and girls came to watch for looters—boy thieves, birds, stray animals—and to sing to the corn like a child and help it grow. Watching season continued until the early harvest moon, when the goldenrod is bright yellow and the green corn-boiling festivals began.

I stooped over [said the Indian woman, speaking of planting] and with the fingers of both hands I raked away the loose soil for a bed for the seed, and with my fingers I stirred the ground so that the seeds would all lie at the same depth. With my right hand I took a small handful of corn from the vessel at my feet, and transferring half to my left hand, plying both hands at the same time I pressed the grains into the soil with my thumbs: two grains at a time, one with each hand, six to eight grains to a hill. Then I raked the earth over until the seed lay about the length of my fingers under the soil. I patted the earth down with my palms and hilled it up.

They said the corn must not be planted close enough "to smell each other" or the ears would not be plump and large.

The very young girls could not go to the watchers' stage but the girls around twelve might, with an old woman to go with them. They cooked their meals there, and while they could not speak to the marauding boys they could sing taunting songs:

> You bad boys, you are all alike,
> Your bow is like a bent basket-hoop.
> You poor boy, you have to run the prairie barefoot.
> Your arrows are fit for nothing but to shoot the sky.

And this one:

> You young men of the Dog Society, you said to me,
> "When I go east on a war party you will hear news
> How brave I am."
> I have had news of you.
> When the fight was on, you ran and hid—
> And you think you are a brave young man.
> Behold, you have joined the Dog Society,
> Therefore I call you just plain dog!

"When the blossoms on top of the stalk turned brown, when the silk on the end of the ear was dry and the busks of a dark green color, then I knew the corn was ripe. You do not have to open their faces to see—then they are spoiled, opened to the birds and the climbing ants," said the Indian woman.

The green corn season lasted ten days. The big pot boiled. When the ears were roasted they popped and everyone laughed saying that the ear had been "stolen." The ceremonies went on of drying the corn for winter, plucking it in the evening at sunset, letting it lie open all night and at morning fetching it to the village, where the ears were husked barehanded and dropped in water, then dried side by side on the drying stage. Some of it the women shelled with their thumbs or a sharp, pointed stick. After it dried they held it in the wind and let it fall from one bowl to another, and it was then ready to be hand-ground in the mortar or sacked for winter.

Big fields were husked collectively in giant husking bees.

The Society of the Dog or Fox was notified by the village crier that a husking would take place, and the young men would come looking for their girls, and the fires for the feast would be started, for the young men had to be fed. The shucking went on all day and far into the night; the best ears were tied together for seed corn.

The final ceremony was a cob-burning. The cobs were kept very clean and heaped in a pile on a fair day. Then in the evening, when in the prairie country the wind dies down, the pile was fired—lighting up the gathering dusk and attracting the children, who made wet mudballs which they swung into the fire so that sparks would stick to them; and they would swing the glowing charcoal into the air like shooting stars. The ashes would burn down dead, and early the next morning before the winds had risen the girls would go to the ash heap and there find a thin crust, which they would break and squeeze into balls and carry home, wrap in dried buffalo paunch, and use for seasoning.

Corn traveled into the wilderness along with independence. A servantless society would have been difficult without the corn titles. You could take enough corn to make you independent in a sack as far as you wanted. A woman alone could sow, tend, harvest, and mill with no need even of the neighbors to thresh or fear of losing it. If you had no market you could fatten beef and hogs and yourself with it.

Corn said to the East when they opposed the Louisiana purchase: We need the Mississippi road for corn, pork, and lard. Open it or we'll secede, take on Spain with one hand, and lick the tar out of the Eastern states with the other!

The north country was built on corn and wheat. The big hog full of corn built towns, railroads, colleges, corn-belt universities open to all. The gilt and plush age was supported by the corn-fed hog. Democracy grew in the hog callings, Grange picnics, Chautauquas, corn huskings; created the man with the hoe who felt the pulse of the earth beating under the ground; nourished him with yellow cornbread, syrup, corndodgers, hoe cake, green corn on the cob, and sweet corn in the can; and corn "likker" made him a hero, a river alligator, rambunctious and hard to beat.

The long green fingers in the wind and the heavy cobs ripening in the thunderous summer heat are a far cry from the Indian maize found here. A boy in Burma writes home, "I'm lonesome for that juicy hot sweet ripe corn." When Bill Chambers died he left one testament, a sack in the attic marked "My corn seed," which made more money than most gold mines. It was the first seed of Golden Bantam corn.

But its meaning for the people has not changed since the Indians made legends about it. Corn is the American Persephone. Down into the Under World, they said, twin brothers descend. One is killed but the other causes the princess to conceive, and she is cast into the Upper World and there gives birth to twin sons who work maize magic of many kinds. Science now matches the legend, for the embryo sac in the ear is fertilized down the fine silk by twin sperm, and the kernel itself is actually twins: one the rich germ, the other the starchy endosperm.

"The Old Woman Who Never Dies," as the Sioux called the moon, demanded of her sons worship, even to their living hearts. Her festival at corn-planting time demands of her children homage to the pioneer "Corn Mother," the distaff side, the earth goddess, the matriarch who has become a giant influence in our lives. America's goddess is the Corn Mother, born on the frontier.

Champion

For farmers in the corn belt the National Corn Husking Contest is a greater sport to watch than a Big Ten football game. People gather in the cornhusking season, when the air is getting frosty and storms come up swift over Pepin, and follow the cornhuskers as they match their skill against each other.

Ed Doggett, Freeborn County champion, does it this way: He stands close to the cornstalk, selects the next ear without looking—with a prong strapped to the right hand he breaks the ear loose. As the left hand flips the husk toward the earth, the right starts the ear upward, pitching it against the backboard of the wagon that follows with an underhand throw which is very accurate. Without a lost motion his hand seeks the next ear. Sometimes he can husk the ear right out, leaving the husk on the stalk.

He's champion husker of Freeborn County.

Golden Goddess

I am more than food for hungry jaws,
I am song of birds on golden straws.

Juggler Joe Brown put in the first wheat near Gray Cloud Island, or so he claimed, but the variety didn't do well in such cold country; it was scant and killed by drought and frost. There are many folk stories of how good wheat was developed in the North Star Country.

One is that a farmer of Ontario, named Mr. Fife, had a Scotch hired man who was returning to Scotland and requested him to send back a Scotch bonnet from Glasgow. The hired man bought the bonnet and was walking along the docks at Glasgow when he saw a vessel from the Black Sea unloading wheat, and filled the bonnet with wheat and sent it to Mr. Fife.

Another version is that it came in the lining of the hired man's coat; and still another, probably authentic, that Mr. Fife was anxious to raise a better wheat than the Siberian wheat he had and so sent to Scotland for it. However, when he got the wheat, it had come from Danzig via the Baltic and the North Sea to Glasgow, and by ocean, lake, boat, and ox team to Mr. Fife in Ontario.

The story further goes that he planted the wheat not knowing whether it was spring or winter wheat; some of it came up. He found that it was spring wheat. His wife saved the few stalks, one with three heads, from the cows, who ate the rest. This Mr. Fife planted the next year—only a few grains—and it produced a bushel of wheat which he divided with his neighbors; and in this manner they produced a good northern wheat, called Red Fife.

This, however, was only a beginning.

Dr. Saunders of Canada planted wheat year after year, in many laborious trials at his small experimental station, trying to get it to ripen a week earlier—which was to make fortunes; or to bear a few grains more on the stalk—which were to overtax the mightiest elevators of the land.

In 1904 he had a few grains in a paper sack no larger than an envelope. He went around the world, bringing wheat from Lake Ladoga in Russia, from the Himalayas in India. He crossed and recrossed his trophies; bred them, waited in summer for the right moment and the right day for the pollen to ripen, artificially fertilized them, picked the best strains; crossbred them, and produced a few grains of what was to be called Marquis wheat—possibly the most valuable food ever grown. In a few years he had a bushel ready to be tested for gluten; in ten years one million bushels of this wheat were produced in the northwest, and in 1918 it would literally feed the world. It made and destroyed millionaires, ruined the land, sent whole counties in exodus from the Dakotas.

Wheat is going north now into the Arctic. Wheat, like people, continues to migrate—from one grain in four years there grew enough wheat to plant five hundred acres. In ten years one grain of North Dakota wheat known as Minnesota 163 actually produced three hundred thousand bushels of wheat.

In the early days it was cut with sickles and bound with willow withes, and threshed on the barn floor with a flail. I have seen it threshed during the depression in this primitive way still, in the villages. It was winnowed with a large scoop resting against the breast. Then it was ground in great windmills, and at last the French brothers introduced the new-process middling purifier at the Washburn mills. The middlings had been thrown away; now the meal from the part of the berry which lies beneath the covering was also used. Flour went up two dollars a barrel in the East. Gigantic combines crushed the brothers and they died, their families destitute.

But Washburn came out with eighty-six sets of rollers—of iron, corrugated and smooth, and porcelain—and broke the grain gradually in six different breaks, and this was the best of all.

The McCormick thresher and reaper made the big bonanza farmers possible—thousands of acres in wheat. The wheat was stacked in wigwams, and the great crews of threshers came, the engine like a locomotive on the road pulling the separator; and behind, the fuel wagon, water tank, and bunkhouse, and a long line of teams; and the throbbing of the engine, the clatter of the iron wheels, the long, thin hoot of the whistle, the harvest hands like a circus, with tall tales and tobacco juice, forming a great seasonal army and later organizing the I.W.W. and riots and agricultural wars—and the boxcars going north black with "harvest crows," with pamphlets on industrial organization in their jeans.

But that's another story as the saying is.

A Whittler

It is very romantic to look at Millet's "Reapers" and to sing, "We shall come rejoicing, bringing in the sheaves," at camp meeting or at revival, but it is quite another thing to harvest prairie acres in the hot August sun, stooping to bind the sheaves—in the field from sunrise and sometimes till after dark, if rain threatens or the season is late. And if you are a young boy like John Appleby you enjoy it less.

He was tired and hot coming in from the big fields, and he lay on the floor watching his mother spin. The McCormicks had designed a mechanism for cutting standing grain, but their binder used a wire which was no good; the cows got it in their stomachs and it caused explosions in the flour mills, sparking the big grindstones, and nobody could get the right kind of knot with twine which the grasshoppers wouldn't eat—which could be applied to the wheels of the harvester.

That night, too tired to sleep, he joined the thought of the inventing men of his time who, sleepless with fatigue and stress of a new country, haunted by a future too gigantic for their rest, turned over in their mind's darkness curious inventions, which in the next century would emerge titanic dynamos of many men's desires and make a new age. He watched his mother tie a granny knot, grasping the two ends of yarn with the left hand and with the aid of the thumb, index, and third fingers tying the knot. He fell asleep in the August night with the sound of giant crickets repeating the rhythm of the granny knot—thrust through, pull, tie—mixing with the sound of the reapers, which became a cricket whirring in his brain.

The next day in the apple orchard very early he fashioned a bird-bill with his jackknife out of apple wood, which by the aid of the hand would tie a granny knot. Years later, after the Civil War, this would be made into steel—make possible the cutting of vast acreages of wheat, banish the threat of starvation through scarcity of flour for the swiftly multiplying population of America.

But first came the Civil War, which had to be fought, and all the inventors shouldered muskets and some did not come back.

John Appleby went, and while tramping with the Army of the Tennessee, in sleepless nights by campfires he developed a cartridge ejector, perfecting the firing pin. When he came back, the war won, industry was a bawling Bunyan ready to grow and a twine binder was still needed, and John thought of his mother and the granny knot. He got financed for a year by his partners and went to the attic over their tiny shop. He stayed there a long time, and his partners would talk down below.

"What's John doing?"

"He hasn't done a thing."

But like many who do "nothing," he came down with something finally, and turned into metal in the shop a hemp twine binder with the needle so shaped as to compress the bundles before tying. A tripping device gauged the size of the sheaf, and all parts received power from one gear wheel. The twine was treated so as to be unpalatable to grasshoppers and crickets.

They went out into the fields with it and told the farmer to get on. "What am I to do?" asked the farmer, leery of such gadgets. "Do nothing," they told him. "Drive the horses." So he started round the field, whipped up his team, and the tidy sheaves kicked out rhythmical, regular as dancers, and when the farmer turned and saw them he let out a yell, threw his hat in the air like a lunatic, and tore around the field, the golden bundles clicking down.

Deering produced the first ones, then sold them to the

Milwaukee Harvester Company, and this was the origin of the combination of McCormick and Deering which made the International Harvester Company.

John Appleby did not get rich. Inventions made him a man who couldn't sleep nights.

Alfalfa Grimm

There was an old German named Grimm, who wanted to raise dairy cattle in the new country, but there was not enough corn. He had brought some alfalfa from Germany but most of it would die of the weather. Do you have to do with people as with seed? Pick out the best, gradually create a hardy breed that will stand the rigors and change and tempers of a new country—and when you get them they survive through thick and thin?

Old Grimm would plant the seed, most of it would die, he would keep the few remaining living grains and at last get a hardy seed. "Grimm's magic" it was called, and he gave it out all over the north until finally dairies could grow and Minnesota could become the leading butter state. Of course, alfalfa knew nothing of states' rights and went over many borders.

Harvest Wars

But hark! the rattling "Reapers,"
Here it comes, with noisy din,
And the grain shrinks before it,
Like good intentions before sin.

One rides upon the "reaper,"
Waving oft the reaper's wand.
And every pass he makes,
Lays a sheaf upon the land.

O band of strong cradlers,
With regular sweep,
Your vocation is gone,
'Tis the Reaper must reap.

There was war between the Reaper Kings. McCormick in an old-fashioned blacksmith shop in Kentucky had worked on the seven points, solving the problem of the reaper.

John Deere, a blacksmith in Illinois, obtaining a broken piece of saw blade, made a steel plow with a wrought-iron landside. This was in 1837. "For years," he said, "I thought of nothing else."

James Oliver was thinking of nothing else in Indiana. John Appleby was thinking of nothing else but how to lighten the awful physical labor of the vast prairie fields. Drudgery was the mother of invention.

The seven principles of the reaper were: straight knife attacking the standing grain by lateral as well as forward motion so gently that the ripe kernels would not be shaken; fingers or guards to support the grain at the moment of cutting; a reel to gather the grain in front of the reaper, and a platform for the severed grain; a mainwheel behind the horse to carry the machine and operate gears and some way to cut to one side of the line of draft, so the horse would walk on the stubble while the cutter bar worked in the standing grain; and a divider at the outer end of the cutter bar, to divide the standing grain from that which was to be reaped. Men lay awake nights in the wilderness thinking how to solve these problems. They would find a way to cut vast acres of grain, too vast for the back of man, and they would show the way to abolish famine in the world.

When they had solved the problem they went from farm to farm selling the idea to farmers who were but one generation removed from the peasant and hand labor. The elder McCormick like a bearded prophet went over the northwest exhibiting his binder, ruthlessly buying or stealing patents.

Wars ensued, legal and physical. Whitely, the Reaper King, would hitch himself to the mower to prove its light draft. The Brothers Marsh with their reaper, unaided, bound an acre of grain in fifty-five minutes. Rivalry took the form of a violent crusade. Reaper Kings led their followers into war. Two reapers chained together back to back were pulled apart to prove their strength. A farmer let it be known that he wanted to buy a grain binder. He was pursued by salesmen from the rival firms, took refuge at last in a hotel, and was forced to jump from the window to escape! A farmer would buy a reaper from one company; the next morning he would find it stolen and the rival reaper in its place.

Another was buying a McCormick Champion and the Deering Company was trying to break up the sale. The Deering salesman buttonholed the farmer. The McCormick man got the farmer up at three in the morning in his old hickory shirt, had a long talk. The next day the crowd gathered from all over the countryside. Deering had a brand-new machine with four big grays decorated with flags. The tangled barley soon choked the binder, while the farmer driving the McCormick was having no trouble. The Deering man claimed the Champion salesman had put straw into the elevator chain, and grabbed him and they both rolled in the stubble. The Champion followers put their oars in and a free-for-all was on in the field. The old farmer came out with a shot gun, cleared the field, and kept the McCormick Champion.

By one way or another, old McCormick began to rule the field, by legal battles, battles with labor, with other inventors and with the Grangers, whom McCormick undertook to lick. The Grangers, banding together, undertook to buy from manufacturers direct, thus abolishing the vicious credit system. McCormick fought them. "No club shall club us," was his slogan. He fought them as he later fought organized labor in their struggle for the eight-hour day, and the result was the Haymarket massacre.

Today the prince heir of the McCormick fortune works in a guarded Chicago tower, rides in a bullet-proof car, lives in a feudal castle heavily guarded.

Oh Susannah, Don't You Wait for Me!

Times went beyond you, too fast, you couldn't keep up or catch up. Some houses weren't even finished in the towns before the people moved out, went somewheres else.
— PIONEER

Language cannot exaggerate the rapidity with which these communities were built up. You may stand ankle-deep in the short grass of the uninhabited wilderness. Next month a mixed train will glide over the waste and stop at some point where the railroad has decided to locate a town, without people, without cattle, then men and women and children will jump out of the cars with their chattels, the building will begin. . . . I have ridden into a Dakota town and pitched my tent. After my supper, lolling upon my buffalo robe I have looked around and seen nothing but a wolf looking down from a hill into the valley. The next spring I saw a long train, a Pullman palace, come down the valley. I camped in the river-bottom of the Mississippi with only a log cabin, a Frenchman and his Indian squaw. The next year I saw there a town of 2,000 people.
— REV. W. H. HARE, MISSIONARY BISHOP TO SOUTH DAKOTA

Something else was always happening, something being invented. I tell you, they were times. A man was on a hot griddle.
— FARMER

It was a mining town of about twenty shanties with a population of about a hundred and fifty people, and a

*hundred of them drank whiskey, played cards, carried
knives and revolvers, and stabbed and peppered each
other. The justice of the peace was one man who didn't
drink. He was also chief of police, superintendent of hos-
pitals, just about everything, being sober. He had all he
could do to carry around his load of dignity. One drunk
could have crushed him to the ground.*

*One afternoon it was his painful duty to go to Wicked
Jim's shanty and remark, "James, it is the sentiment of
this here enterprising town that you git up and git."*

*"Kin you back them remarks?" Jim said, turning over
in bed.*

*"I reckon," said the Judge as he brought two Colts to
bear on the lemon-shaped head not ten feet away. Wicked
Jim surveyed the gats for about seventy seconds and said,
"I'll git. Soon as I kin pack." "That'll do," the Judge said,
and went away to select a site for a college.*

*The crowd gathered to see Jim off as he rode out on
his mule and spoke to them, "Gentlemen, I spit upon
your town. I can build a better one of sand and grease. It
ain't a fit town for an aristocrat noways and I've always
knowed it." At this point three or four citizens began
shooting at him, but he gave them no notice. "The lion
can't partner with the jackal. The eagle can't mate with
the buzzard. Stinks, sluggards, curs, and reptiles, I go."
Here a bullet whizzed through his hat. "But I will return,
and when I do, look out for oceans of gore. In less than
a year I'll dump yer town into the river and hold the site
for a private graveyard. Whoop-yip-yi-yip!" And holding
two shooters on the crowd he galloped off with only two
killed and three wounded.*

*In exactly a year five horsemen rode into town,
Wicked Jim at the head, come to fulfill his promise,
with blood in his eye. "How's this yere?" he said, looking
down from the brow of the hill. He saw buildings where
the Red Eye Saloon had been, gas lamps and streets in
the place of the Can-Can Dance Hall and Opera House
and the Great Hotel. Like men walking on a steep roof
they wound their way down to the public square, where
they saw stores, markets, a railroad ticket-office, library,
and museum!*

*They rubbed their eyes like men who had slept too
long, and finally Wicked Jim said, "Boys, let's give one
old-fashioned yell and break this mirage!" So saying, they
yelled in chorus. No sooner had the echo died away when
men in uniform with stars appeared, rising from the
earth, pulled the wicked one from his saddle with his
companions, and clapped him in a prison. They seemed
to be struggling in the embryo of some terrestrial dream
as they were brought into court, heard the sentence from*

a thin, pale, and dignified judge. "We cannot allow such conditions in a peaceful, law-abiding city. The sentence of the court is ninety days in the workhouse for each of you."

—OLD NEWSPAPER

IT WAS ANYBODY'S GUESS WHERE THE RAIL-road would run. Traders, half-breeds, now important men, wore swallow-tail coats in Washington and negotiated useful contracts. There were reasons spoken late at night, deals made. Mr. Weyerhauser, silent as a mole, might drive through a town one day and it would disappear the next. Mr. Hill, with four other canny Scots, was prepared to water the stock.

People moved like pawns. This side of the river—the other side, wherever they thought the railroad was likely to run. The river ran north and south but the railroad was bound to run east and west. The steamboat and all its cities were doomed. Thriving towns would be deserted and dead in the space of one day.

The railroad sharks, the land sharks came with the locusts, and the depression swept away anything that was left.

One man told it thus:

It was like a fire and famine, a depression, and a bank raid all at once. In our town we had just bonded for the new schoolhouse. The railroad went east and west by another town which meant our town was doomed, the steamboat gone. Old Captain Polly who lived on the hill lost everything. The grain buyers shut the doors on their big mansions and walked out never to return. The hotel keepers and merchants went, but we couldn't go. We had to stay and pay for the schoolhouse. There are a few who sweat heavily, feel grief. They are the few honest folks who know no other way but to pay! Well, we stayed. There was an

awful famine that winter, had not tobacco or flour, made coffee
out of acorns—but we got along. In the spring hope returned to
the people. After all, the producers were left. We started to make
it an agricultural community, all around, with a dairy so we
wouldn't get caught with our pants down again. No use crying.
Well, we muddled through, I guess. We still live here. Towns
are born out of a lot of people's struggle in this country. Some
people make money and leave, but others like us stay on. I
guess we'll always be here. We have nothing but the earth and
we can make that do.

There was a song:

What the black birds leave and the hard times spare,
  few days, few days,
The forty thieves are bound to share.
  I'm goin' home.

You've got our land, then take the state,
And we'll clear out as sure as fate,
  I'm goin' home.

Shan't stay long in the wilderness,
  few days, few days.
To be foxed and fleeced and starved to death,
  I'm goin' home.

A few went back but the most stayed with nothing but
the earth and they made that do.

Citizens!

Elections had to be improvised. Legislatures were self-
starting. In May, 1858, the year Minnesota became a state,
Big Sioux River County in South Dakota was without a
government. The citizens, with unlimited faith in the future
and destiny, had a mass meeting and decided to hold an
election to establish a *de facto* territorial government. The
entire territory was populated by only thirty white people.

On the morning of the election this total population made up parties of three and four to a wagon with a picnic lunch and set off in all directions—wherever a halt was made an election precinct was established. Votes were then cast not only of those present, but of uncles, cousins, and distant relatives long gone. The vote ran up into the hundreds, counted of course by the mutually appointed judges. Afterward a self-starting legislature convened, elected a governor, passed all bills, and then spent the winter trying to obtain recognition from Washington.

There were thousands of constitutions to write. Wherever you were, you wrote a constitution when you founded a town, if there was nobody to witness it but a bluejay. There were more constitutions written in fifty years than ever before in the history of the world. Everyone had a right to make one. Wasn't that what you came to a free country for? Two people took a claim, founded a town, and that night by candlelight drew up a constitution, including rights for women and no saloons on Main Street.

County-seat wars were numerous and bloody, and a good time was had by all. In Spink County, Old Ashton was the county seat, but when the railroad went through it passed by way of Redfield, and the people of Redfield with twenty of its leading citizens—bankers, lawyers, businessmen, and the preacher—marched to Ashton in the night masked and carrying crowbars, looted the county safe of records and papers, and took them to Redfield. The preacher was in his pulpit that Sunday.

Other towns took up arms until three thousand men were armed and the militia was called out. Sixty Redfield militia men grabbed their rifles and fought on the side of the insurgents. An engine was chartered and ran to Watertown for an injunction against the Redfield gang. The war went on, and someone wrote a poem:

Have you heard the story before
Of the war of eighteen-eighty-four?
When the riotous hosts from Olean
Rode forth to battle, then back again.
With flintlock, muskets, and rusty gun,
With hayforks, too, this host war armed
And not a hair of their heads was harmed.

It was finally settled. Redfield won. The county jail was loaded on a truck and toted to the new county seat with the preacher riding triumphantly astride the ridgepole.

While making a campaign speech for Congress in North Dakota, Moses Armstrong was shot through his hat by a cowboy. He went on with his fiery eloquence, but the next shot unnerved him and he called his mentors aside and suggested that he had come for ballots, not bullets. He was told, "Show these damn hyenas the kind of stuff you're made of. If you show the white feather you're a dead duck. Bare your breast and tell them to shoot, and you'll get the vote of every galoot!"

Pembina, one of the earliest election districts of the Minnesota Territory, voted before Election Day so that the returns would get to St. Paul. It was a saying: "Pembina always waits to see how many votes the Democrats need to win!" At this election it looked like a Republican landslide and all eyes were turned to Pembina, whence the election returns had not yet arrived. They were usually brought by Joe Rolette, a man susceptible to the allurements and temptations of society.

Early in the morning, around two, Judge Flandreau was awakened in his home on Pleasant Street by a man named Sweetser who said that he knew for a fact that Nat Tyson (a St. Paul Republican) had just started north with a fast team to capture the returns. The men hurried to Henry Rice, who knew every trader and half-breed. While Flandreau wrote a letter, they summoned a Chippewa Indian acquainted with the country and told him, "Pass Tyson on the road, find Rolette, deliver this letter to him. Go quick and don't stop even to save your life." They gave his horse a slap and he was off, passed Tyson within twenty miles, and found Rolette and Major Clitherell. The latter put the returns in a belt around his person and left Rolette to paint all the intervening towns red; and as he thought that half the Republicans in St. Paul might be lying in wait, he went around by Fort Snelling, leaving the returns with an Army officer. The next day he proposed to a lady to go driving, went to the Fort, and gave her the returns to hold while he drove.

That is how the Pembina returns reached the capital.

Men came to the new Territory to hold office—to get elected by non-existent constituents and then leave for Washington, where they lobbied for their own interests; not to be seen again until the next election. Mr. Goodhue, editor of the St. Paul paper, paid his respects to these anti-democratic forces and probably paid with his life for it:

While we regret the continued absence of the U. S. Marshal and the Judge of the 2nd District from Minnesota we would not be misunderstood to lament the absence of two such men if it were prolonged to eternity. In the present scarcity and high price of whiskey, their absence may be considered a blessing.

The loss of these men to poor washerwomen, barbers, tailors, printers, shoemakers, and all persons with whom that sort of man makes accounts is quite as large already as ought to fall to the share of the poor people in the Territory. We never knew of an instance of a debt being paid by either of them unless it was a gambling debt. And we never knew an act performed by either of them which might not have been quite as well done by a fool or a knave. We never knew either of them even to blunder into the truth, or to appear disguised, except when accidentally. sober, or to do anything right, unless through ignorance, nor to seek companionship with gentlemen as long as they could receive countenance of rowdies.

Will the administration keep infamy upon stilts here, clothe drunkards, blacklegs and unprincipled rowdies with political power, put the premium on vice by placing profligates and vagabonds in office . . . ? We do not complain that we had not a Judge or Marshal, but that we do not have one whose absence is not a blessing. We have had enough officers who are daily liable to arrest under the Vagabond Act, who never set a good example, perform an honest act, or pay an honest debt.

Feeling some resentment for the wrongs our Territory has so long suffered by these men, pressing upon us like a dispensation of wrath, a judgment, a curse unequalled since the hour when Egypt went lousy, we sat down to write this article with some bitterness; but our gall is honey to what they deserve.

The Judge, of course, was not present to defend himself, but a few moments after the paper came out on the St. Paul streets his brother Joseph appeared on the steps of the Capitol to uphold the honor of his family. When he met Goodhue an argument ensued and Joseph said, "I'll blow your brains out!"

He made a pass at Goodhue and both whipped out guns. The sheriff came between them and disarmed Joseph, but as he was taking Goodhue's gun it went off. Joseph, thinking the shot had been meant for him, brought his adversary down with a well-aimed rock before bystanders could pin his arms behind him. Goodhue rose to one knee, jerked out another pistol, and shot Joseph in the side. The wounded man tore away from the bystanders and, flashing a knife, inflicted two wounds on Goodhue, one in the stomach. Friends at last separated them. Both men died the following year.

Bull and Barnum

Local pride mushroomed with the times. In 1850 Minnesota was a Territory with around six thousand whites in the lumber and fur trades, about a thousand gathered around the mission in St. Paul. In 1855 it had grown to fifty-four thousand and the frontier was pushed back two hundred miles. Minnesota began to feel her oats, and when news came up by the weekly mail, by ice along the river, about the Prince Albert in London and the American-organized Fair to be held in New York, Governor Ramsey gave William G. Le Duc three hundred dollars to see what he could do about having Minnesota represented at the Fair. Mr. Le Duc got samples of the wheat that was beginning to be raised there, then went north to get some wild rice from the Indians. There he met a persuasive Frenchman, M. Cunradia, foster-brother of Louis Napoleon, banished for his conviviality and eager to get back to Paris. "I queet this sacrebleu squaw camp and come wit' you."

Mr. Le Duc told him he had only three hundred dollars for the whole expedition and that would hardly keep them in whiskey.

"I show you," said Cunradia, "fine buffalo bool. I geef him, you make money, send for me. Everybody say, 'Meeneesota, where is she?' "

"Impossible," Le Duc said. "I could not drive him to St. Paul."

"Eef I get him to St. Paul before you go, you take heem?" Thinking it impossible, Le Duc said he would. A week later as he was sitting in his office at the corner of Wabasha Street, the door opened and M. Cunradia came in and said, "Haf buffalo bool."

"What? Where—?" Dashing to the window that overlooked the square he saw the young bison, an iron ring attached to his nose, pawing the ground, and drawing a crowd. The bull was hungry and Le Duc and the Frenchman had to lead him through the St. Paul streets followed by a crowd of boys who wanted to touch his jet-black, glossy fur. He was a beauty, a four-year-old with polished horns and a piercing touch-me-not look. At the stable he lay down, but could leap to his feet like a cat, with lowered head ready to meet any attack.

Well, there was nothing for it but for Mr. Le Duc to take the bull, and when they embarked the streets were cleared, bets were laid, the roustabouts alternated between insolence toward the plains beast and fear of his strength.

The steamer got on its way and Le Duc tried to sell the beast in Galena. He transferred to another boat at St. Louis; the river was rising, and the bull shied at a hogshead of sugar unloading, got loose, jumped overboard at the gangplank into the Missouri, and swam to the opposite bank, where he clambered to shore bellowing and shaking his shaggy head. Horses and mules fled in panic, casks of sugar sweetened the Missouri, and it took half the town to get him on board again.

They arrived in Cincinnati and exercised him in the street amid crowds and shouts and questions. "Derned cute-looking beast—slick as a mole and spry as a cricket." "From Minnysoty—where is that?" "You want three thousand dollars fer him? That's a mighty high figure for any cud-chewin' beast."

At last from Albany they arrived in New York with a live buffalo from the great plains of the West; as they crossed Fifth Avenue a horse bolted at the sight and a carriage was wrecked. Mr. Greeley was impressed at the Fair, not only by the buffalo but by the grain exhibit Mr. Le Duc had made (augmenting his meager seed by quantities purchased at a New York store); Greeley wrote a column praising the barbaric country he had once derided and thus helped to start another tide of immigration.

Meantime, men in spats and round bellies and ladies in furs came to look at the buffalo, who was by now eating his head off and costing Mr. Le Duc more and more money by the minute. Also, M. Cunradia appeared and got the splendid idea of taking the bull to his brother the Emperor, who was doing very well as he was; but no French captain would hear of taking a bull buffalo. So then he tried to sell the beast to Mr. Barnum—who had, however, already made a ten-strike with a buffalo on Staten Island and was looking around for some more fabulous wonder. The bull was finally sold to a two-by-four sideshow for three hundred dollars which was never paid.

I Rent Sky Space

It's not invented yet but I'll take your order now. I rent sky space.

—FOLKSAY

*My belief is that the growth and spread of man over the
earth is bringing to light truth. The earth is glad of man.
God has made but one man and that man is still alive
and growing and will never die. He is spread over the
eternal past and will continue to spread over the eternal
future.*

*Man's growth and spread delights the earth. The earth
will grow with her son, Man.*

*Man is made on the looking plan. Being hollow on the
inside and bare on the outside, heat, cold, and hunger
put him into motion. He is forced to look, lean and
learn.*

We were all myths ourselves once and will be again!

—BUDD REEVE

STRANGE CHARACTERS ROAMED THE NEW
country and were looked upon with respect and wonder.
Was not there to be a new man as well as new land, new
wheat, new tools? Violent strains of fantasy mixed with the
colossal labor of the pioneer. Work and dreams alternated
with the violent changing weather. There were new strains

of melancholy, quirks of witchcraft and grandeur, of gaminry and gentleness in the large hands for evening. There were new insights, long as the whip of the northern lights, bright as the far sun setting, reflecting, like winter mirages, a far future, of cities that would rise vertically into the air, of new configurations of democracy.

Old strains showed in men wanting to be kings and emperors; in others wanting only to be left alone free on the prairie; in country workers and wanderers, wood and word poets, earth lovers, those with the itching foot, the wandering eye; in prophets of a new world; and in those who did not sleep of nights, dreaming of inventions, tools and extensions of man not yet known.

These are portraits with their own fantastic touch of myth of country wanderers, workers, prophets, and poets. "We were all myths once ourselves and will be again!"

Mad Emperor

A strange document in Spanish was written in Minnesota. It read: "The army of the Liberator and Leader Montezuma II to his brother of all the lands of Mexico, addressed to the Sons of the Race of Montezuma, sent by God, by Jesus Christ, and the Holy Mother of God, to Sante Fe." This was written by a mad dreamer, General James Dickson, and his dream was to recruit Indians and half-breeds from the North Star Country and the plains, march into Santa Fe, on to California, and proclaim it all an independent empire.

Appearing in Washington fancifully dressed in the grand manner, he was joined by adventurers and disgruntled half-breeds who hated the Hudson Bay Company. They started west. Out of sixty only twenty came through the winter of the upper lake. The Hudson Bay Company was on the lookout for them. An Indian guide got them lost. The main body reached Pembina in the dead of winter. Dickson had heroically and foolishly set out alone and was badly frozen. After this he vanished and with him his dream of empire.

Fishermen Don't Like Kings

Then there was King Strang, the only crowned King of the north. His Kingdom was the largest island of the Beaver Archipelago in Lake Michigan. He ruled for seven years, until his constituents struck him down.

He was a very small man of Yankee Norman stock, sickly in his youth. "My early recollections are painful, make a creeping sensation akin to terror. . . ." An omnivorous reader, ambitious, studied law, contributed to the Smithsonian Institute, he was one of the twelve apostles of Joseph Smith.

When Smith went west, "Thy servant Strang, led by Moses guided by the mysterious cabalistic writings brought by the angel Urim and Thummin," took his followers north and there was crowned King, with ceremonies, burnt offerings of fowl and heifer, and dancing on the greensward.

But the fishermen of the Lake didn't like kings. They had ousted a minister who insisted upon praying for kings and princes.

President Fillmore sent an armed force to arrest Strang, who defended himself brilliantly in the trial held at Detroit, defending his five wives who wore bloomers, and his full Empire.

But when he went back his own followers assassinated him; as he struck the ground, they struck him again and again and thus the only crowned King of the north was dead.

Mr. Dibble, Wanderer

Mr. Dibble is not in any history.

Like a delicate mark of fern found in rock, or the step of a lost animal in glacial loess, the very neat hand of Mr. Dibble is preserved in a few letters, found in a New England attic many years after. He writes to his father, by reflection from the northern lights, or by a sod shanty fire, saying that he would like to enjoy New England apples and cider in the fall, and the company of old friends again, and the little fields of home. "Write a few lines, dear father, to keep intact the bonds of our affection. I cannot at present calculate when I will return."

Return, return, his feet beat out on untrodden prairies. Oh, return never to the tiny house, the little fields, the grasping hands, and the tight skull. He walked always into the sun, canvassing the wilderness, neat as a pin, selling life insurance. He had to walk miles between customers. "If a man had a horse it would be rather pleasanter." But he did not truly want a horse any more than he wanted to return.

He knew in his heart that he would never return to rocky fields, the condemning women, and the tiny fear. He could not get over the joy—and you were not to feel any emotion but guilt and anxiety—but he begged his poor dead mother's pardon—he could not get over the pure joy when he got up in the morning and saw the far horizon, the joyful springing light, and he grinned and hopped like a little New England rabbit, to see the lavish woman earth where he could walk without gun or shock, along with geese, and carrier pigeon, talking with sandhill philosophers.

He knew in his heart he would never return to the girl to whom he wrote, "I am in excellent health, and did gain one pound a day. This is no place for lantern jaws or long lean frames. Here you have to have a wife, good-looking, healthy, kind and strong who can play the piano, sing, dance, talk Norwegian, harness a horse, ride bareback and go afoot."

He would never return to her, never return at all. He would chuckle softly walking alone, loping along the far ridges, with no desires but to love the country, see the hay-cocks, the new sod huts, the husking-bees, and the rosy-cheeked girls getting kissed by the frosty huskers and more corn lost between the wagons than would grow in a New England field. The prairie chickens would walk in the summer chuckling back at him. "Yes," said Mr. Dibble to the prairie, and did not recount this to his father, "everything is plentiful . . . plentiful; a man can walk for a week and not pass over more of a hill than is in the lower meadow at home and so much sky!"

"Wind at your back," said one letter, "and you keep on your feet and are propelled over eighteen miles of very fine prairie, not a bush nor a tree nor a house, just you and the wind. . . ."

In his walking he fell in with many people who asked him nothing and put no fear into him. In fact Mr. Dibble could feel as if he was not watched like a sparrow; he could in his way be important. "The country is democratic," he wrote. "It is upright and outspoken." He rode with peddlers, gamblers, and he helped old people file claims; he slept on fresh hay in sod huts with gay people like himself, growing lavishly in the new air.

Sleeping out in the open—that was one of the nicest things, and not washing in the morning, never getting used to sleeping in his clothes, peeking around to see if his mother might be looking. "It is nice," he writes cautiously, "to sleep in the open. You are always dressed, have plenty of room and air. It is nice."

No, he would never return. He skipped away from the iron trap of the East, skipped merrily away. "Sometimes I think of it at night," he says. "I seem a mystery to myself, that, I think, I should have lived so long and known or cared so little for others. When I am walking over the country then I am happy."

So he pondered, and the old human seemed too small, and full of rot. Once, much later, he saw and heard a tall rangy man from Illinois, and felt great excitement for a moment, catching a glimpse of a man big enough for the horizon, a spirit sweet enough for the light. He fled the old horizon of the heart and the head. "I enjoy going about very much but when I return to a room I feel frightened, alone. It is my worst hardship when I stop walking." But why stop walking? No mountain stopped you. No ocean ended the land. The sun kept going west and Mr. Dibble kept walking after it.

"This year I shall return," and every year he did not return. He kept tripping lightly, disappearing into the myriad activity of the new land.

When his letters cease, he is moving towards the West, moving on, with the partridges, the antelopes, and the little prairie dogs.

"I will keep you informed," he writes, his voice disappearing, chuckling free. "I will keep you informed of my principal moves." A business-like statement of disappearance and flight, a fine phrase to walk away behind into the rich warm folds of the voluptuous land.

A Prophet

For fifteen years they hunted him like an elk in the northwest. He had a dream of a united democracy in the north, including Canada. The courts of the Queen at last caught, tried, convicted, and hanged him.

But standing amongst the bewigged lawyers and the ancient court, he said, "My work is not the work of some days or some years; it is the work of hundreds of years. I believe I am a prophet of the new world. There is in the manner, in the standing of a man, the proof that he is sincere. If I am guilty of high treason, I am also a prophet of the new world."

But he was convicted of rebellion against the Crown. And he had almost succeeded—in creating a confederation of allied democratic nations in the northwest. His name was David Riel. Behind him were the settlers, half-breeds, and Indians whose land was being confiscated by the Crown, whose petitions were ignored, whose rights were trampled. They would seize the land, set up a provisional government, and divide the northwest and Canada into seven nations, of the Irish, Italians, Bavarians, Poles, French, and Indian. They had created an orderly organization, democratically ruled with parliamentary law, reports, minutes, rules for kitchen service, for changing the names of the days, all controlled by the general council called the Exovede: *ex*, from, and *ovede*, the flock. "I was assuming no authority," said Riel. "We considered ourselves a part of society and near to us; another part attempted to rule over us improperly, and by false representation and through bad mismanagement were injuring us greatly. We were being led to annihilation. We recurred to the right of self-preservation. There was no excitement. The people had been waiting patiently and now it was the time."

The priest testified that the petitioned government answered only with the police.

The soldiers testified that the strategy of the rebellion was good, and nearly successful.

The people testified that the call had gone out: Seize arms, gather the people together, take possession of the northwest.

You can read Riel's speech in the court of the Queen beginning: "I will cease now to be called a fool. Do I appear excited? Am I irritable? [They had tried to prove him insane.] My work is the work of some time. My children's children will shake hands with the Protestants, and the nations will be together. I may be declared insane because I seek an idea which drives me to something right and there be hanged by the neck until dead, but I say I am a prophet of the new world!"

I'm Gan to Amaraka, the Morn!

The pioneers kept coming on. New wheat and corn lands opened up, new materials asked for new inventions. Backs were breaking; time was long in the fields. Time and labor-saving machines began to be talked of.

The young John Muir rose at one in the morning, on his Scottish father's farm in Wisconsin, inventing an alarm clock to startle sleep so he could study before going to the fields at four. He saw men and women fall in the harvest fields, destroyed by endless work and worry, cut down by galloping consumption, swamp fevers, and just plain heart- and backache. So he studied how to make machines for saving the time and backs of men.

His father and Jehovah stood in the fields preaching that men and boys must earn their bread by the sweat of their brows, that sin and guilt must be expiated by work, and that every ungathered ear of corn was a rebuke, every weed a devil, and every wasted stalk of wheat a sin. They saw in the awful grandeur of the sky the wrath of Jehovah, and when they threw the brush into the fire their father said, "All boys are sinners. Every branch is a sinner cast into hell fire!"

When he wanted to go to the University of Wisconsin, Jehovah and his father would not give him a dime. So early one morning he took his inventions and went down the road to the tiny station and found that America was in the morn of invention—time- and labor-saving machines. In the person of the station master, the Yankee nation greeted him. "What you got there?" "Inventions." "You must be a down-east Yankee." A crowd gathered and looked at the inventions for keeping time and getting up in the morning. "Mark me," said the station master proudly, "you'll be seeing him in the newspapers." "Where did you get them?" asked a yokel. "In my head," said John. "I'd rather have your head than the best farm in the state," they all said. "Hey," yelled the station master to the engineers, "hoist him up in the cab. An inventor. He'll want to see how she goes."

In his room at the university he invented a bedstead that rose at a certain hour, set him on his feet, clothes that came to him, books that turned on the racks, lamps that lighted. He became later also an inventor of the spirit, a lover of America, a walker from horizon to horizon, seeing that you have to do more than have time, save time, kill time; that flowers have an action and that you can be as well as become, can measure depth as well as space, and that it is not enough to take an idiot around the world at four hundred miles an hour if he remains the same idiot when you bring him back to Main Street.

Prairie Skyscraper

Mr. Buffingston was laughed at but just the same for six years he threw the idea of the skyscraper abroad in the air, from his office on Nicollet Avenue in Minneapolis, until it was picked up. It used to be a joke in Minneapolis, Mr. Buffingston's twenty-eight-story building. The place of any incredible meeting was called the twenty-eighth story of Mr. Buffingston's skyscraper. "I went at it nights, Sundays, other work forgotten," said Mr. Buffingston. He fell at last upon the idea of a shelf fastened to the metal skeleton of every story so the weight was distributed at every floor down the structure of the shell, which was the solution of the sky-scraper. At this time no such building existed on the face of the earth. *The New York Sun* said, "To be sure this is probably the production of a crank, but the cranks of one generation are the prophets of the next." "They beat me out of it," said Mr. Buffingston. "You boys used to laugh at the idea then. . . ." He also designed the West Hotel, a magnificent hostelry combining some of the daring, the Oriental dreams, the extravagance of the time, and he designed the beautiful flour mills. They said then, "When a horse didn't shy at Mr. Buffingston's buildings you knew it was surely broken in."

Civil War

There won't be a damn thing this summer but politics.
I tell you that I can't meet anybody but what they're
puttin' into me 'bout the Little Giant. Southern Negroes.
Old Brown, the Constitution, the Spread Eagle, the Rail
Splitter, and a thundering lot of other names.

Consarn it, why, the bullfrogs in the pond back of our
barn are all on the titter, bellowing out:

Old Abe—Old Abe—Old Abe—
Illinois—Illinois—Illinois—
Put him through! Put him through!
Put him through! Chug. Chug.

—OLD NEWSPAPER

I cannot for an instant recognize that political organization as my government, which is the slave's government
also.

—THOREAU

Now you have seen wheat which was very plump, round,
and good-looking to the eye; but when you weighed it
you found it only came to forty-five or forty-eight pounds
to the bushel. Take a grain of that wheat between your
thumb and your finger, squeeze it, and out pops a weevil.

Now, you good-looking Christian people only weigh
like the wheat, forty-five or forty-eight pounds to the
bushel.

What is the matter?

When you are squeezed between the thumb of the law
and the finger of the gospel, out pops the Negro and the
whiskey bottle.

—CIRCUIT-RIDER'S SERMON

No more peck o' corn for me,
No more, no more.
No more pint o' salt for me—
Many thousand go.

No more hundred lash for me,
No more, no more.
No more mistress call for me—
Many thousand gone.

—NEGRO REBELLION SONG OF THE
CIVIL WAR

THE ABOLITION MOVEMENT IN THE NORTH-west was strong, and in 1848 the underground railroad ran through Wisconsin, moving runaway slaves from the first station at the Illinois border, through Beloit and Milwaukee into Canada. Many of the conductors were ministers, New England farmers, German revolutionists, and Norwegian peasants. Although Southern planters offered large rewards for information for the return of their lost property or for information leading to the discovery of the underground hideouts, they were met with silence and hostility.

Joshua Glover, a fugitive slave from Missouri, found his way to Racine, Wisconsin, and there worked in a sawmill. His owner, Ben Garland of St. Louis, in some way learned of his whereabouts and accompanied by two United States marshals broke into his shanty after nightfall, manacled the former slave, dumped him into a wagon, and started on the twenty miles to Milwaukee.

During the early morning hours the church bells of Racine began to toll and thousands crowded to the court-house, where they were told that Glover had been taken to Milwaukee. A committee of one hundred was elected to go after him. They were stirred to rebellion by the repeal of the slave-catching law, and against the slaveowner-directed federal government.

A Milwaukee editor, Sherman Booth, heard of Glover being in the hands of the United States deputies at the county jail. "I must get a horse," he said, "and ride through the town." Like a second Paul Revere he rode through the streets of Milwaukee, stopping at every corner and shouting, "Freemen, arise! To the rescue! There are slave-catchers in our midst. Be at the courthouse at two o'clock."

At two o'clock the courthouse steps were filled; far into the street stretched the line of angry people. At a signal the crowd advanced toward the jail. They broke down the door of the cell and rescued Glover. A democrat wagon was at the door and Glover stood in the wagon shouting, "Glory, Glory, Hallelujah!" and holding up his manacled hands as they formed a parade and the procession marched triumphantly down the Milwaukee streets singing Abolitionist songs. That night Glover disappeared, spirited to freedom on the underground railroad. The press and people of Wisconsin were jubilant and considered the act justified. Charles Sumner of the United States Senate wrote, "I trust that Wisconsin will not bate a jot of her grand position. She will make history."

But the federal government considered the freeing of the Negro an act of sedition and arrested Booth as instigator of the rebellion. His lawyer was a young man not yet thirty by the name of Byron Paine, and his address before the Wisconsin Supreme Court became a bestseller on the streets of Boston. The court declared the Fugitive Slave Law void, and the prisoner was discharged.

But the slave-owning federal government, which wanted the Northwest states to go slave, arrested Booth again, found him guilty, fined him a thousand dollars. An appeal was made. Resentment stirred the people. "Freemen, arise! To the rescue!" became the catch phrase to announce the secret gatherings of Abolitionists. The people showed their feelings by electing a Free-Soiler and Abolitionists to the U. S. Senate.

After four years of legal battles the federal court once more reversed the state's decision, in an opinion written by Chief Justice Taney, who had written the notorious Dred Scott Decision. Appeal was made, the writ failed, and Booth was jailed in Milwaukee. With the help of his friends he broke jail, caught a train to Waupun, and three days after his jailbreak was found by federal deputies making an Abolition speech at Ripon. He eluded capture and stayed at Pickett station, a stop on the underground in southern Winnebago County.

When a second attempt was made by the federal government to capture him, a posse of angry farmers with pitchforks and shotguns stood waiting silently at the station as the officers arrived. The officers retired.

Booth was advised to flee to Canada, but said defiantly, "Soon I propose to discuss before the people the questions at issue, between liberty and slavery. I intend to remain a citizen of Wisconsin until liberty triumphs or to die in defense of those principles which, unsustained, make life not worth preserving."

He was at last arrested and taken to his cell in Milwaukee. Two days before Lincoln's inauguration he was pardoned.

For six long years the state of Wisconsin had been in actual rebellion against the government, not merely for states' rights, but on the question of enslavement of Negroes in a country dedicated to democracy. The rebellion was broken only after Lincoln's call for volunteers after Fort Sumter. Then Booth traveled over the entire Middle West delivering thousands of speeches, and the farmers who had stood with their pitchforks against the federal officers shouldered guns and marched with the armies who were fighting slavery.

It was during this action against the federal government,

prior to Lincoln's election, that representatives of the old parties met in the Congregational Church at Ripon on March 1, 1854, and launched a movement which was to become the Republican Party, and which would elect Abraham Lincoln and oust the government sympathetic to slavery.

Years later, after the signing of the Emancipation Proclamation, Sherman Booth—who had moved to Chicago after the war—came back to Wisconsin to speak to the Editorial Association. He said, "There was something deeper in the struggle in which I was engaged than questions of technical law. There was something higher than decisions of the courts. It was the old battle, not yet ended, between freedom and slavery, between the rights of the toiling many and the special privileges of the aristocratic few. It was the outlawed right against despotic might; it was human justice against arbitrary power; it was divine mercy against infernal cruelty; it was the refining spirit of humanity."

Gettysburg

As I saw in imagination the bombardment of Fort Sumter, and the hauling down of the flag, it seemed to me that I could see, too, the landing of the Pilgrim Fathers, the "starving time" of Jamestown Hill and Brandywine; Washington crossing the Delaware; the awful winter at Valley Forge; the heroic deeds of Marion and Sumter; the glorious victories of our navy in the War of 1812, every scene of hardship and of heroism that has helped to win for us and to preserve us our proud position among the nations of the earth. . . .—MELVIN GRIGSBY OF NORTH DAKOTA, IN "THE SMOKED YANK."

It did not seem credible that the settlers who had left the East should ever go back to fight a battle against slavery, any more 'than it does today that the sons of immigrants have flown over the areas of the old countries, fighting the same battle from which they fled.

On Saturday, April 13, 1861, Fort Sumter fell, and next day when President Lincoln issued a call for seventy-five thousand volunteers, Governor Ramsey—who was in Washington—pledged a thousand men from Minnesota. Ignatius Donnelly, Acting Governor, after a night of restlessness and anxiety issued an immediate call which the newspapers carried the following Tuesday. Minnesota had then only one telegraph line but the news fled to every village, along the rivers, into the plains, into the woods; by narrow roads, footpaths, buffalo and Indian trails.

So great was the response to that call that the Honorable Henry Clay from Alabama (a state which had seceded), who happened to be in St. Paul that weekend, predicted that the war would be a long and bloody one since even in far-off, primitive Minnesota the pioneers and frontiersmen of that young, poor, and scantily populated commonwealth were thronging forward to fight for the Union and demanding to be led to the battlefield.

They converged upon Fort Snelling, afoot, in wagons, marching together, accompanied by wives, children, and friends. Many had no recourse but to leave their women and children alone with the squirrel gun and the plow. They occupied the barracks that had not been inhabited since Colonel Snelling and Zachary Taylor had been in command. They enlisted for three months, not dreaming of the long and bloody civil war ahead of them. Each was supplied with a frontier shirt of many colors and even decorations of crescents and trefoils; a black felt hat, a pair of black pants, and a pair of socks, besides the knit things the women brought—including havelocks which would soon be forgotten, when long marches and hardships made sunburning the back of one's neck seem of little importance.

Two months later the regiment was ordered to Harrisburg. The news came at ten o'clock on a Friday night and spread to the men, who did not stop to put on their clothing but rushed around hurrahing and hugging one another, wild as a crowd of boys.

At five o'clock on Saturday of the following week the first Minnesota regiment boarded the *Northern Belle* and the *War Eagle*, river-boats. They landed at the foot of Eagle Street in St. Paul, disembarked, and marched through the young city to say farewell and to receive Godspeed. Even at that early hour the streets were thronged. In half an hour they reboarded the boats and went in the summer morning between the bluffs of the Mississippi, stopping at the thronged docks of the river towns, where the women came down to the shore with gifts. The *Northern Belle* went on to La Crosse, while the *War Eagle* went by Prairie du Chien, picking up more volunteers on the way.

They reached Harrisburg on the twenty-fifth and were loaded into cattle trains for Baltimore, where again they marched through city streets. A few months before, the Sixth Massachusetts had been fired on from the houses by Baltimore rebels and several had been killed; the First Minnesota marched through the silent city with loaded muskets and fixed bayonets, and would have used them if one of the scowling populace on the sidewalks had snapped a finger.

They were garrisoned at Washington, crossed the Potomac into Virginia, marched through the ancient town of Alexandria on July 3. The streets were deserted, with grass growing between the stones and only frightened Negroes huddling on the corners and staring at them in dead silence.

They fought their first battle at Bull Run, took part in the Shenandoah Valley and Peninsular campaigns, built the bridges during the battle of the Chickahominy, reinforced General Porter's troops against the enemy at Hanover, fought at the Battle of Antietam—one of the great battles of the war—with five thousand close-marching Union soldiers over an open and fair field, where for the first and only time they had to follow an order to retreat.

The next year, seasoned fighters, they crossed back over the Potomac to their old camp and moved toward Gettysburg, where they would write their names forever in the mightiest battle ever fought on the American continent.

At the dedication of the monument at Gettysburg on July 2, 1897, to commemorate the services of this regiment on the same day in 1863, Lt. William Lochren gave an account of the regiment on that second day of the battle when, as night fell and they crawled back for their wounded, the count showed that of the two hundred and sixty-two men who charged, two hundred and fifteen lay on the field.

We bivouacked long after nightfall about three miles south of Uniontown, and about sunrise the next morning were in our assigned place at the left of the cemetery, our regiment being placed in reserve.

The other troops were then near us, and we stood by this battery in full view of Sickles' battle on the opposite ridge, and watched with eager anxiety the varying fortunes of that sanguinary conflict, until at length with gravest apprehension we saw Sickles' men give way before the heavier forces of Longstreet and Hill, and come back slowly at first and rallying at frequent intervals, but at length broken and in utter disorder, rushing down the slope by the Trostle house, across the low ground, up the slope on our side, and past our position to the rear, followed by a strong force—two Confederate brigades—in regular lines, moving steadily in the flush of victory and firing on the fugitives. They had reached the low ground, where there were then no trees and but very low brush which did not interrupt the view nor impede their advance, and in a few moments would be at our position, piercing our line which they could roll up as Jackson did that of the Eleventh Corps at Chancellorsville.

There was no organized force here to oppose them; nothing but our handful of two hundred and sixty-two men. Most soldiers in the face of the near advance of such an overpowering force, which had just taken part in the defeat of an army corps, would have caught the panic and joined the retreating masses. But the First Minnesota had never yet deserted any post; had never retired without orders, and desperate as the situation seemed, and it was, the regiment stood firm against whatever might come.

Just then Hancock with a single aide rode up at full speed, and for a moment vainly endeavored to rally Sickles' retreating forces. Reserves had been sent for, but were too far away to reach this critical position before it would be occupied by the enemy, unless that enemy were stopped.

Quickly leaving the fugitives, Hancock spurred to where we stood, calling out, "What regiment is this?"

"First Minnesota," replied Colvill.

"Charge those lines," commanded Hancock.

Every man realized in an instant what that order meant. Death or wounds to us all—the sacrifice of the regiment to gain a few minutes' time and save the position and probably the battlefield, and every man saw and accepted the necessity for that sacrifice, and responding to Colvill's rapid orders, the regiment in perfect line, with arms at right shoulder shift, was in a moment down that slope directly upon the enemy's center.

There was no hesitation, no stopping to fire, though the men fell fast at every stride before the concentrated fire of the whole Confederate force directed upon us as soon as the movement was observed. Silently, without orders and almost from the start double-quick had changed to utmost speed, for in utmost speed lay the only hope that any of us would pass through that hurricane of lead and strike the enemy.

"Charge!" shouted Colvill, as we neared their first line and with leveled bayonets at full speed rushed upon it—fortunately it was slightly disordered in crossing a dry brook at the foot of the slope.

No soldiers will stand against leveled bayonets coming with such momentum and evident desperation. The first line broke as we reached it and rushed back through the second line, stopping the whole advance. We then poured in our first fire, and availing ourselves of such slight shelter as the banks of the dry brook offered, held the entire force at bay for a considerable time and until our reserves appeared on the ridge. Had the enemy rallied quickly to a countercharge, its great numbers would have crushed us in an instant, and we would have made but a slight pause in its advance. But the ferocity of our onset seemed to paralyze them for the time, and although they poured upon us a terrible and continuous fire from the front and enveloping flanks, they kept away from our bayonets until, before the added fire of our fresh reserves, they began to retire, and we were ordered back.

What Hancock had given us to do was done thoroughly. The regiment had stopped the enemy; held back its mighty force and saved the position. But at what sacrifice—nearly every officer lay dead or wounded upon the ground, our gallant Colonel and every field officer among them. Of the two hundred and sixty-two men who made the charge, two hundred and fifteen lay upon the field.

At roll call on July 3, the majority of the First Minnesota Regiment were recorded as "Dead on the Field of Honor."

Rise, O Days

Hayseeds Like Me

_____

THERE WAS A BOOK THAT WENT LIKE HOT cakes all over America. It was written in a ruined town called Nininger, on the Mississippi, by one Edmund Boisgilbert, M.D., who turned out to be Ignatius Donnelly, a "Philadelphia lawyer" whose violent, vituperative silver tongue was heard in every movement of reform of the nineteenth century—the original "Great Commoner" of the Middle West. The dream of the fabulous city of Nininger, founded by Donnelly, left the ruin of a thousand houses in the wheat fields and only the pillared house of Donnelly standing beside the river, where he wrote _The Great Cryptogram,_ adding fuel to the Shakespeare-Bacon controversy, and another book which, along with _Uncle Tom's Cabin_ and Edward Bellamy's _Looking Backward,_ influenced America profoundly.

Caesar's Column, the book that farmers read as they rested their horses—that sold faster than the printer could print it—is a work which seems today curiously and terribly alive. It tells of a mighty combat all over Europe in which the human race is entirely destroyed. It warns that the growth of monopoly and oppression will lead to a debacle of monstrous cruelty, with bombing from thousands of planes from the air, poison gas, and long-range guns. And over the millions of dead is erected a new pyramid, "Caesar's Column"—mountains of dead bodies, cemented together.

We will build a monument that will beat the pyramids of all other Caesars. Caesar's Column! Take the million dead, build a pyramid of them, pour cement over them and we'll have a monument of this day's glorious work. Caesar's Column. It shall reach to the skies. If there are not enough dead to build it of, why, we'll kill some more.

Donnelly was leader of the Populist Party, three times elected to Congress. He went from county to county, state to state. When he was beaten back he retired to Nininger and wrote books and broadsides, and speeches that had to be censored before they could be printed.

Farmer

The banker told him the contract would be dated back six months; and that, with the fifty-dollar bonus and forty-eight dollars' interest, would leave him with seven hundred and two dollars. "It isn't my money," said the banker. "Take it or leave it; we don't compel any man to make a loan."

The spring is coming, the baby is coming, the harvest is coming!

He took the loan. He and his wife could work hard, they would have a big wheat crop, the land was new and rich; they hung a lantern on the plow and worked in the dark to the morning. That year the sun shone, the rains fell, and there were no grasshoppers, drought, flood, or hailstorms.

A poem of that time ran:

We worked through the spring and winter, the summer and the
    fall,
But the mortgage worked the hardest and steadiest of all.

Worm or beetle, drought or tempest on a farmer's land may fall,
But for all-round ruination, trust a mortgage 'gainst them all.

Time for the threshers came; all their money was gone,
but the threshers trusted them. A smoky fall day came when
he told his wife good-by and started down the road with his
plump golden wheat to the nearest elevator. In the village
the wagons were lined up for blocks waiting to weigh in,
and as he moved up slowly to the scales he looked back at
the hard, smooth good color of his wheat.

But when it came his turn and the elevator man said,
"Badly shriveled Number Four," he sprang from the wagon,
shouting. The elevator man said nobody was forcing him to
sell his wheat and to drive on, he was holding up traffic, there
was another elevator in the next town.

The farmer's dander was up now and he drove fifteen
miles over rutted roads to the next town, and the weight,
grade, and price were the same there, and he drove to another, and it was the same, and he drove out in the country
and sat in his wagon alone figuring on an old envelope. By
the time he took off freight commission, three pounds' dock-
age, the bum weight—he couldn't believe it, the price he was
offered wouldn't pay for the seed. Gone, his wife's work, his
own work; even the unborn baby had worked. He drove
slowly back to the first elevator, sold his wheat, and was
ashamed to go home.

The next year he defaulted, was foreclosed, lost his
machines, his animals—even his wife and baby, who went
back to her folks; and he went to work on Jim Hill's railroad
for wages.

Banker

It has never been denied.
The North Dakota Bankers Association investigated it.

They wanted to know why two hundred and fifty thousand people had left the state, why the crop was lessening and the land spoiling.

They found out many things the farmer would have liked to know that September day as he sat on his wagon looking at the hopeless crisscross of figures on his envelope.

The three elevators he had visited that day belonged to the same company. The manager had phoned ahead. Even if you took your wheat to the local mill you paid freight charges to Minneapolis. The wheat was short-weighted on the scales. They found that the wheat graded as Number Four would enter the elevators at the Twin Cities or Duluth and miraculously come out as Number One. It was Number Four when it went in and Number One when it came out, and this counted up to millions of dollars. This alone would have changed the life of the northwest.

Then there was the Stock Exchange in Minneapolis, controlled by the Chamber of Commerce. At 10 A.M. the wheat stood in little golden piles and the pigeons cooed at the windows for the grain that would be thrown to them, after its value had been strangely changed simply by a wave of a pencil and a number of lines on paper. The wheat men came in and bought the farmer's wheat, perhaps five cents below the market, assessing one cent for the sale. The wheat man could afford to do this, as he bought the wheat from himself and sold it to himself and took the one cent for the courtesy. For the same concern owned the elevators at both terminals—sold the wheat to its own grain company. The man resold it to the outgoing terminal elevator, paying himself two cents more for the transaction, and the terminal house sent it to the mixing house where it jumped from Number Four to Number One, thus making millions more with no change of value or labor involved. In the course of all this magic incantation, eight to twelve cents a bushel had been added to its value.

But there was further magic: for each bushel of real wheat actually sold and handled at each of these terminals, at least one hundred bushels were bought and sold in so-called future tradings, and this also came out of the real wheat. The cables were open from Buenos Aires, the weather was bad in India, the weathercock of speculation turned this way and that, sweeping away in a morning the years of work of thousands of people.

A Granger paper called it "the productiveness of Nothingness."

The people began to talk to themselves; long soliloquies were overheard at the crossroads, in the fields, coming home from church; debate grew from monologues and a man's mind caught fire and it spread in the wind of disaster. Wagons began passing through the towns going back East with signs saying: GOING BACK TO MY WIFE'S FOLKS. IN GOD WE TRUSTED. GOING HOME.

And some said:

We can't keep on going west. We got to stay now and fight. We got to fight for our homes now instead of making new ones. We made two spears of wheat grow where one had grown. How are we going to get paid for two spears?

They told us to plant crops and we raised big ones, and now corn is eight cents, oats ten, and beef two, and no price at all for butter and eggs.

It costs one-half the value of wheat to get it to Chi. I never saw the beat.

Here's the recipe for Hill soup: take a little stock, six times as much water, and then put in the lamb!

Said a tall, good-looking Irishwoman, Mary Lease, mother of four children, who made a hundred and sixty speeches in one year, "What you farmers need is to raise less corn and more hell."

And other orators:

We will stand by our homes and stay by our firesides by force if necessary. The people are at bay. Let the bloodhounds of money who have dogged us thus far beware.

What we wanted was good fences, good barns, good houses, good schools, good orchards, children enough to gather the fruit. What we got is mortgages.

We are mortgaged all but our votes.

We vote as we pray.

We've voted with our party no matter where it went. We've voted with our party till we haven't got a cent.

Songs were sung: "Good-by, my party, good-by!"—the two parties were referred to as the Pot and the Kettle.

John Burrows of the Farmers' Alliance wrote warningly:

We send the plutocrats a grim warning. The twin of this oppression is rebellion. Rebellion that will seek revenge with justice, that will bring it Pandora's box, fire, rapine and blood. Unless there is a change made, a remedy found, this day is as inevitable as that God reigns, and it will come soon.

Ignatius Donnelly rode through the north from county to county by buggy, train, horseback, with his short, powerful figure, his broad Irish face smooth as a monk's, his powerful voice proclaiming the "Rights of Man." The farmers fastened up his broadsides along the fence posts, on the sides of the barn, in the village store: "From Forge and Farm, from Shop and County, from Highways and Firesides, come and hear the Great Commoner on the mighty issues which are moving mankind to the ballot box in the great struggle for their rights."

Reading became popular. Pamphlets, leaflets, books were carried by the lecturers; town halls were packed. Men came together to listen, debate, talk it over, come to a decision, organize. One said of a Donnelly broadside, "I've read it at the stores, at the corners, at the blacksmith shop. It was good enough to keep butter from spoiling, and Mr. Mason said he'd give five dollars to see it in big type nailed to the bridgehead."

Another said, "The meeting last night was good. Me and the wife went home ready to face the hard toil now, with enough to read all winter while we are snowed in."

There were words now in the skull, strange oratory and rich Biblical speech ringing in the mouth as you slapped the reins over the horse's rump or ran the tractor in the spring plowing:

Shall we face the west, storm the cold, and now pay homage to the wolf?

The wood tick, not the honeybee, has come to our country. It creates nothing, sucks the wood.

A hog in broadcloth has gotten into the corn fields.

Jim Hill is an octopus sitting in St. Paul with you all in his tentacles.

So the questions flew back and forth over the jug, the harvest, in the corn row; thinking came with hunger and drought; despite the poverty books were selling like hot cakes: Henry George, Bellamy's *Looking Backward*, Ignatius Donnelly's *Caesar's Column*, and pamphlets on co-operation, socialism. Thoughts sprang up after them like dragon's teeth, and talk rose like a storm—government ownership—abolition of private property—unity with labor—a thousand desires, a thousand unspoken hopes, contradictions, hotly contested—rumination long and slow, discussion on winter evenings with the Alliance lecturer around the cleared farm table, and the children listening from the cold bedrooms. Talk long into the night, words spoken at the door: Come to the meeting, get the others, organize. Tell the women to bring sandwiches; we must talk it over, thresh it out, winnow it down, mill it, grind it.

Everyone was talking, asking, Where to? What now?

There was talk of combining all the organizations—the

Alliance, the Grange, the Wheel, and the organizations of labor—into one political party, a third party.

A song was sung to much laughter, to the tune of "Save a Poor Sinner Like Me":

> I was once a tool of oppression
> And as green as a sucker could be,
> And monopolies banded together
> To beat a poor hayseed like me.
>
> The railroads and old party bosses
> Together did wholly agree,
> And they thought there would be little trouble
> In working a hayseed like me.
>
> Now I've roused up a little,
> And their corruption and greed I see,
> And the party we vote for next November
> Will be made up of hayseeds like me.

But the one most often seen, clipped, in the cream house, pasted in the lunch box, hung over the washtub, learned by young girls to recite at meetings, was the Thanksgiving Prayer written by Everett Fish in St. Paul:

We thank thee that thou hast given us cunning, craft, callous hearts and knavish souls and sticky fingers.

We thank thee, thou Supernal Cloth of Gold, thou Glorious Diana, that wheat is $1.50 a bushel in Liverpool, because it enables us to pay less than last year, 80 cents a bushel, whereby the outrageous fool farmer is robbed only 35 cents a bushel in his golden wealth and we make a clear profit.

We thank thee, O Glorious incubation of the Civilized, for the pallid cheeks and frost-bitten hand and cry of pain. We thank thee for the daughter of Nebraska who parts with her corn at $2.80 a ton and buys coal at $10.50. We thank thee and so does the Pennsylvania miner who gets 95 cents a ton for the coal and pays $18.60 for the corn before it is ground. Accept our illumined tombstone as a symbol of our great love, dear Syndicate.

In the presence of thy Majesty, O Gelliferous Grandeur of

the Goldarned Galott, we scream for joy and shiver with delight to think that four men can fix the price at which every pound of meat in the whole world is both bought and sold. Like ants we creep up thy breeches leg in glory of Arsenical Asininity.

Finally we thank thee for the Devil and his Satraps. We bend the knee, shoot the firecrackers, for the 25,000 men who own 21 times a thousand times a thousand times a thousand dollars so that the other 65 million who gathered the fuel can light bonfires to their glory. Sing praises! Shout hallelujah! Let everybody whistle!

One-eyed Watcher

Work and more work will make the Northwest.

—"YIM" HILL

At night my old man just takes off his britches and throws them under the bed, rolls over and meets them on the other side, and yells for me to go out and feed the stock.

—FOLKSAY

They said of a farmer whose whiskers hung down like a mattress before his face while his head was bald as a billiard, that it was overproduction and poor distribution.

—ANOTHER FOLKSAY

DONNELLY IN A SPEECH DESCRIBED JAMES HILL, the great railroad-builder of the north who outfoxed, outbuilt, outdynastied all other railroad kings:

When you enter the office of the Manitoba Railroad in St. Paul you see in a corner a door with a sign painted on it, "President." If they permit you to pass through the holy of holies you discover sitting at a common kind of table, and without a touch of magnificence anywhere about, a common kind of man. In stature he is low and though of stocky build his weight is under rather than over the average. His face in repose is dull. Long hair mingling with a bushy beard gives him an untidy aspect, a point of singularity rather than distinction.

Nevertheless, from that unpretentious room as from some murky cave under the sea, and from that seemingly undistinguished man as from the monster of the deep, there reach out the tentacles, unseen but only the more deadly, dangerous for that, which fasten upon you and me to our undoing. We fondly fancy that we live under a democratic government where men are equal before the law and no man has more political power than another except it is delegated to him by the voice of the people.

We are mistaken.

Our government in Minnesota is an autocracy and Jim Hill is the autocrat. He it is who chooses our public servants. He determines who shall sit among the elders of the land and make the laws, what laws will be made—everything in short.

A banquet was given in St. Paul in 1906 when Jim Hill was an old man, his one eye shining, cunning and Cyclopean, upon the great hall of the elite, filled with long tables, which represented a major train of the Great Northern Railroad— the tracks built of carnations, the crack trains of the line complete in roses and carnations, the walls solid with flowers, and the oldest conductors taking the banquet tickets. Speeches were made, while the old Cyclops Jim Hill sat with his massive head lowered like the lost buffalo of the plains. He would rise later and respond sarcastically to the encomiums, and then, ignoring flowers and speeches, lambast them all for their sins.

One speech:

And when your great spirit takes its final flight past the moon station and past the sun station to that final station to which all our tickets read; as you look back over the Northwest, that which will give you buoyancy to your wings will be the consciousness of the opportunity your life work has given to the farmer, the villager, and the city, of great wealth and the building up of confidence and happy homes, sweet and useful lives.

The shrewd one-eyed watcher of the prairie arose and after the applause said bitterly, "Of course, my work has not been entirely a charitable one"; without a moment for flattery he launched into an attack upon them all:

Minnesota is falling backwards. You don't make use of the wealth of the state. Why? You will answer to America for that.

Many years ago I thought maybe I was wrong, but I would do it again if I had to. But I always thought good farming was the best thing for the country. I distributed eight hundred thoroughbred bulls, seven thousand hogs. I took pains. I sent to Great Britain and bought the best that I could buy and scattered them over the state and furnished roast pig to a lot of families.

But now the farmer criticizes us. Now we are just grinding the faces of the poor and taking the last dollar they have got. They are barking curs. We are all honest men and never stole a dollar. (*Applause*)

And now they don't raise enough for a long train to roll down to St. Paul. Tell the people who are on the land they must do better!

And then they take advantage of us; wherever anything is wrong, oh, of course it is the railroad. They sue the railroad!

Now there is doom—doom—the human tide away from the cultivated field toward the factory gate and the city slum. Doom—doom!

He cried it out like some Jeremiah irascible with the unsolvable contradictions of his time, with the sense that he was hated and the glut of his wealth—with the loneliness and emptiness of his later days.

Until he was close on thirty-eight Yim Hill, as he was called by the Swedes, could be seen sitting in an old chair in front of the warehouse on the St. Paul levee, a mud clerk with one eye, chewing the rag with anybody who came up the river or with his partner Kittson about buying the St. Paul and Pacific Railroad, an old rundown line extending to the Dakota border. No one thought anything of these dreams. Wealth was just around the corner. There was land.

Timber. Mines. How was it possible for a poor man like Yim Hill to get hold of a railroad owned by Dutch and Prussian bondholders? Go peddle your oats, they said, tend to your knitting. All except a daughter of an Irish tailor at the Merchants' Hotel who listened to him in the evening.

He was a town character, a good listener, a man who liked the north; came from Canada, a Scot, loved the country, had night and day dreams not only of its wealth but of the boats and trains that might connect it with the outside world —even the Orient—of the magnificent land that would support a nation for a thousand years. He liked the north and when he got rich he didn't go south. He bought a salmon preserve in Labrador and started a winter carnival in St. Paul with a giant ice palace, a king and queen, the people marching in the streets, and winter sports; himself, the true king, in a great fur coat and cap riding in a cutter behind his spanking horses. "The farther north life is developed," he always said, "the more vigorous it is. Some day wheat will be sowed and reaped clear up to the Arctic Circle and it will be the best wheat the world ever saw." The word "north" was in all his enterprises.

He branched out a little with Kittson, got hold of two old sternwheelers, carried goods north to Winnipeg, to Ronald Smith, commissioner for the Hudson's Bay Company, a tall lean Scot with a red beard, already a king over the North country and a valuable man to know.

Another man who was to be king of timber was coming up at the same time, and they later built mansions side by side at the summit of St. Paul, in feudal red stone. He was a German immigrant as poor as Hill had been, who became one of the greatest lumbermen and landlords in the world. A good way then to become rich was to wait until the next crash or panic ruined your boss and then ride in on the following tide of prosperity and take him over.

Weyerhauser and Hill knew how to do this. Both were

creative men, born in great poverty, men of their time—of the roaring, ruthless, but creative era of expanding industry and growing monopoly. Both were later dismayed to find themselves hated, dismayed even at the destruction that followed them, that created wealth and at the same time impoverished the people, laid the land barren.

Both started with nothing. Weyerhauser came into wealth by working from dawn to dark; he created an interlocking web of corporations—mills and railroads and steamboats—so fabulous and intricate that no one has ever followed its threads to their sources.

Side by side on the hill Weyerhauser and Hill worked together, turned up where there was more land to be granted, tried to keep the national forest from being saved; in a thousand unrecorded ways as Mr. Weyerhauser said, working "not for ourselves, not for our children, but for our grandchildren!" And Mr. Hill crying out against the doom of industrial change, "Oh, stand firm for the old simple, immutable things!" And both never missing, getting there, and getting there first.

Getting a railroad then was very much like wolves getting meat. You waited until your adversary was down and you came in swift and drew blood.

At last there came a panic, the railroad Hill had been hounding was going under, the stockholders in Amsterdam were not getting returns; there was panic, bank doors were closing. Hill asked Smith to come down with Lord Mount Stephen, head of the Bank of Montreal, and they tossed a penny in Chicago and it was heads, so they came down to see this mud clerk's crazy dream. The country that year looked like the top of a rusty stove, cleaned by grasshoppers and drought, and the road was a couple of rusty tracks and they didn't see how—it would involve millions. But the next year crops were good, the government was giving out huge land grants to railroads—over two and a half million acres—and the bankers in Canada saw how they could betray both the government and the Dutch bondholders in one stroke that would be called "good business."

This is the way that phony wealth was created: the sale of the land would more than pay for construction; they would water the stock—many times. "We have let in Lake Michigan," Hill cried happily. Wealth was pyramided, the fabulous multiplication of nothingness working a necromancy, rising to an invisible point and boomeranging later to destruction. When you once started it you couldn't stop it.

Hill had ideas. He knew how his road should be run. "Make it plain and simple and true," he said. He claimed the lowest cost of hauling because of his manner of always building with the curve. He laughed at tunneling through a mountain. He believed in the railroad. "Next to the Christian religion and the common schools no other single work enters into the welfare and the happiness of the people to the same extent as the railroad." Engineers said he knew about it. He would turn up on some difficult grade while it was building. The oldest and finest bridge crossing the Mississippi, at St. Anthony Falls, is his best monument: a solid, beautiful, simple and functional span of stone.

He loved the land truly. "I passed this place forty years ago, following three dogs—all I had and all that I needed on a dogsled—and I saw the morning star fading out at Elm Coulee, so that I have seen this country grow from a bald unsettled prairie to what it is today; and it is one of the most satisfactory and proud things in my whole life that I have been able to take part in that growth." He warned of the doom of the land from lack of care, misuse, from not putting what was taken out back into it. That was why he got the pedigreed animals and sent them out free to breed up the stock, so that the land would be replenished.

His wounded erratic roar was heard continuously, like that of some maddened prophet crying out the doom of what was happening yet unable even to stop contributing to it—warning them, in their predatory destruction, of the danger of killing the goose that laid the golden egg, yet himself helpless, catapulted into it, abetting it. At the same time he would cry petulantly, "We have to pay dividends to our widows and children." All his stockholders became to him at least incipient widows and children.

He had certain ideas about how a country should be settled and what nationalities should be brought over for certain functions. His agents brought over the Irish in carloads for the building of the railroad; the German and Scandinavians for farmers and small shopkeepers; the middle Europeans—the Croatians, the Slavs, the Lithuanians, and also the Finns—for the mines on the Mesabi. He had definite ideas about how they should live. His own father was a Baptist, his mother a Methodist, and he married a Catholic girl, sensible, of high principle; he wanted to show the northwest how to have large families, so she bore him ten children, three of them boys, and he built the great cathedral overlooking St. Paul because, as he said, "Look at the millions of foreigners pouring into this country. The Catholic Church represents the only power that they either fear or respect. What will be the social views, their political action, if that single force should be removed?"

There is a story of how he married Mary Theresa Mehegan, in the early days of his empire-building. One day Mary said she was going to get married, and Hill suggested to the boys at the boarding house that it would be a good thing to make a purse as a wedding gift. They took up a considerable collection—eight or nine hundred dollars. Then it was learned that Jim Hill was the bridegroom!

He was a planner. He had many plans. He built a shuttle between Dixie and the Orient and picked up cotton on his trains and brought it over the northern route, then by his own steamships to the Orient and the Arctic and the tropics. He even proved to the Chinese that wheat was better for them than rice, and so opened a new market for the northwest wheat fields.

He drove the railroad through to the coast. He wrote traffic poetry and transportation sagas. His private wires stretched from St. Paul to the world—to every capital of Europe. He sat in the center, watching it all. Once he said, "A panic in September," and converted all his holdings into cash—fifty million dollars—and sat on his money in St. Paul, saved his railroad, outsmarted the other old financial lions, all while multitudes of other men swept down to ruin.

He was a hard man to work for, never knew a holiday or a quitting hour.

He gave a five-million guarantee to Mark Hanna. "Should you need more," he said, "look me up in St. Paul."

In his last days he was given to cyclonic tempers at sight of the devastated plains, the thunder of dissolution, the doom of the land, and he tore the telephone off the wall, fired people because he did not like their faces, roared out his calumny and warnings in the teeth of indifference, and in the last mad swirl before the closing in of doom prophesied the war and the depression, and then another war. He told his sons to get out of railroading. Men no longer ran the railways, but corporations. He wandered around his burglarproof and cyclone-proof mansion with its steel beams concealed in the feudal walls, and the jewels and rare rugs and paintings. "Oh, it was pleasant to get these pictures together. One of the great joys in life—but it is all gone now."

He tried to read, "Now I start to read a book. I don't know a word I have read. Something else has got on top of it, you know." As his wealth accumulated his personality diminished, became a caricature.

"I have left my mark on the surface of the earth," he said, looking at a map of his holdings, "and they can't wipe it out."

"Thank God, I have no pockets in my shroud," he said. "All I can hear now is one continuous complaint." He died on May 29, 1916, from "trouble in the digestive tract."

He ended an era.

They Shall Live

YOU CAN BOIL SOME SEEDS FORTY-EIGHT HOURS; other seeds have been perforated, desiccated, put in a vacuum for six months, and then frozen. They lived.

Seeds have been put in glass bottles and buried for forty years, dug up, planted. They lived.

Seeds in the desert will lie for years waiting for a good season. Energy can be cramped in a tiny space, the shell hardens, life seems to be gone, the finest chemical test does not prove that the seeds are alive.

But they are alive!

To Your Tents, O Israel

The third party was born out of this travail. The paper *The Great West* reported the convention in Omaha:

The party of the common people, the child, is come, and it is a giant at birth. The blood circulated in 10 million hearts which from the depths cry out for a better life. Its sledge hammer swings with the muscles of the toiling army. Its songs will come out of the oppressed.

Men of the West! This is your party. The thrones of despotism are trembling. The rights of man rise triumphant at the convention and decree that the poor shall no longer be the inheritors of toil, nor wealth the reward of man's knavery.

Get into the fight. Trim your ballots. Build your prairie fires where the flickering flames will cast lurid lights in the glassless windows of your sod shanties.

Be ready. Be nervy. Be strong!

"To your tents, O Israel," was the slogan of the Populist paper. In preparation for the convention thousands had joined the party from Iowa, Nebraska, and the Dakotas. Meetings were held everywhere. Men, women, and children came in buckboards, driving in any weather, the women getting up early to fix the picnic lunch, scrub the children, prepare banners and songs, and also to compose their own speeches; to drive to meetings and march in the processions and hear Weaver or Donnelly or Mary Lease or Eva Valish from Minnesota—the "jauntiest, sauciest little woman in the whole coterie of women in the Alliance, as much at home on an improvised soapbox platform on the street corner, speaking earnestly to the toil-hardened Knights of Labor, as in the drawing room, radiating sparkling wit and repartee."

"It was a wonderful picnicking, speech-making Alliance summer of 1890," Elizabeth Barr, writing of that period, said.

It can hardly be diagnosed as a political campaign. It was a religious revival, a crusade, a pentecost of politics in which a tongue of flame sat upon every man and each spake as the spirit gave him utterance. For Mary Lease, Jerry Sockless Simpson, and half a hundred others who lectured up and down the land were not the only people who could talk on the issues of the day. The farmers, the country mechanics, the cattle-herders, they of the long chin whiskers and they of the broad-brimmed hats and heavy boots had also heard the word and could preach the gospel of Populism. The dragon's teeth were sprouting in every nook and corner of the states. Women with skins tanned to parchment by the hot wind, with bony hands of toil, dressed in faded calico, would talk in meeting and could talk right straight to the point.

They came singing across the prairies for miles, over many states, some even walking to the convention at Omaha. The banners of the different states rose above the delegates. WE WANT MONEY, LAND, TRANSPORTATION, their slogans said. The stage was decorated with bunting in the national colors and was occupied by leaders of the Alliance, Knights of Labor, single taxers, prohibitionists, antimonopolists, Women's Alliance, the reform press, People's Party. Across the stage behind them stretched a banner saying: WE DO NOT ASK FOR SYMPATHY OR PITY; WE ASK FOR JUSTICE.

It was a singing convention. Songs started spontaneously and were picked up over the hall; farm women who saw nothing but the horizon from day to day now sat in assembly, now felt each other's singing might.

Literature tables were piled high. The Populist movement had become a vast university of the common people, a debating society. There was a renascence of culture. Everyone could write to the papers, which were supported by his own pennies. All could speak out their minds, write speeches; songs and words came to the silent throat—for the wrong, for the occasion—from the suffering that flowed like the mighty inland rivers from each inward self to that of others.

You stood on the platform and you looked down at the people, and you said things that made your wife wonder if she had really known you—that sent a curious thrill through your own veins, saying, I belong to all of these, not just setting out there hog-tied, fence-high, wire-tight.

Heaven is not over the river Jordan. This is a mighty river nobody can stop. This could be heaven, earth; you could live here, hands touching, without fear.

The People want men. We need leaders who can't be led by the bell ram.

We got to have a pressure of fight about a hundred pounds to the inch.

Go ahead and soak it to them.

The prairies are afire—don't put her out; let her burn rise higher, red and hot.

You need hard blows to split the Devil's head. Give it to them hard! Strike together!

Brush away like vermin the creatures who are trying to distract and divide you and rise up in your wrath and majesty [*that was smooth-faced, silver-tongued Donnelly speaking*]. Rome, thou hast been a tender mother. Thou hast been as the she bear to the lamb!

Is there no light on the hilltops; is there no road in the valley?

Shall we who stood the lion down pay the wolf homage?

Liberty, thy sword is in the pawnshop.

The people are aroused. Never in our history has there been such a union of action among the farmers as now.

A hundred thousand of us banded together now, and members pouring in.

A swift coming of wings beating at the portals of the present [*said another orator, and they all shushed the children and listened*]. It has brooded upon the race for centuries and the lifting of the mighty wings has uncovered the heart of humanity.

But it was not all smooth sailing. There were bickerings, their leaders were subjected to great temptation, many confusions came upon the people. The leaders, "the grange statesmen" as they were contemptuously called, went various ways; some there were whose path was lost, as one Populist paper said accurately, "at the banker's door."

But the program of the people, the speeches, the study, the understanding, the know-why, and the know-how of organization of the heartbreaking nineties was a mighty sea whose undercurrent is still strong beneath the tides.

To list only a few of the reforms which the Democratic Party inaugurated when the Populist Party threw their votes in that direction, forming a coalition, there were the Australian system of voting and other devices for a "free ballot and a fair count." Women's suffrage, election of United States Senators by direct vote of the people, senatorial primaries, the adoption of the initiative and the referendum, first used in South Dakota. The party did much to undermine old party loyalties, since at one time over a million men cast their ballots for the Populist ticket.

Populist propaganda on the free silver agitation is still being studied and a stabilized dollar is now seriously considered.

Much of the rural program was lated adopted by the New Deal: government subtreasuries for grain, short-term rural credits. While government ownership of railroads has not yet come into being, the Populist program of railroad control has long been the pressure behind the removal of many abuses. The creation of the railroad and warehouse commission protected the farmer from bad grading and short weight. Mary Lease, looking back in 1914, was proud: "My work was not in vain. The Progressive Party has adopted our platform plank by plank. Direct election of senators; public utilities being gradually removed from the hands of the few and placed under the control of the people who use them. Women's suffrage—the seed we sowed did not fall on barren ground. . . ."

As an editor of the *Farmer's Alliance* said in 1890:

The cranks are always progressive thinkers and always in advance of their time and they always win. Called fanatics and fools, at first they are sometimes persecuted and abused. But their reforms are generally righteous and time and reasoned argument bring men to their side. Abused and ridiculed, then tolerated, then respectfully given a hearing, then supported. This has been the gauntlet that all great reforms and reformers have run from Galileo to John Brown.

Dakota Blake

It was at the time when the land was going to the devil, when North Dakota started to blow into Iowa, that Budd Reeve, born like a grasshopper from the dust and many years' endurance, built a low wagon and on it he put a log cabin, which he said developed not only manhood but nationhood. With his youngest son driving a span of mules, one gray and the other bay, with a dog of great size named Sparticus, he went forth from the Canadian border to St. Paul, a pilgrim, sent no word ahead, with neither gold nor silver nor brass in his purse. On the cabin door was his flag of the earth and a sign saying, "I am not a peddler. I am a missionary performing a ceremony."

His message, he said, came from Moses: Honor thy Father (God) and thy Mother (earth), that thy days may be long on the land.

He had a book to sell written by himself, called *What I Think After Thinking*. He had been a farmer and thinking through lonely nights and days, worrying about the mortgage, he had come to some conclusions. "There is little difference between a man who can only feed hogs and the hogs he feeds. That man who takes a trip to the moon with a mortgage tied to both legs to pull him back is just as well off as though he spent all his time feeding hogs!"

In his thinking he got to thinking much about the giant hauler, the new northwestern King, the strider over prairie distances, James Jerome Hill. He saw Hill as James, the ruthless empire-builder, and he saw him as Jerome, the prairie saint of hauling. He found himself watching over Hill:

. . . because he was a hauler. It might seem ridiculous this mighty man, a factor in world building and man building, a rich man and me a poor man thinking about him in a certain way. The poor man can think things a rich man cannot. With a poor man the wind is always blowing both ways. I have always been in debt. I have been searching for light. He has been searching for gold. While Hill has been searching for passages, tunneling under, I was searching for the invisible. He is loaded with the world's goods. I am empty handed. He has everything to let go. I have let go everything.

While he was parked on a St. Paul street, his mules with their noses in a feed-bag, whom should he see standing across the street but the state's chief, the visible James and the invisible Jerome! The rich man came over and entered the cabin of the poor man and they spoke together, both agreeing on one thing, that the earth was being neglected and ruined. Hill said, "The farmers are ignorant; they have eaten the pedigreed hogs from England I gave them." Budd said, "Let me try." Hill said, "You can try. I will give you free run of my trains for three days."

So the poor man rode free on the hauler's great and many trains. He saw many people, dirt farmers, professors, grain merchants, and succeeded in calling an interstate grain-growers convention. The rich man and the poor man sat in the hall together planning how to save the land, and the poor man worried about the rich man, the Hauler Hill. He thought, "Thus far he has laid a few rails and built a few lines on the great ball of earth and is carrying around a few people. I don't say he is going to connect future worlds with his railroad, but I do say that through him will be seen the shadow of worlds beyond."

There came a time when many attacked Hill, the ruthless James. Budd sat down town in St. Paul worrying and grieving. He sat down in a hotel and began writing a letter to Hill telling him how he must become Jerome, the Hauler, the Saint, and not James, the waterer of stock, the cinch worm, the locust. When he had finished he rolled it up like a scroll, walked towards the feudal stone house of the Hauler in the early morning, and knocked on the rich man's door saying to himself: "If Lazarus sees me now I wonder if he will say, 'There goes another fool to the house of Dives.'" A servant answered the door and he handed her the scroll and went back to wait word. None came that day so the next morning he went to Hill's office down by the river and stood around, and as no one spoke or summoned him he went away.

He speaks the best for himself. He lived to a great old age, writing his books, publishing and selling them himself. This was done a great deal in the north country. He saw the world in man, in labor, and in growth. He saw the earth glad because of the growth and energy in man.

Another of his pamphlets, printed by himself, was called: *To Those Who Are Put, To Those Who Will Be Put And To Those Who Will Stay Put.* It was his theory that the best thinkers in the world were workers and farmers because they were put, had to stay put. Despite bank failure, depression, flood, and famine, they could not pull up stakes and hightail it to another place.

The man on the prairie for instance [he writes] has to stay put. The wind is howling. It is dangerous. He is lonesome. He cannot move. He has to stay. And that is the reason he is a most powerful man. He will begin to think about solving the light and heat question. He will find out that the drawback shaking his windows and blowing him to Kingdom come, can be used in a windmill. He will stay and wake up!

These are some of his sayings:

Nature: The people have their house in order; it is the suggestion of the natural forces.

The climate demands enterprise and will not accept anything else.

I have seen a weed shake its head at a loafer.

A hog returns the benefits of his peculiarities: ham, bacon, lard and souse.

Man: Humanity is constructed like a barn: granite foundation, braces, timbers, shingle nails, some hair in the plastering, some paint, ornament, the useful and the necessary.

Man is very large from having grown into great nations and many peoples, multitudes of whom are coming and going in all directions, all supported by the mother, the earth.

Man uses time for a glass and space for a book.

Everything is in man, and the future is in him illimitable. The dark and sightless end of him points down to his mother, the earth; the light and illumined end of him points up to his father, God, and he can read from darkness and build from shadows.

Work: I am not here to call attention to great libraries and difficult translations but to that which is constantly before man— to the world as a workshop.

Creation is making something.

Doing it is why it is called labor.

A worker always knows that razors are not made of pewter, nor bear traps of basswood.

There must be more work than talking to accomplish anything. It is necessary to do a lot of hard work to connect man with the world and the world with man.

Man and the earth only grow through labor.

If God made man without labor, who would care to hug or kiss such images. Even flies could not find pleasure in roosting on him.

Getting out of the shell, breathing and growing is the proposition.

Work Ritual

I love my pick and shovel,
I'll paint the handles red,
For without my pick and shovel
I couldn't earn my bread.

You'll be in despair when you wake
Tomorrow in the morn,
But a few days of labor left
And your winter's stake all gone.
                                        —LAKE SONG

With his huge *Blue Ox, Paul Bunyan came west to the
North Star Country. He could log off an entire section
in a day, so that the bookkeeper, Johnny Inkslinger, had
a hard time keeping track. He towered above the trees
and it took seven men to lift his ax. Of course he helped
Jim Hill build the railroad, after digging Puget Sound
and the St. Lawrence River. He got six hundred and
eighty beavers building the fence along the Great Northern Railroad. Paul gave Jim a low price and said he'd
build it quick. The beavers cut the jack pine along the
right of way, chewing them into six-foot lengths. Then he
brought in some Minnesota gophers to dig the postholes.
As soon as the gopher would dig a nice deep hole for his
winter home, Paul would reach down and pull him out
and drop a fence post in it. Some of the gophers objected
and held a mass meeting to complain. You can still see
them to this day, digging holes along the tracks.*
  *Aided by Sourdough Sam, Ole the Big Swede, and the
Seven Axmen, he built a great sawmill to saw up trees so
tall you could only see the tops on a clear day, with bases
so large it took a whole crew to even chop through the
bark with the double-bitted ax he had invented and the
new cross-country saw that stretched for miles along the*

ground and cut everything in its path, and took thirty
men all night to sharpen it. The forests falling raised
such a cloud of snow, the sun could be seen only on odd
Thursdays.
   The trees got so frightened that a whole forest in Bitter
Root Valley ran away.
   But Paul caught them in a net. He cleared North
Dakota in a few weeks, and Babe walked on the stumps,
pushing them down into the prairies so the Swedes could
plant wheat that winter.

—FOLKSAY

They stole into the Territory,
They stole the Territory,
They stole out of the Territory.

—FOLKSAY

Some sailors got shovels and others got spades,
And more got wheelbarrows, every man to his trade;
We worked like red devils, our fingers got sore,
And we cursed Escanaba and her damned iron ore.

—LOADING SONG

VOYAGEURS, HUNTERS, TRAPPERS, TRADERS,
frontiersmen did not care for the wheelbarrow, the pick,
and the shovel. In the new country in a very few years roads
had to be built, thousands of ties cut and laid for the railroad, millions of trees felled and floated down the rivers.
Sawmills piled towns under sawdust as boards were planed
for barns, houses, and fence posts. One guy said he cut
enough timber in one year to build a privy six feet high
and six feet wide, from Saginaw to the other side of the
Erie Canal.
   The great crust of the Algonquian rock that lay, a ring
of iron, under the Great Lakes in the ranges, Mesabi the
Giant, the Vermilion, Cayuna, Gogebic, Menominee, Marquette, had to be shoveled, lifted, hauled to their harbors,

loaded into boats, shoveled into the holds, unloaded at the other end of the journey; by hand, shoulder muscle, the small of the back, the loins, the leg muscles—working ten, twelve, fourteen hours a day.

The bonanza wheat farms grew thousands of acres of wheat which had to be harvested by thousands of men ready to thresh, winnow, store, haul, sack. Canals had to be dug in one year, by mule and man alone.

Thousands of men had to be brought from the immigrant ships, from the Eastern depressions, from the lines of the hungry in the Boweries already created by industry; some shanghaied in the night, thrown into river and lake boats to work on the Sault locks, which had to be finished so that the iron ore could get to the East, to the opening cities of Cleveland and Philadelphia.

There were Germans, Scandinavians, Cornish miners, Croatians, Finns, Slavs, Russians, Irishmen; hundreds of thousands of them without women, home, or children, ready to migrate from Germany, Ireland, the Balkans, to work in the iron pits, the railroads, the wheatfields; to go back in the fall to the Gateway, Minneapolis' hiring center, for a job in a sawmill or in the woods. There had to be thousands of migrant workers with only the back, the naked hands to sell. "Beasts," they were able to name themselves; "timber beasts," the woodsmen said.

There were the handlers of tools and the makers of new tools: the pick, the shovel, the ax, and the peavey, the donkey, the awl, the gimlet. They were the handlers—the diggers, the road—and rail-builders, including gandy-dancers, tie-cutters, and timber beasts, the bull-buckers and bull cooks and punchers, the cat-skinners, the boomers, powder monkeys, whistlepunks; they called themselves sawdust-eaters, river-hogs, boomers, and bloomers; ink-slingers, bulls of the woods, scissorbills.

They were of many races, with names like McDonald, Chisholm, Stewart, McHalle, Mackay, Boles, Jacob, Asa Tract, Emil Munch, Moses Perin, Gehegan, Hanna, McGillicutty, Hanson, Swanson—names you can now read on the country tombstones. They made new languages as well as new tools and industries; they spoke out of the long hours with the hand calloused and smoothed on the peavey, the ax, the pick and shovel, out of the new experiences of accident, fire, sickness, cold, plague, and colossal work; new names, verbs for action were made. The sharp, Celtic mind of the Cornish (called the Cousin Jacks, probably from Cussin' Jacks, for their meaty, salty vocabulary) brought new and old words in their hats; said that the ore was "hungry"—meaning poor; spoke of a "brave, keenly lode," and the "grass captain" and the "surface boss." They brought their "crib" with them—meaning lunch; called a section hand a "navvy" and had their "dish o' tay" after work; called the waste "deads," named the shaft mouth a "collar." A "touch pipe" was a rest, and they became famous for their "taty paasty Cornish cream," and said when you were pixilated you were "picky loaden."

The timber workers made up words with the flying chips. They named themselves the "flunkeys," the "cookie," the "gyppo," "fink"—a word forever in our language, and one we needed. A "boomer," "short staker," "powder monkey" was a dynamiter; "Bible-pounder"—a street-corner preacher; "sky-hooker"—top man on a sleigh; a "stiff"—anyone without a white collar; a "chiseler," "bindlestiff"—a loafer; "brains"—the office man; an "ax-handle hound," a "scissorbill"—a poor logger or a dumb one who will not join the union.

They named the machines they worked with: "cat," "tractor," "donkey"—a small engine which yards and loads; "hootnanny"—a device to hold a crosscut saw while sawing a log from underneath; and the saw itself was a "Swedish fiddle." Then they named the experiences, the actions. "Give her snoose," meaning more power; "driving the pitch"—to drive logs as long as you can see them; "carrying a balloon"—taking your blanket with you; "got her made," meaning a stake for the winter; "mix me a walk," make out my time; "put on the nòsebag"—to feed; "Timberrrrrrr!"—the cry when the tree is falling, to warn other workers. To "Saginaw" a log is to retard the large end, and to "St. Croix" her is to help the small end gain. The "wobbly horrors" were what employers got in a strike; "the long green" and "hay" for money have become part of our language; a "widow-maker" is a tree blown down by the wind, which might fall on a man; "snoose" or "Scandinavian dynamite"—chewing plug; the "bull pen"—a jail for drunks; "packing a card"—belonging to a union.

They were walkers, and still are—the long country-bred walkers, from the old chief Kichiwiski who paddled to Buffalo, left his canoe in the bushes, and walked four hundred miles to Washington. John Muir walked to the source of the Mississippi. Stefansson the explorer walked behind cattle in Dakota, thinking of far worlds. All the anonymous bindlestiffs walked from camp to camp, from job to job, all they owned in the bundles on their backs, following the sound of the ax, the thresher, the hammer, and the pick. They were mighty wanderers in those days, and still are. They walked from Detroit, Grand Rapids, Chicago. They walked into Minneapolis for the weekend to see Swede Annie on Hennepin or to Nina Clifford's in St. Paul, and they walked back on Monday; they went from the Menominee Range down the shore of Green Bay to the Brule, the Sturgeon, the Paint, the Iron and Little Cedar Rivers; from the Sausaukee, Pike, and Pembina; the Rum, the St. Croix, the Mississippi. After the country was logged off they went west into Oregon, Washington, California. They kept on walking until they stood at the ocean's edge, and then they walked back.

We Cursed Escanaba

Her smokestack's back and her whistle's blown,
And I wish the Lord I'd stayed in town.

Oh, we're bound down from Marquette—
My two hands are sore,
I've been pushing a wheelbarrow
And I'll do it no more.

Oh, maybe you don't believe me, lads,
And maybe you think I lie,
But ship in this starvation town
And you'll see the same as I.

The *Ward's* bound up, the *Moran's* bound down,
And the *John M. Nichol* am hard agroun',
And the *William H. Stevens* lying roun' the bend,
And all she's a-doin' is a-killin' good men.

George Stuntz, they said, was "tough as a juniper bush and stubborn as muskeg." He went to the head of the lakes in the blunted hills of the Chippewa country when he and a Negro named Bonga were, as the Negro used to say, "the only white men in the country."

It may be said this man was haunted by the iron cities, the long boats of iron ore, the steel that nobody dreamed about. He came up from the south to the tamarack swamps, the granite glacier-scarred hills, the blue waters. He was a surveyor, always traveling in the straightest line to the future.

Sometimes the solitary surveyor got so excited by what he saw coming toward him, all alone there in the wilderness, he had to get up and tramp all over the north, fighting the black fly, the swamps, the bitter cold, seeing occasionally the broad-nosed grisly Bonga with his big fur cap and pine staff.

Stuntz lived on a spit of land at the site of the future

Duluth, which he knew as certain as day would be there. He staked out the town lots by himself and he talked in the night to the people who weren't there yet.

He pushed the building of the Soo Canal while Henry Clay in Washington scoffed at such a project as ridiculous "in a place beyond the remotest settlement of the United States if not in the moon."

Seven people finally came and built seven shanties on the site of Duluth. They set about building a road with axes, crowbars, and fourteen men. Stuntz miraculously cleared a road fifty-seven miles from St. Louis Bay to the St. Croix River so that more people could come up. He brought back with him three yoke of oxen and two cows, who all had to live on sand grass, deer moss, and hazel thickets. But now there were fourteen men, some oxen, and two cows for Stuntz to talk about in Philadelphia, where he went to see a man as crazy as he was by the name of Jay Cooke, and there showed him a hunk of iron, and Cooke came back with him in a silk hat and cloth-topped shoes and gave him money so he could hire eighteen more men and build a road to Lake Vermilion where he thought the iron was.

After the panic of '73 which wiped Cooke out, Stuntz went to Philadelphia to look for another millionaire, and found one, and built the Duluth and Iron Range Railroad to run in easy stages from the Vermilion to Two Harbors— Now Stuntz heard the tooting of trains through the iron hills where before he had heard only his own dreaming and cursing, and the deermeat frying in the pan for one person to eat.

He kept on ahead of his dreams and the laughers forgot to laugh. On a clear day in July, 1884, he saw the steamer *Hecla* clear Two Harbors deep-laden with Vermilion ore.

Before he died he saw the Lakes fleet carrying a greater volume of maritime trade than the entire foreign commerce of the United States, and he saw the people coming of whom he had dreamed: the Cornishmen, the Finns, the Swedes, the Germans, the Irish, Scots, Yankees, Czechs, and Croatians.

Now in the Oneota Cemetery in Duluth he lies above the sound of the heavy traffic, day and night, of iron-ore barges, carrying ore that makes the steel of which he did not dream.

High, Wide, and Handsome

Benjamin Franklin, looking through old French archives in Paris, saw reference to copper on Isle Royale and managed to shift the boundary in the Louisiana Purchase north to the Pidgeon River. Thus he brought the Vermilion, the Mesabi, and the Cayuna into the United States, a region destined to remake the continent's life and give the name to a whole era: the Age of Steel. This iron ore lay close to the surface and not fifty miles from the greatest inland sea of the world. The Steel Corporation said, "Buy every pound of ore in the northwest." Rockefeller led the fortune hunters of Cleveland to rich rewards, while Judge Gary grabbed the lion's share and the Morgans and Carnegie and Frick got a hand in. Hill was early and others were late, but bankers and steelmen are still fighting over this rich country and most of the ore, they claim, is bespoken by them forever.

The metal had to be portaged to Sault Ste. Marie and then reloaded into Lake Erie. That was when workers "cursed Escanaba and her damned iron ore." The men had to load the boats in the cold wind; their skin and beards became red as iron; they had to reload and wheel the red dust to another boat. They sailed in the icy wind of the lakes, known by all seamen to be dangerous and treacherous—first the steamers, the freighters, then the flat iron pigs. The life-line was taut above the open hatches, and when the load shifted you had to go down into the yawning pits to trim the ore and square the ship, sweating in the icy hold of a pitching vessel amidst the shifting ore.

Now the ore is loaded in chutes from towering trestled docks, and three days later massive electric scoops whine at the hole to disgorge it on the Eastern landings, eating seventeen tons at a bite. But then the iron ore was moved solely by the might of thousands of men, and the Soo Canal had to be built—the Sault Ste. Marie, once the largest canal in the world, between Lakes Superior and Huron. It was built not by an engineer, but by a twenty-five-year-old Deering Scale salesman—opposed by the American Fur Company, which did not want iron ore or settlers; opposed by Eastern statesmen who laughed at the idea of a canal in the middle of the wilderness; opposed by Henry Clay and Congress, circumstances, financiers, cholera, incompetency, bribed engineers, and at last the Army.

The salesman's name was Charles Thomson Harvey. He later built the first elevated railroad in New York City, but then he was worrying about how he would get two thousand men out west to work on the canal. He was wondering how he would get the Michigan Legislature not to think him crazy to want to build locks 350 feet long and 70 feet wide. He finally got an appropriation of land, some backers, and four hundred men who came on a lake steamer straight off immigrant boats from New York. Barracks were built, and the first load of dirt was taken out by mules and men in 1853. Harvey wore out three horses a day galloping from one end of the locks to the other, solving unsolvable problems. He made them work all winter. The building of America was being held up for lack of a canal. They froze in the pits, chopped their meat with an ax, the mules breathed ice, the picks stuck in the frozen ground. A man posted at the head of each wheelbarrow runway rubbed snow on the gray faces of the workers as they went by, to prevent frostbite.

A reef that was supposed to be sand turned out to be a

ledge of rock. Two thousand men struck for their pay.
Harvey hid their supplies and refused them food until they
went back to work.

Cholera broke out, and one out of every ten men died.
A new pit was dug in the woods and they were buried at
night so the others wouldn't stampede. Hundreds more in
the East were herded into boats, and the picks kept swinging.

An old burial ground of the Indians was dug up, and the
Indians came beating their war drums on the hills, making
everyone nervous. Yet twelve and a half months later the
mules were hoisted out of the cut, the last of the thousands
of wheelbarrows came up the runways, the gates were
opened and Lake Superior flooded into the locks. The job
was done, and the men who stood watching knew that they
would have to go on down the narrow roads into the wilderness, to another job, into timber, the railroad, wheat.

"What's opening up?" they asked each other, turning in
their wheelbarrows and their picks and shovels, with possibly
their names carved on the handles, but not belonging to
them.

"I hear they want men south."

"I'm goin' north."

"West is the place to go. There is land; roads are being
built."

"The railroad is goin' west; follow the railroad!"

Some stayed for the iron locos soon to be hooting in the
pits and shafts, moving into the Mesabi now the way was
open and the Steel Age was beginning. Cemeteries would be
moved, churches lassoed in log chains and hauled away,
graves moved up "reverently" with scoop shovels, and the
greatest railroad traffic in the world then would open up on
the Duluth, Mesabi & Northern Railroad.

Sailing ships ended; the pig-iron ships came with new
machinery, elevators, derricks, electric scoops, and dippers.
Towns rose and became ghosts. Ironwood and Hurley mush-

roomed, passed laws against alley rioting, false fire alarms, and smoking on the dynamite wagon. There were barrel-houses, where whiskey was sold by the barrel, and variety houses; women were furnished in stockades with wire fences for a dollar a head. There was a monkey who would steal your wallet—one night he knocked over a lamp and burned Wakefield to the ground. Duckboard sidewalks were pitted by the boots of loggers and miners, and over everything and in everyone's skin was the red dust. From Saginaw to Duluth they said, "The four toughest places in the world are Cumberland, Hayward, Hurley, and Hell." Riches and ruin and boom and fall, drivers, millmen, and miners made towns and left them ghosts when the timber was gone or the copper or iron ore. Millionaires were made and ruined. A house was built of solid champagne bottles, mortised as a wall.

> It's the story of how, under kerosene lights,
> And far into the dark of the long winter nights
> Of the snow-drifted north, by the unsalted sea,
> Man dreamed of the day when he would be free.
> Free of his toiling from early till late,
> Of the second-rate chuck on a hungry man's plate,
> Of the gyppo's lean wage at the end of a strip,
> Of the rotten conditions, the crack of the whip,
> The choice of a bunk that was crawling with scum,
> Or cold nights in the jungle, hot days on the bum.

I Been Working on the Railroad

The new foreman was Jean McCann,
By God, he was a blame mean man!
Past week, a premature blast went off
And a mile in the air went big Jim Goff.

When next payday came around,
Jim Goff a dollar short was found;
When he asked "What for?" came this reply,
"You're docked for the time you were up in the sky."

And drill, ye tarriers, drill!
Drill, ye tarriers, drill!
It's work all day for the sugar in your tay,
Working on the U. Pay Railway.
And drill, ye tarriers, drill!
And blast!
And fire!

—EARLY RAILROAD SONG

THE BUILDING OF THE RAILROAD IN THE
Northwest was one of the great sagas of man's enterprise,
labor, and heroism. To span the great West with railroads
seemed like an impossibility. A railroad moves by human
muscle, by the clang of the sledge, the laying of rails weigh-

ing four hundred pounds—each stroke the work of a living
man who has a past, who dreams of his life, wishes he was
someplace East where the Indians didn't drop the man next
to you and the sun didn't burn down with such ferocity;
wondering if he will manage to stay alive tomorrow or if his
bones will be left like those of so many others. There was a
saying that a man was buried under every rail.

The gigantic enterprise lived in the imagination of men
in cities, the newspapers carried banner headlines as they do
now of football games, reporting how far the road had pro-
gressed. There was rivalry between gangs. How many miles
today? the papers asked. In 1869 seven miles were laid in one
day by Jack Casement's army of Celts. Charlie Crocker's
Chinese raised it a mile. Jack Casement's army challenged
the Chinese. On the day of the contest the whole nation
waited eagerly; in one city ten thousand dollars were bet on
the Celts. The Celts set a record, laying 25,000 ties, 3,520
rails, and 7,000 plates, which took 14,000 bolts, 55,000
spikes.

The Indians tried to stop it. They tortured captured
workers, shot them from ambush. Rifles lay beside picks
and spades, and at any moment you had to drop the spade
and shoot at nothing in the brush. At one place a Sioux
gang tried to stop the train by drawing a lariat across the
track and holding it taut from both sides. The engineer saw
it, opened the throttle, hit it running, and spread Indians
along the track.

Nothing could stop it. Tent cities sprang up along the
roadway: saloons, dance halls, even bands that played around
the clock for the day and night shifts. Games of chance went
on, day and night, with tremendous stakes.

The *Fortnightly Review* describes the process of laying
track:

On they come; a light car drawn by a single horse gallops up
to the front with its load of rails. Men seize the end of a rail

and start forward, the rest of the gang taking hold by twos until it is clear of the car. They come forward at a run at the word of command, the rail is dropped in its place right side up with care; it is taken hold of on the other side and in less than thirty seconds to a rail for each gang. So four rails go down to the minute.

Close behind come the gangers, spikers, and bolters, and a lively time they make of it. It is a grand anvil chorus that the striking sledges are playing across the plains. It is triple time, three strokes to the spike. There are ten spikes to a rail, four hundred rails to a mile, and eighteen hundred miles to San Francisco. Twenty-one million times those sledges are to be slung. Twenty-one million times they are to come with their sharp clang before the great rail of North America is complete.

When at last the two rails met and the golden spikes were driven the whole nation rejoiced; whistles blew in Washington, thousands paraded in Chicago streets, and the Liberty Bell was rung in Philadelphia.

And the thousands of workers moved on, walked west, rode the freights back east, went south with the birds, were chased by the bulls off the trains. Here is a song written by one of them about an old rider of the trains. It contains some of their language:

> The lingering sunset across the plain
> Kissed the rear end of an eastbound train,
> And shone on a rusty track close by
> Where a dingbat sat on a rotten tie.

> He was ditched by the shack and cruel fate,
> The con high-balled and the manifest freight
> Pulled out on the stem behind the mail,
> And she hit the ball on a sanded rail.

> Nothing in sight but sand and space,
> No chance for a bo to feed his face;
> Not even a house to bed for a lump
> Nor a henhouse there to frisk for a grump.

And another:

> If you want to do me a favor
> When I lay me down to die,
> Plant my bones on the mainstem
> So I can hear the trains go by.
>
> I've handled a pick alongside a spick,
> Laying steel on the M. K. and T.
> And I've hit the heavy on the N. O. levee,
> Sailed on an oiler to sea.
>
> I've juggled a tray in a Bowery café,
> Hopped bells for a hotel in Chi,
> Carried a pack along the B. & O. track,
> Glommed red-ball freights on the fly.
>
> All my life I've roamed without friend or home,
> Up and down the old cinder trail,
> And now it seems all I have is my dreams
> Of days that were spent out of jail.
>
> He built the road.
> With others of his class he built the road.
> Now over it many a weary mile he packs his load—
> Chasing a job, spurred on by hunger's goad,
> He walks and walks and wonders why in hell
> He built the road.

Live on Hay

> You will eat, by-and-by,
> In that glorious land above the sky,
> Work and pray, live on hay,
> You'll get pie in the sky when you die.
>   —JOE HILL

In the days of the big wheat crops, the boxcars going north would be black with harvesters sitting on the top, going to the fields. In Minneapolis, where employment agencies lined one of the biggest labor marts in the world then, they gath-

ered to get jobs. In the early days farmers went to the harvest
from their farms in Kansas or Nebraska to pick up a little
cash.

The folksay here becomes confused because railroad songs
and harvest songs became the songs of the itinerant worker
generally as he moved from job to job, from camp to camp,
farm to farm, walking, catching the highballs.

> The sun is bright, the skies are blue,
> Honey, I'd like to stay with you,
> But there ain't no work for me to do—
> My private car is waitin'.
>
> Your kissin's sweet as new-mown hay,
> Your smile is like a sunny day,
> But, honey, I must be on my way.
> I'd like a house near a shady tree
> An' a bunch of kids upon my knee,
> But, honey, the good life ain't for me—
> My private car is waitin'.
>
> There ain't a thing on earth I've got,
> Even if I had a six-foot lot—
> They'll give me that when I'm left to rot.
> Just call it quits and say good-by,
> You'll get another man—and I,
> A bunch o' stars in a jungle sky—
> My private car is waitin'.
>
> My car has a roof an' a slidin' door,
> O Lord, when I lay on that hard wood floor,
> 'Way down in the guts of me I'm sore—
> Honey, someday the time will come
> When a workin' stiff don't have to bum,
> An' a man's a man, not a jungle crum—
> My private car is waitin'.*

And this one:

> You advertise in Omaha,
> "Come, leave the valley of the Kaw,"

* Irene Paull.

Nebraska calls, "Don't be misled,
We'll furnish you a feather bed."

Then South Dakota lets out a roar,
"We need ten thousand men or more.
Our rain is turning, prices drop,
For God's sake, save our bumper crop!"

In North Dakota, I'll be darn,
The wise guy sleeps in a Hoosier barn,
The Hoosier breaks into his snore,
Then yells it's quarter after four.

Oh, harvest land, sweet-burning sand,
As on the sun-kissed field I stand,
I look away across the plain
And wonder if it's going to rain.
I vow by all the brands of Cain
That I will not be here again.

Good-by to Bay Shalore

Pilgrims!
The silent pilgrims of the winding trail, whose lives are
a constant ramble. These pilgrims are perpetually in
motion like the comets in the sky.
Pilgrims!
They are simple, sincere and artless children of toil,
and there are so many of them. They live outside of the
world proper; forgotten and discarded. The forests of
the West, the vast acres of Minnesota, Michigan, and
Wisconsin know these men and their iron grip. Behind
them in these places they have left the label of their toil.
These pilgrims have laid their calloused hands on the
virgin breasts of our nature, and they have devoured the
pride and dignity of our forests.
For whom have they done this? For themselves? No!
They have just helped to fill the coffers—not even the
trifle that has been paid as wages has benefited them. It
has gone to support the moonshiners, the speakeasies,
and the fellow victims, outcasts of the world proper, the
women of the streets.
These simple men of the crude world, the world of
toil, have no means to select company. They go where
they are welcome, where they are known. Through the
winding paths they have traveled, and in the forest—on
these winding trails one meets them, singly, in pairs, in
groups. One sees heads that are bowed low, feet that are
weary and tired. In their packsacks they are carrying their
worldly goods: underwear, a shirt, crumpled and stiff
from dried sweat, and perhaps a picture—or some treas-
ured keepsake.
Not a great accumulation for decades of misery and
toil; it is not heavy to carry—
When an ax bites into a tree or a saw grinds through
wood, a peculiar emotion gropes for freedom within the
breast of the woodsman. Ever reaching outward, it brings
bitterness and pain. Or when a lonely traveler treads the

*trail, returning from a trip to the city where his few days
of freedom were spent ingloriously, a bitter lump rises to
his throat—*

What is the end of this winding trail?

Death—

*The scythe of death finds a fertile field. Here it is easy
to persuade the victim—physical resistance is gone, unnatural diet and cheap spirits have paved the way—a man
in thin clothes has slept in a snowbank or in a fall rain,
he fails to make camp, the whispering pines witness his
death.*

*Others die in filthy beddings of the camp, where
vermin fight for a meal from the last warm drop of his
blood. Death is always around, like a bloodthirsty coyote,
through the hazards of work. The companies do not com-
pensate for these deaths; relatives are seldom known.
They are sent out to be buried.*

Where? Somewhere.

*There is nobody asking questions. No wreaths are laid
on the graves; no one will be looking for these graves.
No tears are shed at these burials. Johnny and Jimmy remember, but they are unable to decide which is luckiest,
he that is buried or he that is continuing the journey on
the winding trail.*

Remember?

*They are sometimes remembered. They are given a
name to separate them from humanity. When one of
them is jailed or commits suicide, the press remembers
this name.*

*Their work is hard and hazardous and important. Why
are they forgotten? Society will continue to need these
toiling hands.*

These men are going to arise!

*Arise in the eyes of themselves, in the eyes of society.
The day is dawning!*

> —FREE TRANSLATION FROM THE FIRST PAGES OF
> UNHOTETUJEN MAAILMASTA, BY MICHAEL
> RUTANEN, A BELOVED FINNISH POET WHO
> WORKED TWO DECADES IN THE WOODS OF THE
> LAKE STATES

THERE WERE THIRTY-ONE MILLION, FIVE HUN-
dred thousand acres of virgin forest in Minnesota. In the

Big Woods grew maple, basswood, balsam; in the north, the red Norway and white and jack pine, white spruce, balsam fir, white cedar, and tamarack, mixed with hardwoods: white birch, aspen, elm, basswood, maple, and ash. Lumber was needed and lumber was here, and everyone wanted the land timbered off so they could plow it up for wheat.

It was a very exciting time, with all the wealth and speed necessary for land grants to "cut out and get out" for railroads, roads, canals. Timber barons wore white beaver hats and lobbied in Washington. The biggest land grant ever recorded—totaling forty-seven million acres, a tract larger than the whole of New England—was about to be made. Cattlemen, mining men, lumbermen, and saw-long statesmen were after a slice of the public domain. The West was being parceled out in poker games at the Willard. Towns were rising, railroads were being built, timber cut in the night. One farmer tells this:

Yes, sir, I told the lumbermen they could plumb go to hell, that I wasn't selling my stand of timber. I wanted to keep a little stand of timber and I wouldn't sell to God himself. I chased 'em kit and kaboodle off my land. But I guess they was more powerful than God, leastways more persistent. I went to town to get a writ forbidding them to cut my timber. I was gone only a day and a night, and when I come back and come around the bend, it looked like a plague of locusts had gone right through my land. It was bald as a baby's bottom, nibbled right down to the root, every last tree gone, the sky standing there naked as a jay. They took away every stick, gnawed it down and took it clean away, slick as a whistle. That's what they done for a fact, and there I was, standing there legal as hell, waving my writ at a bunch of stumps!

There were professional homesteaders who got title to the land and turned it over to the lumber kings for cutting. There was "sugaring-off"—buying some portions, holding them, cutting the cream before anybody knew it. The slogan was: Cut out and get out. There was the "round forty" business. A man might buy forty acres, send the boys in to log around forty acres; so the boys would cut around forty—first the forty to the north, then to the south, then to the east and the west.

The National Conservation Commission found that solid townships in northern Minnesota "had been acquired under the Homestead Law, the timber cut off, and not a single voter or inhabitant could be found in the townships." Certificates were given to half-breeds establishing ownership to eighty acres, which were then signed over tc the companies.

Nine million logs went down the river in 1851, and in the next year forty-four million board feet, until the sawdust piles heaped over the streets of the towns. Mansions went up in the Twin Cities and along the rivers, built by the new empire-builders: wheat, lumber, and railroad barons.

"Were the lice thick?" the lumberjack was asked.

"Times were hard for them, too; only the fittest survived. They died from famine by the millions when we were laid off, and we were laid off plenty. When the cutting started again they would get thick."

"Weren't the blankets ever washed?"

"Not during the pine days. I've heard that they were washed in the spring of 1937, but the boys claim that after the dirt had dissolved into the water the blankets vanished!"

A thousand million dollars in timber was extracted from Minnesota alone. The earnings of a lumberjack were rarely more than thirty dollars a month. Often in the spring he left the camp without a dollar; the books of a bogus contractor, working under a bigger company, showed a loss and rooked him out of his hard-earned pay. Employment agencies conspired to rob him.

In return for this insecurity the lumberjack walked sixty or seventy miles to camp, got up at four o'clock, hiked a couple of miles to the timber, waited for dawn dodging the frozen branches—"widow-makers"—which cracked many a skull. He had to be skillful of eye, nimble and precise, with power, hardihood, and strength. There was a saying that the lumber industry took "a Swede a day."

He slept in what were called eight-blanket camps. Sleeping platforms ran the length of the side walls in two tiers, holding eight men. Balsam branches were thrown on top and a continuous blanket ran the length of the bunks, nailed to the walls; the men crawled in and were covered by another, also nailed to the wall. These were not as bad as the muzzle-loader bunks that allowed forty inches' width for two men; the sleepers crawled in from the foot until it was loaded. It was the duty of the bull cook to see that they crowded close enough to allow room for all.

For entertainment on Saturday night if they were too far from town, there was an evening stag dance with the "ladies" marked by a handkerchief around the arm.

The teamsters and choppers felled the trees, cutting a notch or "calf" in the side toward which they wished it to fall and then sawing into the opposite side with a crosscut saw until the blade went far enough so that an iron wedge could be driven into the gap. The tree was then lifted over toward the side where the calf had been cut. The loaders put the logs on the skids, marked them with brands before they were put into the rivers—the Willow River, then the Apple, the Wood, the Clam, the Yellow, Loon Creek; then the famous Namekagon, Hay Creek, Bean and Potato Brook, the Fox, the St. Croix, and the Chippewa, and at last the broad flood of the Mississippi.

At first the men birled the logs with cantdogs or peaveys, wearing heavy driving-boots with calked heavy soles and steel pegs to keep them from falling into the water. The main body of logs was sluiced out, the stragglers brought in, and the oversized logs, called "drummers," released. It was dangerous riding the twirling log, revolving and cuffing it with the feet until it spun many revolutions a minute; then they would stop it suddenly, hold it stationary in the water, keeping their balance. They rode the logs even through the sluiceways, where they held them at an angle of thirty degrees, riding them like broncos.

Later the logs were rafted down the rivers, lashed together and managed by large oars some forty-five feet long, one oar on each end of a string of logs. Rafting was without parallel as a feat of navigation—piloting the rafts through the treacherous Mississippi, in the dark, without mark or channel, especially through dangerous Lake Pepin where storms rose instantly and the channel shifted with sand and wind. By cordeling (hands propelling the rafts from shore) they made two to four miles a day. The raft pilot was paid well, wore French calk boots, black cassimere trousers, red flannel shirt, and a large black necktie with flowing ends, together with a wide soft-brimmed black or white hat. His crew were often tough men—"alligator horses"—of short lives and violent ends. The steamboat pilots threw newspapers down to the rafts and sometimes—with their compliments—a demijohn.

A relative of Abe Lincoln, Stephen Hanks, was one of the best pilots on the Mississippi—was shot at during the war by rebel guerrillas.

The many tough, roaring, hard-working, and fast-living men "cut their brag in the bark":

I'm the toughest goldarned alligator in the North Woods, I'll swear by the Mackinaw Jesus I can outskyhook, outfight, outwork, outdrink any knights of the trail within the sound of my voice.

Roll out, daylight in the swamp!
Rise up, snakes, and bite a biscuit!
This is the day you make your fortune.

I hollered to him to throw a Saginaw into her, but he St. Croixed her instead.

We worked all the holidays. We worked as long as she run.

You could fight like hell when you couldn't stand it any longer.

Or get you a session with John Barleycorn.

Or high-tail it to Swede Annie's, or Nina Clifford's, under the hill in St. Paul.

They was looking for you on the skidrow. They'd take you to camp in your sleep.

It was a hell-roaring time all right.

God, how we ranged and roved in them days! I been from Saginaw to Muskegon to Marquette and Escanaba. I been to Green Bay and to Chippewa and to Stillwater, and I don't know where-all!

They got hot ponds so we can work all winter.

Took seven weeks to break the Angle Rock jam—two hundred men and a hundred horses, two donkeys, and a steamboat.

In the fire hundreds of us burned in the trees, fell out charred to ashes.

The timber is gone. The hunters are shootin' loggers for deer, the whiskey's gettin' weaker, and there are signs in the saloons: CALKED BOOTS NOT ALLOWED. Time to move on.

Time to go down that narrow road, on further, west—to-morrow.

> We shed no tears for yesteryears,
> Good-by to Bay Shalore!
> Farewell to you, old midnight crew—

Struggle

Folks Say

---

*This is the country, yes, toward which they shouldered
the daily suns.*

*This is their children's land:
the double winter of human agency,
insecurity's ague, chills that eat us poor.
Hopes gaunt in kennel no longer trace
that once warm scent, love's quiet early deer.*

*The dead here made their choice,
We too must choose—
dispel the frost of spirit and come forth
under the strange, familiar trees of home.*

—RAY SMITH

Fourth of July, 1944

THE VILLAGE HAS BEEN GAILY ALIVE, BELLS
ringing, boys and girls in their Sunday-go-to-meeting suits
and bright dresses swinging across the fields, and the hot
sun shining on the old men, the young children without
memory, upon the full-bosomed women who wipe their eyes
at the parade, remembering. At the cemetery the meadow-
larks and the mourning doves sit on the graves of men and

253

women who came to this country when it was spired with pine masts and it took three days to go to town. In the light of modern day—in an age of tractors and four-motored bombers—old muskets are fired and the militia shoots off new ones over the graves, and the sounds turn in the sun and the echo of the shots moves around the valley in contrapuntal, shifting space and time for a moment, into a thousand pieces, reflected, shifting, moving together again.

This year the young girls look frightened and hold each other tighter around their bright waists; the old men, bent like sticks in water with the mark of their long labors, look up with blind eyes, the past falling back into them; and the women with their strong, willful look to go on after every war—after this war, after any war—putting the pot on the fire, borrowing an egg, lending sugar, crocheting a quilt.

On such a day questions rise from the eyes. They are bound in time, rusty with disuse, buried in the obscurest dreams. What did Silas do then after the Civil War and why did his wife kill herself, and what happened to the boys who later went to Alaska? And what does it all mean, all the work, the loss, the speech that has no record, the bodies, faces, hands that have sunk away; the whispered speech in the next room bordering on horror? But there will be no answer, only silence full of murmurings, a rambling story, broken pictures.

The album will come out to the parlor table and you see again the pictures of lost men and women, leaning their chins upon their hands, the grim women in imposed repose, the children who died young, all the mystery and identity in their eyes, the mouths opening to speak, the hands for touch.

There are picnickers all afternoon along the river, cars stand in front of the beer joints, everyone full as ticks of food and memory, the pleasant sensations of family reunions, talk of crops, the new children, the sons in Africa, the Pacific, scattered over the world; the long struggle marked in the farm houses standing in the countryside, in the bodies of men and women, marking all the myriad strong ways of the people, lanky, powerful, containing and making true history.

Down at the river tavern, women and children stay up late to see the holiday fish come in. The country women have elegant fingerwaves; the children play the slot machines. There are pleasant ribaldry and badinage. A boy like a fawn plays an accordion, and later a flute and a banjo join him. The musicians wander up and down the river. An old man dances with a baby in his arms, humming like a cricket, and the fat bready women elbow each other, laughing behind their hands.

The moon comes up; across the river rockets begin to hiss into the sky bringing everyone to their feet with low moans and little cries. The fishermen from the boats watch and when the light breaks after the zooming arch the river reflection shatters and then darkens. Young bucks aprowl in the woods yell and the girls are set astir.

"The fishermen are coming, Charlie," someone says. The boats come slowly down the moonlight strip, "Right in here." The lantern swings, the black boats nose in, men rise stiff and grope for land. Fish talk and excitement agitate the darkness, cries of, "Look at that now! Ahhhhhhh what a beauty!"

The fish are lifted into the shifting light, hanging from their bloody mouths, their eyes opening in a stare—strings of glittering darkness, turning the river shine from their sides. "Aren't they beauties? Aren't they dandies?"

The midsummer night deepens. This is the time you remember. We have lived and known the history of these hills and villages. We sleep in these hills. Every valley in which the night deepens is known; you have worked in it with hope and sorrow. Sometimes you did not get your salt back.

History both personal and communal lies in these hills and valleys, living in this tide of the moment. The bright wreath of girls sing in the night now not knowing what tomorrow will be. The old farmer dances with the baby in his arms.

And the voices of the young girls unseen now, lift from the dark earth.

By the Icy Lake

I came to America when lots of immigrants came because there was lots of work in America, because they were building then and talk of coal, iron, railroads, wheat, corn, digging, building, needing lots of laborers and you could get an education.

In Sweden when I was a young girl, not too plump but nice and round, I sang on Christmas Eve and everyone stopped in the snow to listen. Yes.

In America I was like drunk for years, a child coming every year, lifting, scrubbing, polishing, pulling, shoving, planting, chopping, birthing, the cold shooting into me, the child not born gnawing me, and famines, panics, depressions coming and going.

I come to the north country and married my husband who worked on the ore docks high up in the icy wind and we lived down on the sand spit where my children never saw green grass.

I had six children in so many years and then my husband took sick from the hard work in the cold and the next fall at thirty-six he died. The docks killed him and the company gave me a sack of flour.

My children was getting bigger and they wanted a nice house, to have it, and with all my children working we started to build a house. It takes always a lot of blood and work to build a worker's house. First the frame and then the roof, and we moved into it, building inside like spiders. In that house we have lived in it. My mother and two sons died inside the walls we raised. In that house I have suffered and we have remodeled it. With my children all bringing in the money it was many years before we got the floors upstairs and then the basement and the furnace, and we had a house, then the first World War came. The boys went to war and never came back.

I now have all my children married and those that are dead. I have one daughter who sticks with me till the end. Somebody

else now lives in my house and I cry to think of it, besides paying one hundred dollars taxes, but I cry to sell it because it's all
I got to show.

I like to go back there before I die.

I have now all my children and those that are dead.

—AMELIA FRIEDELL

American Boy

What I have to tell as to what happened to me on the streets
of America is very hard for me to tell. Perhaps all the people
who have come to America have had a like experience. They
have come from an old country into a new, and so they have
died a death and been born into a life.

In St. Paul there was the Mississippi, my ancient father, my
Uncle Moishe and his family, who owned their own house
already. My Uncle Moishe said to me day and night, "That's
what you have to do, become a real American boy. Forget about
Russia and become a real American like my sons."

They came home every night with their shoe boxes, whistling
and talking nothing but English, and talking very loud. They
were trying to forget everything about the old country, my uncle
said.

After supper we sat down and my uncle went on talking.
America was the land of opportunity, he said; why, you could
be President. "Give me," he said, walking up and down with a
big cigar, "give me a boy with brains and the education and
Napoleon wouldn't have a look in. Everybody is the same in
America, and the fellow who makes money is the merchant, not
the farmer."

"What kind of education, Moishe?" my father said.

"Education is business," Uncle Moishe said. "Education is
how to do it. I know what kind of Gemara student this boy
was. I know he was the best in his class in the Talmud. Then
why can't he learn a business course in America, I ask you, and
own the railroad?"

My father had hidden his face in his beard; his eyes were in-
scrutable. Afterwards when we were going to bed he said, "Uncle
Moishe has grown a long tongue in America."

Through the city, at the base of the warehouses, ran the Mississippi. Every morning I went across the iron bridge that spanned it and into the city. The river came to mean something to me—something that I was trying not to remember, so in the mornings and the evenings I hurried across it, not looking over the railing into the broad, slow, tenuous, moving water.

"The first word I learned was 'greenhorn.' That was what I was called. In order not to be a greenhorn I knew I must forget Russia, land of dreams, and the river Bug of my childhood.

"When a boy calls you a greenhorn and you don't believe it, you got to fight him, and if you win you quit being a greenhorn," my cousins said.

When I was called a greenhorn I said, "Come into the alley." And shook my fist as I had seen other boys do, but when I began to fight the gang all jumped on me and yelled out that I wasn't fighting in the American style. I thought there was only one way to fight, with teeth, fists, everything. It did no good to tell them that they should fight their way and I mine. When I told them that, they all yelled out a kind of dog-laugh and one fellow shoved his fist in my face and said, "Once a greenhorn, always a greenhorn!" Then he hit me a blow and the gang went down the alley still laughing that kind of dog-laugh.

I came to think that what my Uncle Moishe meant by an education was thinking and being in style. There was a way of doing everything, and if you went your own way you were called a greenhorn and you did not make money. You had to dress a certain way, look a certain way; you had to whistle and you had to smile. My uncle would say again and again that my face was too sad—it was enough to hurt business.

I sold papers and shined shoes and wrote on the inside of my shoe box, "America is business and style." I found out you did not make money by working but by scheming.

One night a newsboy going home found me looking down into the slow water beneath the bridge. "It's foolish," he said, "to worry and look like an old man. I'll take you where you need to go."

That night he took me down a side street to a saloon. We went through the bar to the back room and there on the pool table under a light I saw a crap game. Around the table, leaning over it, were the white and black boys and girls, and a big Negro kissed the dice and boomed out, crooning and shouting: "What

you gonna do for me, baby? Come on, pretty bonzies, step out,
honey, give us the black dick every time! eeeeeeeleven! A pair
of snake eyes for forty bucks!" It was underground American
poetry, of love, conquest, battle, prayers and supplication, rivaling Isaiah.

After that every night I went to the saloon. I had to cross the
bridge but I always took a streetcar and closed my eyes. I knew
the river was right underneath the bridge but I kept saying to
myself that there was no river. I went around with the gang now
and to all appearance I was now an American boy. I had something to do every minute and I was no longer called a greenhorn.
I could talk to the dice now, and I discovered baseball—to rise
and yell with a thousand throats, to shout out violent poetry of
action and motion, learned from the pink sports sheets, spelled
out and yelled across the field; it made you forget that placard
"Smile" in your shoe box. It made you forget the education you
would have to have to make you "think in big money."

One night I shot craps and made what is called a killing. I
went home and my father was waiting for me. "Do you want to
break my heart? Whistling and with your pockets full of money—
is that education? Uncle Moishe has the ambitions of a Russian
baron. Do we come from Russia and the Czar to be the slave of
something worse?"

I couldn't stand to see his face and I went back to town,
picked out the darkest streets, and walked. Then I came back to
the river. There it was. I could no longer deny it: a live, black
river, moving on and on. A moon above and a city asleep, an
American city sleeping. The lone steel bridge hung over the
river, beneath were the railroad yards and the boys moving out
on freight cars. My hands gripped the steel railing. I had felt
the same years before when my mother told me we must tear
Russia out of our hearts. Other things must be torn out, too. A
strong black river flowed under the bridge. I could no longer
deny it: a dark river flowing beneath American life, like the crap
game, baseball, and women.

A train came into the yards, snorting in the moonlight, full
of power and speed and American style, and for the first time I
began to understand what my uncle meant by owning a railroad
and by education. For a few minutes I felt that I could do anything in America. I felt the strength of the bridge, and the rails,
and my own body. I, too, felt strong. Had I not slept on the

ground with land dreams? Now could I not become a money-dreaming American, with my strength and my brains?

Then the train pulled out and everything was still. The old river flowed on beneath the bridge. I felt the river rising toward me as if many hands were held out to me from the dark rising water, and I felt afraid. I shouted with terror. I ran home and found my father sleeping. I took off all my clothes and lay down beside him wondering how to become an American without entering into the conspiracy against her.

—Y. ROBONOFF

Drought

─────────────

Because the ground is chapt, for there was no rain in the earth, the plowmen were ashamed and covered their heads. Yes, the hind calved in the field and forsook it, because there was no grass. And the wild asses did stand in the high places, they snuffed up the wind like dragons; their eyes did fail, because there was no grass.

—JEREMIAH, 14: 6

Instead of fraternity you will get isolation; instead of inalienable peasant alotment the land will be drawn into commerce; instead of a blow at the grabbing speculators, the basis for capitalist development will be expanded. But . . . it is historically good, for it will frightfully accelerate social development and bring much nearer new and higher forms.

—LENIN ON KARL MARX'S ANSWER TO KRIEG AS
TO THE OPENING OF FREE WESTERN LANDS IN
AMERICA

THAT YEAR, IN THE EARLY DAYS OF THE DE-
pression, after the bank holiday—what has come to be known
as the "crash"—came the drought. I drove through the country trying not to look at the ribs of the horses and the cows,
but you got so you couldn't see anything but ribs, like
beached hulks on the prairie, the bones rising out of the

skin. You began to see the thin farmer under his rags and his wife lean as his cows.

This was not something sudden. It had been happening a long time and came sooner than Hill had predicted. In the spring, after the terrible winter, added to mortgages and low prices, there was no rain. The village where I lived did not exchange money for two years; they bartered and exchanged what produce they had.

I drove to Dakota in the bus through the hot, stifling country, with dark clouds of dust moving steadily eastward into Illinois and Ohio; Dakota walking east. Everyone talked about horses, cattle, seed, land, death, hunger. The bus went steadily through the bleak country, and they pointed out the window at land now owned by the insurance companies, and we saw it splitting open like rotting fruit after years of decay and erosion, exposing the gashed core; it was the fifth year of the depression.

We stop at a little town and some drivers get on, space-drunk young men, their skin pocked, burnt from the dust and wind, driving from Dakota east, driving trucks back and forth. They like to drive swift and mad over the country, a girl in every city. "We went three hundred miles yesterday," one of them says, slouching down, sleeping on the go—huge half-man, half-boy; mid-American faces lolling.

There is something about the American earth that is curiously loved. Even like this, with this dark doom of ruin over it, everyone sees it as it originally was: lovely, green, eldorado, with clear streams and broad pastures beside the still rivers.

The country looks so lonely and silent; I realize with a start that the ground has not been plowed or planted. There was no seed. A farmer answers me before I have spoken, "You can't get you no seed. Last year the drought ruined everything and this year they ain't no seed. My farm plumb blew away. The land is sure ruined this year, and mine for a sight longer. It blew right out from under me, clean as a whistle. The fields packed against the barn so you couldn't see the top, the thistles and tumbleweed caught the dust at the fences so you could walk right over them on solid sand. That there land won't grow a Russian thistle."

"What's going to happen?" another says. "People from my home town, pioneers, mind you, gone to Alaska now. Pioneering some more. It beats the Dutch."

"Holy mackerel!" says the grieving men. "Whole villages ruined! What will they do there?"

And the man talk goes on:

This is the bread-basket of the world going up in dust.

Yes, sir, we were starved, stalled and stranded. Dried out three years runnin'. My wife and child jest dried up and blowed off.

Did ye hear this one? A Dakota farmer was waitin' at the hospital for his first baby. The nurse announced an eight-pound baby to the man waiting with him and to the Dakota farmer she announced a three-pound one and to the surprise of the other he seemed very happy. "Man," said the father, "three pounds is a smidgen of a baby. Don't look to me that baby's got a chance. Why are you so happy?" "I'm a farmer from North Dakota." "What's that got to do with it?" "Why, everything. In North Dakota we're darn glad to get our seed back!"

Got to keep movin'. Jest lookin' fer a home. We didn't stop to shut the door.

Dust got so thick the prairie dogs dug their holes right into the air!

Yes, sir, the government bet me a hundred and fifty acres against my belly that I couldn't stick it out. I won.

That land now jest fittin' to hold the world together.

We seen many a time, many a season. We come a far trek and we'll go farther yet. We'll ride through more seasons and buck more journeys yet.

And the folksay echoes back from the years:

My whole place dried up and blowed away.
I didn't sell out, I give out.

Tractors and the wind is our enemy. Should never have plowed up the buffalo grass.

An Indian turned back the freshly plowed prairie sod and said to the new settler who was showing him how to plow, "Wrong side up!"

Another Indian about to be hanged said, "The land you now take by force is the flesh of my fathers."

The conversation continues in a beer joint when the bus stops for lunch. A man in a tattered coat and split shoes joins us in hopes of a free drink, and the young man has been tippling from a bottle in his pocket and makes a speech. The Constitution is a good one, he says; there's a difference between the Constitution and the government, you can bet your bottom dollar on that. According to the Constitution there is no such thing as sedition and the Constitution permits life, happiness, and shall we say the pursuit of freedom—yes, we will say it. "Your mother told you you were going to be President. That's the bunk. Who in hell *wants* to be? All I want is to find some water to go fishing in. Why didn't she tell you you were going to live a good life, that's all—just that stuff, a good life? That's what the Constitution says for a man: life, liberty, and the pursuit of happiness."

The man in the tattered clothes waves his hands surprisingly. "But what about private capital," he says, and you could have knocked us over with a straw. "Yes, sir, what about private capital? Suppose," he says, "I want to put up a skyscraper, or build a railroad, what about it?"

The bus fled through the country and the sun was obscured by the moving dust. The women put wet cloths over the children's noses. And you could see the kind of terror that had grown in everyone. The winter wheat had died; the peas had gone in and fallen down as if mowed by a hot scythe. The corn never came up. The onion seed blew away.

And it was too much, at last. A high wind is an awful thing; it wears you down, it nags at you day after day, it sounds like an invisible army, it fills you with terror as something invisible does. It was like the flu terror. No one went outdoors. People shut up their houses as if from some horrible invasion, some massacre on the streets. The radio took to announcing that there was no danger in the dust, which was not true; many children died of it, of dust pneumonia and other diseases that were never named. When you looked out the window you saw the black cloud of dust going over, you saw the fields whiten and die and the crops creep back into the ground.

At first the farmers kept on plowing, first with two horses, then you had to use four to rip the earth open, and when you did a fume of dust went up like smoke and a wind from hell whipped the seed out.

Every day the pastures got worse. The grass was dry as straw and the cattle lost their flesh quickly. You had to look for a green spot for them every morning. Children were kept out of school to herd the cattle around near streams and creeks. Some farmers cut down the trees so the cattle could have the poor wind-bitten leaves. Some farmers have turned their cows into what was left of their winter wheat, which is thin as a young man's first beard.

Then on Decoration Day all hope went—the wind started again, blowing hot as a blast from hell, and the young corn withered as if under machine-gun fire; in two hours the trees looked as if they had been beaten.

We pass mules hauling a light wagon full of barrels, and with a start I realize that they are hauling water. The wells are dry. The hills are bare and we see no cattle. We pass a freight taking John Deere machinery back to Minneapolis. It is being repossessed. We begin to pass old cars loaded to the gills with household furniture and the back seat full of waving children. They are going west again.

When late afternoon came down not a soul was in sight: the houses closed up tight, the blinds drawn, the windows and doors closed. There seemed to be menace in the air. It was frightening—you could hear the fields crack and dry, and the only movement in the down-driving heat was the dead writhing of the dry blighted tumbleweeds.

There was something terrifying about this visible sign of disaster. It went into your nostrils so that you couldn't breathe: the smell of hunger. It made you count your own ribs with terror. You don't starve in America. Everything looks good. There is something around the corner. Everyone has a chance. Is that all over now?

The dust now becomes so thick, the driver must drive very slowly. It grinds against the windshield. We drive as if going to a funeral; the corpse is the very earth. The houses are closed and stand in the haze hardly visible, unpainted, like the hollow pupa when life has gone. But you know that everywhere in those barricaded houses are eyes drawn back to the burning windows, looking out at next winter's food slowly burning.

The whole countryside bears not only its present famine but its coming hunger. No vegetables now and worst of all, no milk. It is monstrous with this double doom! Every house is alike in suffering; hundreds of thousands of such houses from state to state.

An awful thing happened. The sun went down behind the hot rim of the horizon, and the men and women began to come out of the houses, the children lean and fleet as rats, the tired, lean farm women looking to see what was left. The men ran into their fields, ran back for water, and began to water what was left of their gardens with buckets and cups, running, pouring the puny drops of water on the baked earth as if every minute might count now. The children ran behind the cows, urging them to eat the harsh, dry grass. It looked like an evacuated countryside with the people running out after the enemy had passed. Not a word seemed to be spoken. In intense silence they hurried down the rows with buckets and cups, watering the wilted corn plants, a Gargantuan and terrible and hopeless labor. One man came out stubbornly with a horse and plow and began stirring up the deadly dust. Even the children ran with cups of water, all dogged, mad, without a word. There was a terrible madness in it, like things that are done after unimaginable violence.

A farmer gets on and says he's going anywhere. He's got to get away from the sound of his cows crying for food. He says that the farmer across from him yesterday shot his twenty-two head of cattle and then shot himself.

When I shut my eyes, the flesh burns the eyeballs and all I can see is the sign visible now of starvation and famine, ribs, the bones showing through the skin, rising over the horizon.

In the small town, Main Street is crowded and the farm woman and I look in the window of the grocery store. "A few nubbins of corn," she says, "is all that come up. Nobody in our parts could use the tractors, no gasoline, we got out the old mules. We'll be goin' back to the hand plow and the sickle. We lost our mule then and sold the hogs to feed the chickens, and ate the chickens ourselves. Now our place is bare as a hickory nut. I don't think you want to come out. Listen, I haven't got— Oh, it would make me feel bad."

"Never mind," I said, and she looked at me with her bleached eyes, with a touch of strange awkwardness, and bowed quaintly and we got in the old surrey driven by the only son left at home now. The old nag walks through Main Street and the men lounge far back in the shadow of eaves, the street looks stripped as if buzzards had been at it. We move out into the prairie, through the sulphurous haze; the ruined earth slopes into the sun and, strangely, a young cycle of moon shows white in the scorched sky.

We drop into the smoky pit of prairie and have to cover our faces against the blowing sand which will cut into your skin. The bald prairie, without a blade of grass, is mounded unfamiliarly, some houses almost buried, the marks of fences sticking up. The grasshoppers are ticking like clocks.

We drive in on a road marked out since their departure by shifting sands and one side of the two-room shack is banked with sand. The mother scrapes open the door and I go in with her while the son puts away the horse. It is early but she has to light a lamp to see, and the shivering light falls through the yellow dust onto the chairs, and over a bare table covered an inch with dust, which she quickly wipes off. There is a picture on the wall of a strong man with black mustaches; perhaps the man, her husband, who plowed this land. The mother moves around the room, her shy eyes on me, her body taking on the grace of a hostess, "I tell Joe not to hang the towel on the line—the grasshopper'll eat it clean out. They are mighty powerful hungry this year, like everything."

We move closer to each other, spreading the scrubbed wooden table. We become tenderly acquainted in the room as she begins to get excited, in the way of lonely people, telling about her husband—birthing her children right in there, she says, right on that bed without hide or hair of a doc. She is like a drunken person, recounting now her lonely pain, bearing children that are gone and will never return. "There was a time," she said, "when I was afraid to look out the window down past the lower forty—afraid they'd be a-comin' to take somethin' away from us. But that's one relief now; we ain't got nothin' now and nobody is a-comin'!"

We ate dinner, the boy shy at first; then he too is hungry for talk and tells about working on the road, about how he wants to work—he's real strong, about the Knutsons, and he gets up to show me their light eerily spread in the dust down the coolie—they are leaving tomorrow for the west, the whole kit and kaboodle of them. They're getting off that farm where they been all their lives.

"Yes," the mother said, "where all their children was borned and raised. It's shameful. It's a terrible thing."

After supper we can still see the eerie light and imagine the Knutsons moving in their sad tasks. The mother can't keep away from the window and I know she is thinking that they could be put off, too. The boy goes outside and I know he's looking up the hill. He comes in, cracking his knuckles, "They shouldn't do it. They oughtn't get out like that without kicking up a row. What about their money? What about the years of work they got in there? What about it all? You don't hear nothin' about that. The mortgage ain't nothing to have in that land to what they got there, their whole endurin' lives."

"Be quiet," the mother says. "God'll punish you. We are law-abidin' and that's the law."

We go into the lean-to. I am to sleep with the mother. Joe on the floor where he always sleeps. She tells me shyly she hasn't sheets, but her blanket's clean. She blows out the light modestly and we undress in the dark. I feel good to be near her. We lie side by side in the old bed and I know I am sleeping on the side of her dead husband. Accidentally I touch her dry hand and she clutches me, "Do you think they will take it away from us?" I am startled by the fierce vitality of her hand, like a strong bird grasping my fingers. I grasp her hand warmly and she is shaking—not crying, just shaking like a bird captured and straining.

In the morning the sun came up naked as a hot plow in the sky, and there truly seemed as much of the earth in the sky as below it. We start out early for the Knutsons'. Their old Ford is packed and an old rickety trailer sags beneath their household goods. Mrs. Knutson has a baby and is with child, and there must be eight children in the back seat. We stop and we all get out and stand in the dust looking at each other. Nobody knows what to say now. They haven't lived all their lives for this moment. We drive down the hill again. "They have a lot of children," I say inanely, and the mother says bitterly, "That's one crop that never fails—never a crop failure of babies."

The sun is already hot. Before us, standing in the dust, a clot of men are gathered at the gate of a farmhouse; the gate is half buried in dust; the dust sits gray on the clothes of the men, on their slouching hats. The sheriff and three men are standing on the stoop. A man stands in the center of the group of farmers, speaking. As we drive up he calls out, "Join us, brother." Joe stops the horse. "We can't back down," the man is saying. "We can't be afraid. Let him post the notice of auction; we'll be here. Now is the time to do it. You got rights. We got to begin to go forward. Everything is dry as a contribution box, you can see that. You're willin' to pay but you *can't* pay. We got no wheat, no hogs, no nothin'. We got time to think about it, to figure it out—"

Just then the Knutsons come down the hill and drive by without stopping, the children peering back around the sides, Mrs. Knutson not looking back, not waving; and we watched the old gas buggy go down the road and pass out of sight in the dust.

"They's no use going off now," Joe says, "for the West, for Oregon, for Alaska— They's no use goin' off now—"

The Farmer is the Man

This young snort from the agricultural school came out there to North Dakota to look over my land and my stock. He said he was goin' to appraise everything on my farm for the government. He said he was goin' to make a report on everything there and help me pull out of the red.

Well, he looked over everything, wrote it all down on the record neat as a pin; stuck his nose into everything there.

He thought he just about had everything when he saw an animal looking around the house. We keep the old goat because we had him so long. "What's he," the young squirt said, "and what's he for?"

I said, "You're the expert here. You tell me. I ain't supposed to tell you."

"Well," he said, "I don't know what it is. I'll have to wire back and find out what it is so I can put it down on my report."

"All right," I says, laughing, "you do that."

So he wired clean to Washington to Secretary Wallace, I guess, and he said, "There's an object here and I don't know what it is. It's long and lean with a bald head, chin whiskers, empty lean stomach, a long sad face, and sad cadaverous eyes. What is it?"

And Wallace wired back, "You wet-behind-the-ears, mewling baby jackass! That's the farmer!"

We are at the crossroads of history. We don't want to be railroaded through. We don't want to fold up like a jackknife. There are things solemn and dear to us. This is a grave situation and we must stand together. Where are we to stand upon the future?

The farmers are on the march.

—FARM HOLIDAY MEMBER

Don't let a man scare you about a strike or being radical.
If a man isn't radical today he hasn't enough red blood
in his veins to stain a handkerchief. Take steps or lose
your homes. This is your last stand. You'll either win or
put on the wooden shoes.

—MILO RENO, LEADER OF THE HOLIDAY

THE LEADER OF THE FARM HOLIDAY IN MINNE-
sota said, "I don't know how many will come. They have
deputized all the merchants in town. We have a meeting at
the farm first and then go to the courthouse; then they
change the place and have the auction before we get there.
They keep us from getting meeting places—we have to meet
in the woods along the river. We are going to meet the
leaders of the County Holiday at the pavilion."

Riding along the country road, it suddenly became dangerous; the country looked different, menacing, unfamiliar.
The light seemed to brighten as over some catastrophe and
you wondered if, after all, you knew your own country, if
you had ever truly lived in it. The land became more than
the land, and the shut, silent houses—many of them deserted—were a hieroglyph you tried to decipher. Everyone
leaned forward in the car, silently now, scanning the road.
Was it imagination, or did the roads look peculiarly empty of
traffic, and who was that on the side road—a car stopped, a
large car full of men, perhaps with guns?

There had been many penny sales in the country then.
The farmers gathering at a neighbor's whose farm was up
for auction; packing the yard, standing there without arms,
just packed loose together, and when the bidding started
with pennies, buying the farm farcically for five cents. It
was a kind of passive resistance so far, the farmers simply

massing and standing silently close together—simply damning the sale so nobody dared stop it; even professional bidders did not dare to shout out in the midst of that tenuous, lean silence of hundreds of men determined not to lose their land and their stock.

Having bought the farmer's farm they gave it back to him. This was the time of the milk strikes in Iowa, and the farmers of the Dakotas and Minnesota sent their backing. Platforms were set up at crossroads and speaking went on in the light of bonfires; in Iowa also, when an insurance-company lawyer came with a judgment note to take over a farm, they assembled at the courthouse and told the sheriff he could not sell the man out. Then they asked the lawyer, "Have you got a judgment note? You are not going to use it to bid with."

They took him out and stood him under a tree, "Will you write a telegram to your company to withdraw that note?"

"No," he said, "I can't do it or I will lose my job." So they slung a rope over the tree limb and asked, "Will you send the telegram?"

"Yes, yes!" he shouted, and wrote, "Withdraw the note. My neck is in danger."

"Here it is," the Holiday leader said. We came to the pavilion on the river and no one was there; it was threateningly empty. A boy was sitting under a tree tying knots in a rope. When he saw us he ran over to the car. "The deputies were here," he said. "They went on to the courthouse where the public sales is going on. The Holiday crowd said to come there."

We drove on faster now, into the county seat, which was quiet until we came in sight of the old courthouse with its curious New England steeple, red brick and solid. And in the yard packed solid were the farmers, standing silently.

We got out and the solid pack parted for us and we got into the courthouse, which was jammed up the stairs into the court, where the county treasurer was reading each item on the list—each one standing for a farm, a small property, and at each one he paused and waited for bids. There would not be a sound; the silence was menacing as a gunsight. Then the clerk would read the next on the list, but the farmers stood silent, their hats on; occasionally you saw a curious smile but there was not a sound.

We stood closely packed in. Groups of unemployed also were in the room, I was told, in case the farmers needed help. The sales would have to be postponed until spring if there was no bid.

I squirmed around so I could see the county clerk, an amiable little man, strangely pale and obviously frightened at having to stand up in that deadly silence and read off these names and places. Toward the end he stopped, looked around as if something had been prearranged, and sure enough, a voice from the left said, "I bid a hundred dollars." There was a single moment, then the solid mass seemed to break at a point over our heads, seemed to eddy, and then above the massed heads the kicking body of a man rose in the room, his arms and legs squirming; and he was heaved up—without moving, they handed him upon solid outstretched arms to the door, and he was emitted on a solid band of lifted horny hands down the stairs, and I do not know what became of him after that. He didn't bid any more. Neither did anyone else. The clerk came to the end of the list, made a gesture that he had done his duty and to hell with it. The solid, persistent mass broke now and began like a tortuous river to pour out into the countryside again.

Old Andy Comes to the North Star Country

*This opulent city, cradle of enterprise from the first
settler in 1856, is now a bankrupt, instead of being the
seat of wealth and independence as its advantages dictate.
It only serves as a monument to identify the spot where
"wise" men were mistaken; where the man of industry
took a recess, the speculator knocked him down and the
five per cent ate him up. You didn't cultivate land, you
speculated. All this arises from the impudence not the
necessity of man. It is a nightmare.*

*I saw a beast, dreadful and terrible and strong exceed-
ingly and it had great iron teeth. I saw him devour the
healthy merchant, break to pieces the farmer, mechanic,
and everything that fell between its iron teeth. At last I
saw him force entry into our little home. I saw my wife
weep and the children cry and we were turned into the
street without covering for our backs. My tongue lost its
action and I was in great distress.*

*All we pioneers have suffered in life are comforts com-
pared to this vision. The bitter fruit of three and five per
cent mortgages. Three and five per cent is the fourth
Beast seen by the prophet Daniel in his vision of the
night.*

—REMARKS OF J. E. MC KUSICK AT AN "OLD
SETTLERS' " MEETING

IT WAS IN A HOTEL ROOM IN DULUTH THAT Andy Carnegie first came to the North Star Country, representing a faceless new kind of giant—the monopoly. It was there that the financial East met the West for a showdown. On one side of the table were the battery of lawyers—many bought up by Old Andy—a preacher, and poker-faced speculators. On the other side were the people represented by the Daniel Boones of the Northwest—the seven surveying Merritt brothers.

The sons of tiny Hepzibah Merritt didn't have the chance of a snowball in a blast furnace. They were old-fashioned Americans and they still believed that there was enough for all, and they thought the people in a country should own it and wanted the claims to the richest soft-ore basin in the world to be taken up by the common people, wanted to make Duluth the steel capital of the world and thus create wealth for everyone.

They had traveled every foot of the range, misery bands holding the packs suspended from their foreheads, struggling through with ax and compass. "I understand woodcraft better than anything else," Leonidas the strong one said. They were tough, they had all the guts of the frontiersman, pioneer, woodsman, but they were lost from the beginning amidst the roaring sound of Eastern blast furnaces opening their maws for iron ore.

They were lost because the first year they came to the range Henry Bessemer learned how to burn iron into cheap steel and Mr. Carnegie needed cheap ore to support the vast consolidations of his monopoly—forcing the cost of steel down and down. America was bawling for steel for skyscrapers, giant bridges, railroad ties, steel plows for the growing wheat harvest. The seven brothers were lost because they believed that the rich resources of nature were for the use of the common people. Mark Hanna shocked Leonidas by saying to him, "The common people be damned!"

And they were lost because of the kind of men they were—sitting across from the poker faces, from Mr. Frick who, as Leonidas said, "cut me off short and bulldozed me"; and because just when they could have cashed in hands down, made them a pile, retired as nabobs, they were still digging, working, turning up new claims, busy as beavers struggling through the woods with axes and compass. These were men whose every adventure and effort was a saga, part of the heroic struggle of men of all times to make new paths through the wilderness, create new tools, take the earth's wealth and put it back again.

At midnight in his office in Duluth Leonidas, the bush-wacker, appealed to the citizens to save him from the eastern capital:

> Put some cash in the Mis-sa-be,
> Lend a helping hand to others,
> Others who are working for you.
> Let us bind with bands of iron
> The Mis-sa-be to the Zenith.

But they would not.

Carnegie was at his hunting lodge in Scotland when Oliver, the plowmaker, told Frick about cheap ore in the open pits of the Biwabik which could be loaded into cars with one scoop of the shovel. "No shaft, no air compressors, no upkeep—" Frick had been wounded two days before by an anarchist who thought it his duty to call attention to the offensive power of steel in the Monongahela. He was so excited he forgot his annoyance at the striking workmen at Homestead. He had blast furnaces and rolling mills, and he needed cheap iron ore. And he got it, beating the Homestead strikers, and skinning the Merritts.

The hotels in Duluth were full of frenzied speculators, incorporating to the tune of five million a day, secret bargaining, backstair deals, the stock watered, doubling, zooming.

At last by devious devices of chicanery the Merritts came back from New York stripped, without, as Alf put it, a "soo-markee." Their backs to the wall, they had been forced to sell their entire consolidated stock to Mr. Rockefeller. They had barely enough left to get home and then were without streetcar fare.

Eighteen years after their discovery of iron ore—when thirty million tons had been shipped out and Charles Schwab testified that probably three hundred and thirty-three million dollars would be a fair estimate of the value of the Mesabi property—in 1911 Leonidas sat in a long room in Washington, facing notables and authorities in a silence that was full of strange askings, defenses, challenges, accusations, and the sorrow of Leonidas, who at times could not speak. He remembers that he and his brothers found the Mesabi—he remembers the thirty years that preceded their discovery. He remembers those great days of cold and hardship and excitement and their fantastic belief that iron ore lay under the lake country and that they would find it. The touch of the Homeric storyteller is in the way he tells it; the dignity of their labor, the greatness of their faith, and the belief still that he was right in the way he wanted to develop it, so that the earth should belong to the people that he knew.

Leonidas says that he has cultivated a forgetter. He says that when he came back from the journey to New York, where he sold the consolidated stock of the entire Merritt clan to Mr. Rockefeller in 1894, he nearly lost his mind. His family didn't have streetcar fare. "I could not conceive that I could go down with millions—how in hell I could within those few months, without spending a cent above my board bill, have lost all those millions."

"I blame myself," he says.

Congressman Stanley cannot stand the beleaguering of the big woodsmen by the brilliant lawyers. "I went to the state of Minnesota," he says in Leonidas' defense, "I went to the city of Duluth, went to the range, went among the lumbermen with whom they, the Merritts, had explored in the snow, and found that not one man but the people of Minnesota regarded these men in a way as we regard Boone of Kentucky, and as they regard Houston in Texas, with gratitude, with reverence."

The Merritts were poor after that and they stuck together. Their mother Hepzibah said, "Have you done anything wrong? Then the Lord will care for you."

Mr. Rockefeller said, "Probably the most generous people in the world are the very poor, who assume each other's burdens in the crisis which comes so often to the hard-pressed!"

So an era ended.

In the early days, industry, mills, timber, and mines were often owned by individuals like the Merritts or George Stuntz, but when the Rockefellers, the Fricks, the Morgans entered the North Star Country contending for the vast mineral resources, bespeaking the ore "forever," the pattern changed and produced a new alignment of forces.

So the political supremacy of agriculture was broken and a new industrial dynasty was born having its own night talk, jokes, back fence badinage, and argument high up in office buildings:

A timber baron claimed: We took the backwoods, cleared the land in less than fifty years; our efforts transformed the wild timber lands into a modern economic state.

The farmer heard about the bank crash while he was in the hay mow. He jumped five feet into the air, slid down the rick and took off across the field. By the time he got to the north forty he stopped and asked himself, Why am I runnin'? I haven't got a dime in the bank!

Do you know the banker has a glass eye? Do you know how you can tell it's the right one that's glass? There's a gleam of kindness in the glass eye!

I've been blackmailed and hoodooed. I cut my own hair, shave myself with an ax. I'm a blacksmith, a tinsmith and a barrel-maker. I am anything from a bushwhacker to a Methodist preacher. I've made millionaires and I don't want to be one myself. I got two fifty in my pocket right now that I can spend if I want to. I wouldn't change places with Rockefeller. I can eat and sleep in peace. Someday I'm gonna die and when I'm dead someone will say, Herbert is the man who started the production of tin in the Black Hills.

They went on looking for more iron. Visionaries, they still saw rich treasures; optimists, they still believed in the impossible. Always looking forward—Leonidas lived to the last in a little grimy house near the ore docks, the Mesabi Railroad running at his door; he died in 1928 and was buried on an iron-ore hill overlooking Kitchi Gammi. The earth of his grave trembles now from the loaded cars that run day and night down to the lake with the red dust that will go to the furnaces of the East to make guns. He left no debts, no will, some household goods, a hundred and fifty dollars in cash. His brothers now lie near him.

And the children and grandchildren aplenty have founded co-operative creameries, fought in wars, are aviators, geologists, dredgers, farmers.

I walked under the black frosty range sky; the villages squat desolately, old mines like graveyards of old machinery, tar-paper shacks in the cut-over of families thrown out by the introduction of machinery in the mines, or blacklisted from strikes and those who wait for death from silicosis of the lungs; the great open pits, lighted now, gleam at night and the ore cars move continuously down to the fiery furnaces past the graves of Stuntz, the Merritts, and the thousands of the unnamed workers who created this great empire.

Industrial Struggle

―――――――

Business men realized in 1903 that something had to be done. We organized the Citizens Alliance. I telephoned eight men and asked them to meet me on Sunday morning instead of going to church. I told them I did not believe in breaking the Sabbath but I thought this was more important than going to church and they met me. I told them what we had to do and in ten minutes these men underwrote the Citizens Alliance for twenty thousand dollars.

—A. W. STRONG, CHAIRMAN OF THE CITIZENS ALLIANCE

There's an epidemic craze here among farmers and those who receive wages and salaries.

—JIM HILL TO MORGAN, SPEAKING OF AN ATTEMPT TO ORGANIZE

The Citizens Alliance was one of the first big organizations in the country for breaking strikes and eliminating unions. They organized the most complete undercover spy system in the U. S. which became the model for all others, and for thirty years they fought to keep Minneapolis open shop—the worst scab city in the United States.

—MINNEAPOLIS LABOR REVIEW

THE GROWTH OF CORPORATIONS AND ABSEN-
tee ownership of natural resources brought a change in

human relationships, shifts of group allegiances, a new pattern. Pioneer days were marked by thrift, economy, and simplicity. But now mutual co-operative aid and the simple relationships of an expanding democracy were shattered. A new pattern was forged, a separation of interests; groups fell into those who possessed natural resources and tools of production, and those who, on the other hand, sold their labor.

The pattern sharpened by the further impoverishment of the land, depletion of forests, erosion, and destruction, so that the land also began to fall into the hands of Eastern financiers; there was the vanishing of old ways to make a living, marked by ghost towns, dead areas, loss of farms, migrations of whole sections, and there was even a partial exhaustion of high-grade ores. The development of aluminum alloys, the refinement of steel, sharpened the conflict of the big dinosaurs. Judge Gary leased Hill's ore properties and broke the government's back, then contended with the Clevelanders who still owned large strikes on the old Michigan ranges, and contended with Carnegie and Rockefeller; but they all united against the nation-wide struggle of labor for the eight-hour day and the closed shop. In 1937, during the Farmer Labor regime, the division of groups became so sharp that the mineowners, refusing to pay taxes, quixotically threatened to move the big ranges of the Mesabi out of the state!

Ten monopolies representing only about a thousand holders monopolized 1,208,800,000,000 square feet of timber. The price of lumber and ore and coal increased during the first World War; lumber increased from $16 to $116, with the government paying as high as $1200 a thousand for spruce.

And Paul Bunyan was still sleeping in muzzle bunks, on lousy straw, working in the cold up to fourteen hours, and coming to the end of the season with hardly a penny in his pocket. He got the idea then of industrial democracy, of the vertical union, and of other simple things, like money instead of company scrip, warm clothes, clean bunkhouses, and food without maggots in it, and perhaps something to wash in besides tins hung over the fire.

Such primitive and simple desires began a reign of terror in the North Star Country. Thousands of gunmen and deputies were imported, skimmed from the city slums; scabs were brought in of different nationalities, so that confusion of language was added to the confusion. Strikes spread from coal to ore mines, to timber and harvest fields. Many men worked at all of these to make ends meet. But now thousands of men and women were thrown in jail, union meetings were closed, labor papers suppressed.

Big Bill Haywood and the I.W.W. were on the range now, in the wheat fields and the mines. Men got together riding on boxcars, waiting at Gateway Square for a job.

The struggle against U. S. Steel began on the range in the strike of 1907 led by Tapilo Petreila of the Western Federation of Miners. Men came out of the pits in droves. Not a steam shovel moved in Hibbing and Chisholm. But the company brought freight-train loads of Italians, Montenegrins, Croats, Slovenes, fresh from Europe, unwitting scabs, unable to speak English, and the men went back to the pits fearful of losing their jobs for good.

In 1917 Big Bill Haywood declared war on the U. S. Steel in eleven languages. For three months the I.W.W. kept the ruthless, armed forces of the steel corporation at bay. But not until 1937, under the influence of the New Deal, the Wagner Act, and the organization of the C.I.O., was the range finally able to break the feudal terror, the spy system, of U. S. Steel.

In 1917, if you wanted to ride on the freights from coal to ore mines, from timber to harvest fields, your pass was an I.W.W. card. Minneapolis' Gateway district was the hiring center for the northwest. Ore miners began to meet steel puddlers come from the mills; itinerant workers told many stories in the evening of cheap labor all over the United States.

Along the old Buffalo trail from Enid, Oklahoma, to Northern Alberta, fifteen hundred miles, the I.W.W. organized the itinerant worker, controlled the flow of labor on the jobs for the first time, moving the thousands of workers northward with the ripening crop, spreading like a fan through Kansas, Nebraska, the Dakotas, and Minnesota, then on to the Colorado beet and potato fields, then westward to the orchards.

Organized gangs of gamblers and highjackers had preyed upon the harvest hands. White slavers, gunmen, stools, and dicks in cahoots with the police ruled the freights which were the only "private car" of the bindlestiffs. Heavily armed and organized, these gangs stuck up the jungles—the workers' hotels—drove them from the towns. The saga of this bloody war is a picture of midnight stick-ups, exaction of tribute, beaten forms thrown in the darkness from moving freights. The I.W.W. train and jungle committees stopped this leeching. There were many pitched battles in inky box cars, on the tops of swaying trains. The I.W.W.'s organized and moved their workers for the first time in an orderly tide.

Meeting in 1920 in New Rockford, North Dakota, general officers were elected and in that year, 160,000 leaflets were distributed, 40,000 pamphlets, thousands of copies of their own papers, of which they had three, classes were organized, and a thousand-mile picket line stood behind every worker. The so-called "red card" became, in the northwest, pass card, railroad ticket, job insurance. Schools were organized. When the frost came and the fields were picked in the west, I.W.W. poured into Kansas City and went to school all winter.

Shocking standing grain in the broiling sun is a terrific job. Men on the binders, threshers, the shockers, haulers, cornhuskers, pickers learned of solidarity, sent delegates to the Soviet Union, fought for free speech, studied in the evening, wrote short stories, music, poetry, articles for their own papers, later saw them in print, carried them into the lumber camps, jungles, and fields. Son of an English Lord, Charles Ashleigh was seen walking down the highways, carrying a cane, writing poetry. Ralph Chaplin, Joe Hill, and thousands of itinerant workers became part of the nation, contributed richly to the cultural heritage.

When trouble broke out finally on the range, the companies hired Pinkerton thugs, who arrested thousands. Union halls were closed, papers suppressed, men sentenced from one to fourteen years for simply reading a paper. One man was shot on his front porch because he was reading a Finnish paper. Campfires burned beside the roads, warming both strikers and gunmen in the bitter north winter. When the men were arrested faster than they could be replaced, women and children marched in the picket lines carrying signs: WE ARE HUMAN BEINGS. WE WANT OUR FATHERS TO LIVE. OUR FATHERS STRIKE FOR US. WE WANT TO LIVE TOO.

A young man named Ormi started running over the range from mine to mine calling, "Come out. Come out." He ran to the Biwabik, to the McKinley, to Virginia; twenty miles he ran along the range and the men came out.

The strikers held a meeting in Finnish Hall in Virginia and the armed chief of the Oliver Mining Company, Dave Foley—head of the Citizens Committee and a dead shot— ordered the leaders to leave the state. When they refused, rioting broke out.

A plug-ugly named Nick Dillon, a bouncer from a Duluth house of ill fame, deputized during the 1916 strike, together with another gunman named Myron, entered the home of Philip Masonovitch, near Birbik, and beat up Philip and his boarder, saying they were searching for illegal liquor. They were beating the women when one of the miners lifted a chair and knocked the pistol from Dillon's hand, which so enraged him that he began shooting, and a soft-drink peddler outside the house—Latvala by name—was killed, along with Myron. A boy said Dillon fired directly at the man on the pop wagon. No one carried guns but the deputies. The boarders had also all been shot and lay in jail wounded for days.

Immediately the strikers, along with their leaders, who were twenty miles away in the town of Virginia at the time, were arrested and sent to Duluth charged with murder in the first degree.

Another striker, John Alar, was killed on the streets in Virginia. No arrests were made.

Stories are still told:

A miner walking along the street during the strike was arrested, and a friend asked the cops, "Where are you going with my friend?" The cops said, "It is none of your business," and when the friend remonstrated at this unjust arrest, invoking the Constitution of the United States against seizure and arrest without warrant, they arrested him, too, and took him to jail. There was a trial, and a jury found the miner who had come to the aid of his friend guilty.

But the judge, one of those rare ones not owned by U. S. Steel, said to the jury, "Gentlemen, if I may call you that, will you please stand." They all stood, and he said, "You have condemned a man who has risked his own safety for that of his friend and for what he believed to be right. This is the expression of the highest citizenship. I want the defendant to stand up so that all in this courtroom can see a man, and a citizen of the United States."

He broke his leg in Arizona, where he went then because twelve hundred miners from Bisbee had been deported in boxcars like cattle and left on the desert to starve. He went north again to a strike in the mines of Montana. Here they came at three in the morning to the Finnish boarding house where he stayed, dragged him into a car, drove to the railroad bridge, dragged him out, and hanged him by the neck until he was dead. The papers said: "So far as is known, he made no outcry."

His name was Frank Little.

A slender young man used to sing on summer nights at the Gateway in Minneapolis, and on the range, walking along the roads, making up songs in the harvest fields, and singing in miners' meeting halls on the range . . . "songs which came to be the songs of all wandering, struggling men. He made them up for whatever happened, hot off the griddle."

> Halleluah I'm a bum, Halleluah bum again,
> Halleluah give us a handout and revive us again.

> Work and pray, live on hay,
> You will eat pie in the sky, by-and-by. (It's a lie.)

When he was later executed in connection with a shooting in a strike, and the Swedish Government along with President Wilson's protests could not save him, he wrote his last will and testament:

> My will is easy to decide.
> There is nothing to divide.
> My body? Ah, if I could choose,
> I would to ashes it reduce,
> And let the merry breezes blow
> My dust to where some flowers grow.
> This is my last and final will:
> Good luck to all of you, Joe Hill.

Some say his last words were, "Don't mourn—organize."

Two other men were mightily hated by the big monopolies.

A stocky man sat alone in the Senate, a cigar in his mouth, one foot in the aisle, and voted alone against the imperialist war. His picture was taken from the Wisconsin state house but not from the hearts of the north country farmers. He was Robert M. La Follette, Sr.

Another man, tall, with a sad stern face, together with his long rangy son, drove around the country speaking and throwing out handbills, and this man also voted against the war. As he was about to speak in a Minnesota town, vigilantes came after him with tar and feathers and his friends smuggled him out the back door, down to the railroad tracks. A freight was just pulling out and the brakeman, who belonged to the Non-Partisan League, let him ride in the caboose until they got to safety.

This was Charles Lindbergh the elder.

With soup and gas and club and gun they tried to make the system run.

Fifty thousand lumberjacks for fifty years packed their own bed, but never will again.

The only way to gain your liberty is one big industrial union.

"Yaas," said the farmer, "all the I.W.W. fellers I've met seemed to be pretty decent lads, but them 'alleged' I.W.W.'s must be holy frights!"

We are striking partly for wages but more for the eight-hour day. When a man goes to work at six and quits at eight what chance has he to educate himself? We say eight-hour day is enough.

If we lose there is no place for us in the north country. We are forced out of the old country—out of the West. We got to stay here.

And the talk went on, a little different in a different time:

Ain't got a word to say. He took my job away and chiseled down my pay.

The wolf don't bother me no more. He starved to death right at my door.

Casey Jones, get busy shovelin' sulphur! That's what you get for scabbin' on the N.P. Line.

Strike

We are assembled during the most crucial period in the history of our nation and the state. An army of unemployed, homeless and wandering boys, thousands of abandoned farms are evidences not only of an economic depression but of failure of government and our social system to function in the interests of the common people. Just beyond the horizon of this scene is rampant lawlessness and possible revolution.

—FLOYD B. OLSON, FARMER LABOR GOVERNOR OF MINNESOTA (1932)

WATERING HIS LAWN ON A HOT JULY ON THE first day of the strike, the head of the organization of employers, the Citizens Alliance, said, "We have already collected over fifty thousand dollars to break this strike and continue open shop in this city. We don't care about anything but to break this strike."

The *Strike Daily* said, "Fight like one man till victory. We are not fighting an isolated cause. Ours is the cause of the whole labor movement. Should we be defeated, other unions would be chopped down one by one. Fight like one man until victory—until victory."

Between these two elements a subtle barrage of words—

289

conferences—cars speeding with ultimatums, with agreements and disagreements. Words like ghouls to cover an old viciousness. Words about rights, justice, freedom. Heirs to nineteenth-century liberalism said they would deputize and go down and pick off like rabbits these strikers who dared ask for bread: Do they think they can control our streets, tell us how to run our business?

From the strikers' headquarters in the heart of the city, straight across from the swanky club, the pickets go out every hour, covering the city in a systemized network which was worked out before the strike began. The newspapers say trucking is normal. In reality not a truck is running.

From the windows of the office buildings towering above strike headquarters, which is only a flat two-storied garage, liberal doctors, lawyers, peer out. "Nothing will happen," they say to each other, but there is expectation in their eyes. "Nothing can happen. This will all be settled square and above board. Why, this is the twentieth century! This is a civilized city! This will all be settled over the table."

Women said it was a shame that they could not get things delivered from the stores. The stores put up elegant little signs saying that owing to the strike, they thought it best not to deliver goods. This gave the strikers a horse laugh, since in the preceding strike they had broken the heads of hundreds of scabs!

The thermometer registered 90°, 98°, then 102°. Not a truck moved.

On Thursday the mayor and the chief of police and the employers got nervous because nothing was happening. Picketing was peaceful and effective.

Then on Thursday afternoon the police staged a show, with the ragged pickets looking on from their squad cars. In front of over a hundred cops, before reporters and cameramen, they moved one hundred and fifty pounds of merchandise in a five-ton truck. This was a decoy, supposedly a hospital truck, and the intention was to get the pickets to attack hospital supplies and make good publicity. Surrounded by a crowd of bystanders and picketers they loaded this truck with one box and it was convoyed, amidst the clicking of cameras, by thirty automobiles filled with cops, guns sticking out like pins in a pincushion.

The picketers did not fall into this trap. The fake movement was a failure. The strikers wanted to arm after this. The president of the union said, "I can't understand a word of any of these elegant negotiations. Speak in terms of bread and butter. I'm through listening to words."

The words continued.

Strike headquarters is a dark old garage that must have been a stable once. A roadway runs through the center of it, where the picketers wait the call that comes from the loudspeaker above the door. One side is roped off. This is the hospital, fitted with one plain table, six cots, and an operating table. Buckshot wounds take lots of operating.

An old wooden stairway leads upstairs to an improvised auditorium where meetings are held. Here also the loudspeaker penetrates incessantly: "Calling car 31. Calling car 31. Calling picket car 20. Wanted, a driver and a helper. Wanted, a driver and a helper. Calling Danny. We might as well announce right now that we can't call husbands unless they have been away four nights running. Wives, remember that picketing is no grounds for divorce."

The loudspeaker also throws the voice down into the street, over an area of one block, which is packed with people standing in the hot sun hour after hour, listening to the strike broadcast, watching the picket cars swing out of the black doorway, packed with hot, wild-looking boys, drunk with fatigue.

Upstairs also there are cots on which lie sleeping boys and men. In the rear is the commissary where, at a small counter with two hundred tin cups and fewer plates, over three thousand men are fed daily.

If you think that the commissary is organized like a church supper you are mistaken. Most of these men and women have spent years in industry: specialization, organization, and efficiency have been ground into their bones.

Women are making sandwiches. Two are pouring coffee and buttermilk for the men who are passing rapidly by, filling their cups, getting sandwiches, passing on to squat down in the hall, eating. Somebody shouts, "For Christ's sake, look at that!" The stout forewoman bawls out the offender who has thrown his coffee grounds out the window.

The heat is intense. An old man mumbles, "I wish I was out in the country." "No, you don't," a young buck tells him fiercely. "You wish you was right here where you belong."

A sign on the wall says: No drinking. You'll need all your wits. The afternoon edition of the strike paper is passed out. It tells about a market that has been set up for the farmer to bring his produce to the strikers. The paper says: "Every farmer is interested in our struggle." The strikers gather with the farmers to help butcher, working by auto light, lubricated occasionally by some wonderful home brew. A farmer writes:

We folks in Polk county have put up some brave fights. The paper don't tell you city fellows the truth about us but we assure you we are brothers to you; we will fight together to the end.

A humorous serial letter runs every day from one Mike to his "dere Emily." It goes:

Here i am at strike head¼ an' its plenty hot. These here bosses we got in town keep yellin' in the papers that communism and payin' 54½ c an hr is one an' the same thing. Well, if thats what it is I guess I'm a communist an' I expect most evry one in the world except a small bunch of pot bellyd and titefisted bosses must be to. eneyways we got the town tied up tighter than a bull's eye in fly time.

It is one o'clock now. Something is going to happen. Nobody is tired or hot now. The pickets have been pouring down to the market now for an hour. Women, feeling something in the air, begin to pour down to headquarters. In the country thousands of farmers sit at their radios waiting.

Hundreds of men are poured out of the building, hundreds pour in filling the ranks as fast as they are emptied. The hall is very quiet now. The excited, steady voice of the announcer calling cars, calling men. You cannot see men any more, only the forward-going body, the face marked by one emotion. Reports spread like wildfire. The announcer says that hundreds of cops are now in the market area, armed with sawed-off shotguns.

At five minutes to two the pickets are still silently pouring out onto the line.

The doctors and lawyers were looking out of their office windows into the street saying nothing can happen. They were drawn from their chairs like dummies on steel wires, by shots that lasted continuously and thickly for five full minutes. Two blocks away at the hotel, the negotiators stopped their words. The women shopping on the avenue swerved, moved, listened. For five minutes the cops fired into unarmed pickets and bystanders.

What happened was this: Police and pickets gathered at the market because a truck was about to be moved. The chief of police said, "We're going to start moving goods. You men have guns and you know what to do with them. When we are finished with this, there will be other goods to move."

The design moved toward a crisis, clotted in centripetal movement, congealed, twisted together with horrific fury. When this movement was over every person within a hundred miles would be changed, the shape and substance of everything different. Words would no longer have any meaning, for the distance is shortening between the word and the catastrophe. With a hunger now for the real happening, men and strikers gather at the market. Clusters of them standing protective on the street, yet all moving within themselves, the cops moving in an outer circle of known authority, the picketers moving within the mass of townsfolk, a glowing mass, without visible command yet bound together in a powerful impulse, following a design in their movement which goes from seperateness, congealing swiftly into a massed and integrated form.

The police, pointing their shotguns, tried to hold the circling crowd back and the pickets away. It was 102° in the shade. The sidewalk bubbled. An area was made by the police in the center of the street for this visible action which was about to show a real temper and a known intention. In that area it was about to happen.

A squad car of pickets waited in an alley for the truck to move. The truck drew up at the warehouse, was loaded, began slowly to move, surrounded by police and pointed shotguns. The picket car moved forward to stop it, jammed into the truck, and the picketers swarmed off, but instantly, stopping them in mid-movement, the cops opened fire, spraying them with buckshot. The movement stopped—severed, dismayed. Two boys fell back into their own truck. The swarm broke, cut into; it whirled up, eddied, fell down soundlessly. One's eyes closed as in sleep and when they opened, men were lying crying in the street with blood spurting from the myriad wounds that buckshot makes. Turning instinctively for cover, they were shot in the back. And into that continued fire flowed the next line of pickets to pick up their wounded. They flowed directly into the buckshot fire, inevitably, without hesitation, as one wave follows another. And the cops let them have it as they picked up their wounded. Lines of living, solid men fell, broke, wavering, flinging up, breaking over with the curious and awful abandon of despairing gestures; a man stepping on his own intestines, bright and bursting in the street, and another holding his severed arm in his other hand.

Another line came in like a great wave and the police kept firing. As fast as they broke that strong cordon it gathered again. Wherever it was smashed the body filled again, the tide fell and filled. Impelled by that strong and terrific union they filled in every gap like cells in one body healing itself. And the cops shot into it again and again. Standing on the sidewalk people could not believe that they were seeing it. Not until they themselves were hit by the bullets. Three blocks away business was moving thickly, women were shopping.

In ten minutes the militia appeared over the bridge, swarmed out of their trucks with orders to "deploy as skirmishers." They stretched across the streets and sidewalks. They carried bomb guns, automatics, rifles with set bayonets, sub-machine guns, and mounted on the trucks were machine guns.

The food truck and convoy only then began to move. The strikers stirred. From each police car shotguns were trained on the pickets. The truck rushed by.

At headquarters the wounded were brought in. "This is murder!" the announcer shouted. Men were lying on the floor. Forty-eight unarmed workers had been wounded. There were only two doctors and two nurses.

The skirts of the women had blood on them. The floor of the strike headquarters had blood on it. Already myth was growing up around the afternoon. "Black Friday," the men called it. The boys made designs of a kind of dagger to be made with an ice pick and a bit of leather. A line formed outside the hospital to give blood transfusions to the wounded.

On Saturday Henry Ness, father of four children, war veteran, died with thirty-eight slugs in his body. The temper of headquarters changed. In black letters the *Organizer* said, WORKERS' BLOOD IS SHED. THE FIGHT HAS JUST BEGUN. THE FIRST MARTYR. Four times as many pickets massed as there had been before. Night and day, workers carrying their children held them up to see the body of Henry Ness.

The following Tuesday, labor followed the funeral cortege that took three hours in passing. Six solid blocks of over-alled men, a solid block of women and children, four abreast. Thousands of women looked out of their windows at the cortege. Thousands of men stood on the sidewalk. Children stopped skipping rope, ball in hand, and watched; and there was not a sound. There was a silence slowly being filled with the awful condemnation of thousands of people.

A grim silence stood in the afternoon that frightened the city. Thousands marching in meticulous order, in a strange pattern, without coercion, the drama forming from deep instinctive and unified forces of real and terrible passion.

Silently, with the delicate muffled sound of many feet, past the "Stop" and "Go" signs that clicked mechanically, went the muffled crowd. Not a policeman was in sight. Some said the chief was out of town. They directed their own cortege with miraculous, with spontaneous order. Where there was a gap, a man sprang into it. No one had a name except the name of sorrow and the name of action.

They marched straight through the heart of the city, holding up loop traffic for over three hours. Streetcars lined the city for blocks. Conductors got out of their cars and directed traffic in the streets nearest them.

A man with a number of badges tried to break through the line with his car at one point, where the cortege had stopped for a moment, and instantly the car was covered like a rotten thing in fly-time and men with baseball bats ordered him back, saying that no man was going to break the cortege of labor. A man did not dare put on his hat until the whole silent march had passed, or he was in danger of having it knocked off.

Some told and retold the story of the shooting to each other, the women marching, men and women on the sidewalk. They said over and over, repeated, echoed, carried down the long line of march: "We won't *never* forget this. We won't never forget this—"

Stride On, Democracy

Cradled Hercules

Paul Bunyan, the Mighty Lumberjack,
He logged the timber tall.
The years have no effect on him;
Tho' his hair is white as snow,
He's just as young a giant
As a hundred years ago.
He has always led us forward,
And we've come to realize
That he'll always be our leader,
For Paul Bunyan never dies.

—PINE CONE

With single screw, triple expansion, and steel crosshead;
with brass oil cups, blue burnished bolts and the connect-
ing rod the huge shinbones of the giant, the knuckles
transferring the vertical motion of the piston into the
rotary motion of the propeller and the tandem pedaling
the screw, one wake, sixty-five strokes to the minute, clip-
ping like scissors, an absolute beat, the great web cranks
flying in orbits of oil, up and down, beating down the
North Sea, driving to the apex of the sky, to the core of
the earth and the arc of the ocean, six times as tall as a
man, the new giant, the new Bunyan.

—CIO NEWSPAPER

Only the wilfully blind can fail to see that the old style
of capitalism of a primitive freebooting period is gone
forever.

—ERIC JOHNSTON

THE MOUNDS OF MY VILLAGE HAVE BEEN TER-
raced against erosion. The young men and women have
gone to far lands. Our past is usable today. Restless, we
sense new frontiers, in vast and intricate combinations,
using the democratic legacy in new extensions of old and
barely realized forms. We of the north have agile practice
in swift equilibrium in forever changing forms. We are
agile, acrobatic, and dogged, living on the curve of movement, in the groove, on the ball. Our hope is real and hon-
ored and we move forward to great ends, in new configurations of life.

Man has his hand on a new and powerful tool. From the
hand loom, the ax, hoe, and peavey, to steam power, then to
the dynamo and man's hand turning the dials, pressing the
buttons of a new power—of the juice-peddler, hot-box, light-
ning-snatcher; of the gut hammer, bulldozer, the Stilson
wrench, air hammers, compressors, the giant auger and the
earth auger; tools of a thousand horsepower, instruments by
remote control, mechanical interrogators, differentials, mul-
tipliers, solving instantly and continuously problems in solid
geometry, producing perpetual answers.

The men of the north country who have come through
this turbulent gap into the vent of the future, in so swift
a time, are grandsons of Norwegians who married the daughter of a German forty-eighter, whose father's mother married
a Polander, whose daughter very likely married an Irishman
whose father was a Finn. These tall sons, and they grow tall
here, fold up in the cockpit of a plane and get a bead's eye,
not only on the enemy but on the future.

The village has new life. At four during the harvest the
town closes up, everyone goes out to save the pea, corn, and
wheat crops. Merchants, bankers, housewives, high-school
kids put their shoulders to the wheel in new forms of co-
operation, developing from the machine and from necessity,
expressing itself further in pooling of parts, collective use of

machinery, and county planning. The engine is coming, dragging the separator between the barns and the granary where the grain is waiting. Far into the night, by arc lights the hum of the thresher is heard, the yellow chaff stacking in the light.

Freezing units are owned co-operatively so you can now eat strawberries in November from your own garden. Industry comes to the village bringing with them the newest inventions and giant projects of power. Yes, even trade unions have come.

Wheat is no longer shipped miles but is put in elevators, many owned and operated collectively, or it is taken by river to the south on the streamlined Mississippi with its many locks.

One hundred thousand bushels of grain can be loaded in an hour, not by a thousand backs but by power shovels or scraper rigs, only two men scraping the grain from each end of the hoppers under the cars. No more do the men stand on the docks, the red ore freezing in their beards.

The labor of the Hullrust mine—and if work should stop there for a moment it would be felt around the world—is done by giant steam and electric shovels plying the black, brown, red, and yellow ore day and night, having no need of rest. The volume of their excavation exceeds the cuts of the Panama Canal. Scarcely touched now by men, augers driven by high-speed compressed drills make the dynamite holes in the underground mines. In the open pits, miles of tracks carry the ore loaded from electric shovels picking up sixteen tons to a dipperful, and from belts and conveyors loading on four-hundred-foot grades at the rate of seven hundred and fifty tons an hour.

Black Forest Village

Christian Burkhardt, from the Black Forest, built a badger mill town in Wisconsin, planted seeds from his native forest, built mills and water dams, and a solid house of hand-cut stone and hand-made brick whose foundations after fifty-six years shows not a hair line crack. But something has changed.

The Midland Co-operative Wholesale bought the whole community lock, stock, and barrel except for the church and the tavern, and under the direction of Mr. Westhoff, a good business man, experiments will be made in a new kind of future. Mr. Westhoff says, "That which affects living will be given an opportunity to prove its present rules. If the rules are improperly drawn because of social, financial or political errors, the residents here will get the chance to work out different ones."

The plans, which are of great magnitude, will put into a giant co-operative test tube all phases of rural and village life.

Cradle of Democracy

The North Star Country's long cradling of democratic institutions, the peculiar largeness and boldness of its structure has always demanded new techniques and laws of common and individual rights, suggesting always the necessity of broader forms of democracy.

Our future stands in real and sunlit shapes ahead in all the gloom. Grit and gumption are still ingredients inbred in fertile stock. Now planes headed for far countries fly over; messages not yet decipherable are myriad in the air. Much has been lost. Much found. There are new surveys, new maps, new records made of space and time and man upon the earth.

Speech is being created. Now the young men barely seen in the depression, in the dust storms, who migrated on freight trains, the horn players, ball players, the sharpshooters, hunters, mechanics who were barely seen on the desiccated horizon, surviving hunger, desolation, but surviving, are now the young men returning to luncheon looking out laconically, players of practical jokes, comic characters, inventors, who always say, "It was nothing," at the greatest wonder. They are those whose sky pieces have tall spires of the future in them. They are those familiar with TNT. They are the bulldozers, surveyors, choir boys, and cat skinners, the longshoremen, stevedores, ore loaders, gyppos, the mechanics, butchers, handlers of trucks, rivet tossers from swinging caissons, muckers under compressed air, the hooded on steel mill floors, the welders, torchers. They are on the night shift, the day shift, the swing shift. They are the users of gadgets, dynamite, earth augers, standing on steel gratings to work gauges, dials, indicators, to turn valves, regulate burners, turn the switch on electric motors, conduits, connections, and controls to send the roaring crescendo of a thousand metals in motion, of turbines, evaporators, condensers; a concordance of thunderous pumps, motors, generators, of tens of thousands horsepower, the new Giant turbine, the potential convertor of steam into the torque, expanding, unleashing titanic power, a potent generator, delivered into the naked palms of man alive in a new era.

Early one morning a boat was launched in the middle of a cornfield, the high prow of an ocean-going Navy tanker rising out of the flat country and nosing into the cradled Hercules of the Mississippi; before the freeze sets in it will be safely below the frost line, headed down-river to Orleans and the Big Drink.

The first boat was called the *Bataan,* and moved through
new locks, new connections, new canals. Man makes new
portages into new worlds and never stops. The ships are
nosed down a nine-foot channel to the Minnesota, into the
Mississippi. The first one was launched with shipyard workers cheering from the shore.

"Mark twain," calls the man swinging the port lead line.

"Quarter less twain," calls the starboard man as the boat
is nosed through the shallow channel.

"Twelve feet depth to port!"

"Two and a half feet here—"

She noses into the soft mud after going 6.9 miles. "Six
feet," calls the lead man, and the water clouds as the high
prow noses into the inside shore. Slowly she is swung round,
the twin rudders of the tow are speeded, one ahead, one
astern, and then full astern on both engines. The boat clears;
the bend must be cut back, says the pilot. Near Fort Snelling,
she slides into the Minnesota and the lead song sounds from
the bridge: "Maaaark twaaain!"

And she enters the Mississippi, that floats her easily down
to St. Paul, under the many bridges.

The prairie and the ocean now are one, another impossible has been accomplished; the circle is complete, the hundred years of search, of conquest, have ended. The long trek
turns to the extension and defense of man's free labor and
his land and machines, to the further and perpetual war
against his destroyers.

Waiting for the engine to warm up, for the take-off, for
the next shift, man looks over a far horizon, his speech
matching speed and precision.

My machine looks lonesome when I leave her. She can't do
without me.

I got to see my old girl. I got to tell her goodnight. She's down
there in the dark. I just want to put my hand on her metal nose,
her wing spread, her mermaid's tail.

She's a sweet engine, fourteen thousand horses. I oil her pistons and she could crack your back running at open throttle.

When the huge cranks are galloping in the pits and the long bright shafts are spinning in the shaft tunnels, I'm happy.

What are you gonna be, *if* you live?

My engine was named Alice and she fell out over a daisy field in France, and that night I cried.

Heck, all I did was freeze my finger to the trigger until she was hot enough to boil eggs and they kept coming.

I been down under, I been over, I'm goin' to the Alcan Highway.

I hear they'll deepen the St. Lawrence river, open the midlands to the Atlantic.

I hear the northwest will be the aerial door to the orient.

It'll be opening up all over now—all over the cockeyed world.

Milk Train

IT IS ALMOST A YEAR SINCE I LAST CAME ON
the slow milk train down from the north. Last year I met
Bud, who was going back to submarine duty in the Pacific.
He had a bottle of wine and we rode all night on the slow
train, the ghostly conductors coming through the darkened
coaches with their old-fashioned lanterns. It was Bud's last
night inland and he was taking a good long whiff of it. He
had come home to shuck some corn before going back under
the sea. That night, all night long I watched him as he stuck
his pug nose against the window and looked out on the snow-
locked land. He looked funny in his uniform. He was an
inland kid really, a farmer's kid.

"Lord," he kept saying, along with some stronger language, "that's the earth there under the snow. The sea's like
the prairie sometimes on a still night, but the sea you can't
get your spurs into. The prairies now, you can get your
knees in. There she is—America!"

I thought it was the wine then. A year later, now, it is
different. It has been different all evening, coming from the
harbor, men swarming the docks, still light at nine-thirty
war time. And the women in overalls coming from work,

and now the train is half-full of women going to the city for war jobs, each looking anxiously into the dark windows. It is different now.

This is America, now, at war.

And Bud is reported missing somewhere in the Pacific, in a submarine engagement which took place around March.

The train has jerked to a stop. I saw him coming down the aisle and I don't know why I did it but I ducked down in a seat and pretended to be asleep. It was Bud's old man, a farmer from upstate. He came down the aisle confused, like a man used to a wide horizon caught in the confines of a train. He was so tall he had to stoop for the train lamps, and you wouldn't know what hinged his bones together in the tight sheath of his skin; his big nose rode his skull like a prow. He was burned to parchment and I heard his sundried bones pop as he folded into the seat opposite me, his long hands strong between his knees as haying hooks. His hawk eyes marked me off.

"Well, ain't you out of bounds?" he said.

He is a great talker, a man seasoned in weather, canny as a fox, and a heart like a red haw.

"How are you getting on?" I said. This is the first question you ask a farmer and you know the answer.

"It's all right," he said, pursing his great mouth, empty of teeth. "The A.A.A. was a short blanket; you pulled it up to warm yer ribs and yer feet stuck out. But the huntin' has been good this year and never a better fer fishin'. I guess we ain't set a trap yet good enough fer that wild animal, Hitler. Jest cribbed me five hundred bushels of corn without Bud this year. He would've liked the sight of the corn, knee-high a week before the Fourth."

"Where are your sons now?"

"Bud was the last to go. Five now in the Army and the Navy. Leaves me on my land like my grandpappy in the

Civil War—then nobody left but the women. He lost five sons and got wounded hisself. He volunteered from Minnesota, Abraham Lincoln's first volunteers, organized by Ignatius Donnelly; and he got a medal for 'brave and meritorious service,' that's what it said on it, but when he come back to the farm alone, he never put no store by it—left it lyin' around. That's the way with my boys. Like Bud, up and volunteered— The Irish got a hankerin' for freedom, seems like—" He grins in his empty mouth and his eyes cloud with a film of distance.

"Can you run the farm yourself?"

He spit long and accurately into the tall brass gaboon. "Hell, I can run it now, and in a couple more wars, if they're the right wars. I got a feelin' in my bones this here is a right war."

I wouldn't ask him how old he was, or how many years it had been since he hewed the farm out of the woods.

"The way I figure it"—he was settling for a long tale—"is that everything ain't perfect. Like I always say I got the best up-to-date, equipped, and mortgaged farm in these parts. You're pore. You're milked from both ends, but I figure in this war the people are going to rare back and give it a whirl. You feel it like a good season. Now, Bud tells me in Africa they hate to dock and see the people there starvin' and beggin' the way no hum'n being should. Sometimes, though, you feel mad as a hornet at the slow way they're goin'. I write me a letter every Saturday night to the President or somebody down there. I tell 'em what I think. I got a right to tell 'em. I got a duty."

"Where you headed for now?" I said.

"I'm goin' down to see about them soy beans the gov'nment is wantin' us to put in now, and raisin' milkweed seems like a good thing, effen it floats like they say." He talked a long time and I listened, and the train went meandering on and after a while the coach was darkened and the night rose, visible in the windows on both sides, and you could see the tiny main streets and the church steeples and the closed and sleeping houses, and then we would take off into the low wide prairie with the wonderful swinging arc around us, and the sky swinging above in another arc, and the evening star bright and low in the fox fall.

The old farmer gradually lapsed from the saga of his life, from the long, toothless rumination into a sleep which was as just as his speech.

But I couldn't sleep. I listened to the call of the switch-man, to the signal of the frogs, and I kept thinking of that other night a year ago, coming down from the north with Bud; that night he didn't sleep like his old man now. He slept fitfully and in astonishment. He was astonished at what was happening to him. He knew it then.

We didn't know it, laughing at him because he looked so ludicrous and because it was so funny and melodramatic to see a sailor far inland, on a snowy night, who couldn't tell us where he was going.

We were all saying good-by at the station and kissing each other, and there was this cocky little sailor like some kind of gay bug with a bottle in his hand from which he boldly tippled. "Kiss me," he said. "Kiss me too!" And I said, "Why, it's Bud!" And we all kissed him, laughing, till he was spinning and hooting amidst the girls, and it was very funny seeing him then.

It was winter. The first snow had fallen early, in a blizzard. And what was he doing in that frost-locked, moony land? He was going to the Twin Cities. He was taking off for parts unknown; he couldn't tell us where. And that was very funny, too. It all sounded funny then and he looked very funny.

That was early in the war.

He knew it then. I saw him knowing it. His eyes opened wide, looking at me, and the pain lay back in them like some shadow when the sun is low, cast far before. He knew then. He was ahead of us.

"I come back," he said, "to shuck me some corn. I got mighty lonesome to shuck a crib of corn, and hear a good old jig-time tune, at cornhusking time. I wanted to crib me about a hundred bushels of corn and that's what I did. Just wanted to come from that old salty brine and rip off the husk of a big juicy ear of corn and see the milk come out." He showed his broad thumb, thick as a spat. "Good big-knuckled corn too, and now I got to see my Uncle Sammy, got to see the world. Sounds funny, but it's true now we're walkin', fightin' on the earth, sailin' on it, sailin' in the sea, touchin' it, makin' love to it. Flesh and earth, you find out they're everywhere. You look down our valley, in the middle of the U.S.A. and the snow now, and the Dog Star, well, you know without sayin' a word what the people of Poland felt, the farmers of France, the people in China who fight in the rice fields. You got to work the earth to find out—maybe you got to fight in it—maybe—"

I'm not saying that he talked like this right out, in one spurt. It came out slow through the night, with sleep, and drinking, and walking on the milk-station platforms. Talking comes out in the night, and American talk is very beautiful at night. It's most often on the ledger in the daytime. Night talk is very different from day talk in America. Perhaps it is so everywhere.

And the talk of men about to become part of a world struggle is something you listen to all night long.

"This is my land!" He shouted so the conductor stuck his head in and put his finger to his lips. "My land, and I'll talk about it, you old coot, it's my land and I come back here a thousand miles to shuck me some corn—got anything to say about it? Put up the old dukes, world, let 'er go! I'm a south-paw and I'm rarin' to go!"

He seemed to sleep a moment, and then he opened his

eyes and leaned over, tapping my knee with his finger. "You know, that Fascism tears up the earth, it's hard on the earth. It's hard on people, but it tears up the earth; it's very, very hard on the earth."

Another time he told about his great-grandfather coming over from Ireland during the famine, and he began to sing, "Give me a grain of corn, Mother, only a grain of corn."

"I been workin' all my life and that's what I like—work."

He talked seriously then, with all the deadly accuracy of a man who's living quick and chewing the cud of his life. He knew, what was going to happen then. You could tell by the way he didn't sleep, but would just close his eyes and spring alive like a man with a job to do in the morning. "This is going to be a big fight," he shouted once, half crying and half laughing. He said he had not expected such a big fight— the Golden Gloves maybe, or even the Twin City League, but this—

Then he told jokes, those silly wonderful jokes about the mongoose, about the horse that talked, and the shaggy dog stories, and dozens of moron stories. He looked out the window at the American night and thought of his boyhood, and the sights and smells of the day, newly cut grass and your first corn-silk cigarette under the house, and the fights and the girls. Toward the "shank of the evening," as he called it, he seemed suddenly in the midst of speech to sleep, but in a peculiar way, bolt upright, and his whole body rode the train expertly. I finally took his bobbing head and drew it to my shoulder, thinking to hold him still, he looked so fragile and I had a sense to comfort him, but he sprang instantly awake like an animal used to danger, and looked at me and grinned. "I suppose I was riding the wild waves. In that sub when the depth charges go off you think that you are going to cave in. When you eat dinner, the plates go by you quicker than porpoises. I've eaten off seven different plates in the course of a meal. I've drunk out of ten cups of coffee passing by. You get so you can't sleep without bouncing. Anchored in bed is torture. I could sleep best in a hay wagon going over an unplowed field. I got to get me some air. Let's take this one walking."

The train had stopped and it was just before dawn. The chill wind blew and I saw him lean over and touch the frosty earth. He saw me see him, and grinned. "The sea is awful deep," he said, "but somewhere at the bottom must be the earth."

"Yes," I said.

Then he pretended to throw a curve, winding up with his left arm and letting the ball go. I'll always see him like that: his lean, wild Irish body, tragic and cocky, his hat hanging like a bat on the side of his great unfinished head, his big ears like pitcher handles, and his wide child's eyes, and yet the look of something the world is just knowing. He knew it then. In a gesture like the pitcher uses when he reaches down and gets the dust on his mitt—or even touches the earth for luck, dusts his spit—so he reached down and touched the earth. I'll never forget him crouching there, looking up at me, grinning that twist of a grin that is the same for pain or fun. Just for a moment he beat his left paw in the socket of his right palm, then wound elaborately— spinning, lifting his foot, swinging his short strong body back, he let fly an imaginary ball into the frosty night.

We were coming into the lowlands of the river city now and I did not look over at Bud's old man. I looked out on the long and tender dawn of the flat lands. The early morning earth was smoking; low down on the turf rose the mist out of which the cows lifted their horns. In the sky hung a star, yellow as a daffodil, shining now not in the dark but in the long swath of dawn sky.

The train wailed long and parted the wisps of mist and fog in the lowland and along the steaming river; it passed the dark horses standing in the mist, which flowed along the dark loam like the hair of women sleeping.

My skin prickled and I knew Bud's old man was looking at me with his hawk's eyes, and I had to turn, and he was pointing one long cant-hook finger at me. "He'll turn up," he said as if he had known every thought of my head. "He'll turn up, captured or rescued. You can't tell but he'll turn up. He's my last man. I lay my bets he'll turn up. Pitch over the hay and there he'll be. He's my youngest, my last man. I told you he was a southpaw, didn't I?"

I moved over to be near him.

The Shapes Arise

Did you too, O Friend, suppose Democracy was only for election, for politics? I say Democracy is only for use, that it may pass on and come to its flower and fruit in the highest forms of interaction between men and their beliefs.

—WALT WHITMAN

And now who shall use these accumulations,
Give them back purpose, give them life this year—
The young eager dreaming men? The pioneers again?
—RICHARD LEEKLEY

Anything in reference to the future of man should not be a surprise. Some people have long faces. Things will be destroyed, they say. But when the pine is used up there is enough clay to build skyscrapers; when the clay is gone there is enough sand to build cities that will never die.

—BUDD REEVE

THE HOT DOG MAN TRIES TO STOP THE freshet of people flooding past him at the Fair:

Hoy-Hah, Hoy-Hah,
Got 'em all ready and they're all red-hot,
Got tomatoes, onions, and pepper on the top!

316

But he cannot stop them. They flood past him: the buxom farm women, the Norwegian women with their plaited hair, and now the young strong girls in pants, the factory workers, learning to handle steel and bullets, one generation from the peasant, the soil. The older men burnt from the year's harvest. And coming on, the endless children, clinging to the hurrying skirts, rooting themselves in the precarious flesh, tossed on the wave of courageous flesh that keeps thundering in.

There are no young men this year. The young girls swirl in eddies of bright laughter together.

There are again, even in war, the exhibits of embroidery, spinning, canning, lacemaking, leatherwork, wood-carving, baking, witness of the vitality, craftsmanship, and courage of the north country people; in disaster, in struggle, taking pride in the work of the hand, invention, and prowess; faith preserving them, and the believing and the expecting necessary to any work—always present in the darkest days, arousing slothful or despairing time.

Arousing also liberty, in which they have never lost hope or belief. To walk in the fall glut of harvest close to the flood of hip and breast, in the rich talk and discussion, is to be with health—to see it in the strong neck and the sleeping hands, big as hams—in the young sprouting flesh; to hear it in the flood sound of their feet, in the low talk, with the jaw showing the intensity bred now—it is cheer to the heart and a terror to despots.

And "Is liberty gone out of that place? No. Never!" Even the wonderful gyp of the midway carnival has lost its bite. What are lions on motorcycles with blondes riding them, what are two-headed ladies and rubber men to a people who wait for news of sons lost in war; who have now, daily, an experience so strange and violent, it cannot exist in the cranium or heart alone?

What are the naked ladies this year and those who drive nails through their noses, in the face of a world whose global happenings beggar dreams! So also the gyp games, the rolling ball, dice, hoops, mice that run into colored holes, the corn game—they have lost their power of the gamble beside this colossal gamble of the world.

The Glory Gang

The young men of these mothers, missed at the dances, in the drugstores, on the Main Street corners, have turned up now on old ancestral paths, flying over the lands their fathers fled, landing in far countries not marked on the map, smashing geography, canceling space. In these far places they remember New Prague, Bohemian trading post, a little village founded by their Czechoslovakian fathers; they remember now in far places the white spires of churches rising in the heavy green of summer. The Polish boys in the evening in Saipan yearn for Polish *czernina* made of duck blood and wonder who brings the cattle in along the valley floor. The letter from home said that the girls drive the tractors, bringing in the heaping loads of corn from the mechanical picker, filling the huge cribs for the steers and the hogs. Father said they worked harder this year and must keep on working; everyone helped bring in the crops, he said; it was like the old days when you had a house-raising, or a quilting-bee, and everyone came in to help you. It was good to know these things still lived.

The boys from the Icelandic settlements of the North Star Country—Minnesota and Ghent—have letters from their mothers reminding them that Iceland fought a long time for freedom and has the oldest parliament in the world. Danes from the rutabaga country take pictures of their loaded tables of vegetables to send to sons in the Aleutians, and the Hollanders say there are no young men this year to play rolly-bolly, a Dutch game of horseshoe.

Many young men, like the Indians before them, think with nostalgia in a far country of the broad valleys of the Traverse des Sioux, home of the defeated Sioux nation—remembering the river towns, pleasant cities, a productive empire now, feeding the hoppers of war.

In the north the Cornishmen, Slovenes, Croats, Serbs, Lithuanians, Italians, Finns, work day and night breaking their own records in the pits, loading ore directly to the railroad cars to speed down the Merritts' railway and past their graves to the docks, to drop into giant hoppers and into the holds of waiting ships. Soldiers guard the mine shafts and the docks. Six hundred boys are gone from one small town.

They have a double fight. They remember two countries.

The timber workers make a plan for speeding up their production, and the unions organize the villages and cities for scrap drives. Windows in every village show the service flag, usually with more than one star. Headlines in the newspapers tell the story: 3RD MIDWEST ARMY ADVANCES. FIRST ASHORE IS IRISHMAN FROM SOUTH DAKOTA. MINNESOTA DIVISION IS "GLORY GANG."

At the Fair in the rest rooms, women open and read to each other letters with foreign postmarks; men talk about their sons, leaning against the stalls of the giant Percherons or combing the marcelled curls of the sleeping bulls; girls whisper to each other, resting on the grass in front of the grandstand, waiting for the band to play, and the children act what they have heard from letters and brothers on furlough: shooting from behind trees, lone heroes in the fall sun, pretending the pigeons are enemies.

Words are repeated, a new poetry is being made, reasons are stated; there is the flavor of the broad common stock and the struggle and pride in it, the true anonymity of a world event, fraternizing all speech:

"I brought both kinds of music," he said when they landed, pointing to his rifle and his guitar.

When we was sinking, the skipper wanted to go back for his false teeth.

I said to my buddy when we was on that raft, "I got a stronger stomach and can heave farther."

As for the crew, I can't say too much: they were men.

"I fight," he says, "in the hope of a new democracy, embodying the law of the common man."

We have the tallest buildings, greatest cities, hot dogs, Main Street, the Yanks and Dodgers, movies, zoot suits, automatics, and colleges. This is what I am fighting for.

When this war is over I want to own a black Morgan stallion, have two slack combinations, and go to college.

I fight for my friend Bob, killed by the Japs. We used to hunt and fish and race each other up and down the river in our canoes.

So the talk and the letter-reading goes on—low, laconic, with song and higher register and screams rivaling those of the prairie plover or the birds that cried over this land before man. So solid growth arises, from man, more enduring than the stands of pine, cedar, or hemlock; broader than the prairie, deeper than the ancient stands of iron ore, harder than the skull of the Mesabi. "As if men do not make their mark out of any time."

The screen doors of Main Street houses are opened softly at night, and a man or a woman creeps out from the sleepers and looks up at the fall Pleiades asking: Where to? What now?

They can only be answered by the chemistry of their own courage, endurance, the everyday common doings asserting always their high nature and originality; rising now, gathering speed and force, hurling again into action:

We failed many times; we'll fail again and we'll keep on pitchin'.

We got in us the river, the hills, the real things, past and present. It takes workers, carvers, stonecutters, riveters, and patternmakers to hew out a nation. There are solid forms we are going to cut in the future.

We have fought before this wild boar of power, and escaped the scaffold, garrote, cannonball, and slavery many times, and we will again.

I heard of a road from Tierra del Fuega, across South America, North America, crossing the north country in Canada, across the straits to Siberia, into Russia. Why stop there? Why not drive through Europe and home across the Bering Sea?

We got the know-how, and the derring-do, the get-up and the go, the got-to, will-do, must-do and the can-do! Let 'er go!

> O saa vona me, manddommen varar
> At den aukar seg aar etter aar.
>
> And so I hope that our strength may endure,
> And grow from year to year.

And again at the time of harvest there is the roar, the rich tone, precarious and noble, ignominious and human, ahum and indestructible in the fall solstice.

The people are a story that never ends, a river that winds and falls and gleams erect in many dawns; lost in deep gulleys, it turns to dust, rushes in the spring freshet, emerges to the sea. The people are a story that is a long incessant coming alive from the earth in better wheat, Percherons, babies, and engines, persistent and inevitable. The people always know that some of the grain will be good, some of the crop will be saved, some will return and bear the strength of the kernel, that from the bloodiest year some survive to outfox the frost.

Afterword

North Star Country by Meridel Le Sueur first appeared in a series of regional studies called American Folkways. Conceived of and edited by Erskine Caldwell, it was to be written, he said, "by authors well acquainted with the localities in which they lived." Each of the volumes would "describe and interpret the indigenous quality of life in America . . . the cultural influences implanted by the original settlers and their descendants . . . [and so] reveal the ingrained character of America." By 1945, when *North Star Country* was published, there were thirteen American Folkways books with such varied titles as *Desert Country, Blue Ridge Country, Golden Gate Country, Town Meeting Country,* and *Deep Delta Country.*

Among these *North Star Country* was unique—like Meridel Le Sueur herself, a brilliant maverick. True, it conformed to Caldwell's definition of a regional study by presenting indigenous material, providing historical perspective, and describing "ingrained" American characteristics; but the perspective was highly personal, the material idiosyncratic, and the history utterly fragmented. Unlike Gertrude Atherton's *Golden Gate Country,* for example, *North Star Country* did not tell a continuous story, one that would make the past an evenly chronological series of events dominated by notable figures—governors and generals and their glamorous ladies. Rather, its author recovered from forgotten newspaper files and secreted diaries and letters the stories of anonymous people; she had let them speak for themselves in their own dialects and with their own poignancy or humor. Her book gave as epigraphs both the Bible and anonymous quotations, each a "folksay" or fragment

---

This essay was originally written as a Foreword for the Bison Books Edition of *North Star Country,* published in 1984.

of a work song. It presented interminable lists of places, nationalities, animals real and imaginary, tools, foods, special kinds of words. It was a strange mosaic of bits and pieces—highly political and yet poetic, disjointed in structure and apparently haphazard in selection of material, a barrage of quotations rather than a narrative. It had, however, an underlying unity of theme and imagery, and it was stamped by Meridel Le Sueur's special sensibility as a writer, social critic, and iconoclastic woman.

Reissued in 1946 as a Book Find Club selection, *North Star Country* had at first bewildered and intrigued its reviewers. Their descriptions of the book were accurate but conflicting, each concerned with pieces of the complicated mosaic but missing its grand design. To contemporary readers for whom this new edition of *North Star Country* is intended, their conflicting reports may serve as an informative if puzzling introduction to an extraordinary book. One reviewer said, for example, that *North Star Country* offered "good reading" and "valuable facts"; another, that its facts were in error but it had "poetic truth," and was "suggestive" and "haunting to the imagination." This disparity may explain why a third called it a "factual, passionate book," and a fourth "neither straight history nor description, but rather an impressionistic sketch." Yet another reviewer presented seemingly contradictory versions of *North Star Country* as a story "told in the everyday speech and idiom of the people" and also as "a series of poetic explosions, of emotional and lyrical outbursts." All were insightful remarks, though when gathered together they fit another accurate appellation of the work as "scattered, random, helter skelter"—a "scrapbook." Its eclecticism may have led one reviewer to conclude that *North Star Country* was "truly a folkways book." However, another ended by asking, not disingenuously, "What is a 'folkway,' anyway?"

At issue in understanding *North Star Country* is not an anthropological definition but Meridel Le Sueur's concept of American folk. Obviously, it was a term Le Sueur considered synonymous with *tribe* when she wrote plangently of Sioux Indians driven from the plains. When she described homey country stores and country fairs, labor unions, dusty roads traveled by peddlers and truck drivers, and farms where families toiled, then folk meant everyday working people. In its most inclusive and typical meaning, the word referred to all those against whom the rich and powerful in America were polarized. *Folk* was thus a class term; and the reviewer (a Harvard University professor) who asked cogently enough why "it was not a 'folkway' to have lived a middle-class life in La Crosse, Wisconsin," as he had, was both discerning and dismissing Le Sueur's class consciousness in *North Star Country*. The legends, tall tales, ballads, slogans, slang, songs, and excerpts of letters, diaries, and speeches interspersed throughout the book—or rather, comprising it—belong either to Le Sueur's folk or else to the powerful in America whose words reveal how far they are removed in sentiment and interest from working-class people. Language itself thus becomes a folk *way* in *North Star Country*, the discriminating *means* by which a diverse group scattered in time and place expresses a consciousness of shared dispossession.

Time has given the contemporary reader an advantage over the book's early reviewers, for *North Star Country* may now be placed within the context of Meridel Le Sueur's lifework (still in progress) and the historical period that illuminates its fragmented form and its unifying theme. By the time Le Sueur was invited to write for the Folkways series, she enjoyed a considerable reputation as storyteller, radical activist, and reporter. She had won literary awards for several of her stories, among them "Persephone," her first published fiction, and "The Horse"; she also took a prize for an autobiographical essay on the Midwest called "Corn Village." In her journalism she created a unique style that made her work highly visible and highly esteemed. Such emotionally charged reports as "I Was Marching," "Women on the Breadlines," and "Women Are Hungry" combined autobiography, journalism, and social criticism; graphically detailed, personal, they were, for all their lyricism, sternly condemning. Hers was the only woman's voice heard speaking out at the American Writers' Congress of 1934, an international meeting attended by American writers of distinction. As it turned out, the kind of pronouncements she triumphantly made at the Congress, typical of her reportage, was to impede her literary career. As a Midwesterner growing up in the center of populist, socialist, and radical labor movements, she believed, as she said at the Congress, that "revolution can spring up from the windy prairie as naturally as the wheat." Such statements would in time set Senator Joseph McCarthy upon her trail. In the late forties, she found herself summarily blacklisted, her manuscripts rejected. She could publish little except historical books for children, and even these were politically suspect. *North Star Country* is thus her major work of the period and, in ways that remain to be seen, an expression of her protest against forces which for three decades would deprive her of a reputation and an audience.

Like other writers in the American Folkways series, Le Sueur was particularly qualified to describe her region. Though she had spent some childhood years in Texas and Oklahoma, and as a young woman lived briefly in Chicago, New York, Hollywood (where she was a stuntwoman), San Francisco, and Sacramento, she was deeply rooted in the Midwest. Born in Iowa in 1900, brought up in Kansas, and established permanently in Minnesota, she identified herself indissolubly with the North Star country, which, she says, "occupies the exact geographical center of North America." She would define it also as the center of American dreams of democracy. Geographically, the central Midwest described in her book includes Minnesota, Wisconsin, and parts of the Dakotas—the mountains, rivers, prairies, and farmlands within a hundred mile radius from St. Paul, the city she calls home. Though she has written poignantly about hard and hopeful times in St. Paul in her novel *The Girl*, her profound emotional affinity is for the prairies. In her work she recurrently describes a sense of communion with the prairie land and a symbolic union at once mystical and erotic. Her brooding, haunting evocation of Kansas in the 1930 essay "Corn Village" shows her intimacy with a landscape she finds mysterious and elusive, imbued with beauty, not without terror, and capable of inspiring tenderness and a "sense of ruin and desolation." Even a short passage suggests the authority of Le Sueur's style and the lyrical quality of her voice when she sings of and sings to the Midwest landscape. Her image of the land as a raped virgin, recurrent in her work, expresses her mythic identification of woman and earth and political outrage at the exploitation of both:

Oh, Kansas, I know all your little trees. I have watched them thaw and bud and the pools of winter frozen over, the silos and the corn-blue sky, the wagon-tracked road with the prints of hoofs, going where? And the little creeks gullying with delicate grasses and animals, the prairie dog, the rabbit, and your country with its sense of ruin and desolation like a strong raped virgin. And the mind scurrying like a rabbit trying to get into your meaning, making things up about you, trying to get you alive with significance and myth.

In *North Star Country,* Le Sueur continues to try to make the Midwest come "alive with significance and myth." That, indeed, summarizes her purpose. For this reason she retells the stories by which common folk sought to mythologize their heroes and their history. The tall tales interspersed throughout the book show the exaggerating power of a people who wanted to see things as bigger than life: sheer gleeful lies made ordinary swapping fabulous and familiar animals strange, comic, or horrific. Songs also convey significance. They memorialize the workingman's stupendous labors, his loneliness and disappointment, and his death: "Work and pray, live on hay / You'll get pie in the sky when you die." When repeated in a later chapter, Joe Hill's workingman's song has a parenthetical addendum—"(It's a lie)." There are lies and lies in *North Star Country,* those that fabulate and amaze, and those that deceive, like the advertisements of railroad builders recruiting labor from abroad or the promises of landgrabbers fleecing the naive homesteader. Both kinds of lies have significance for the folk: one to endow their daily life and labor with a sense of wonder, as Paul Bunyan's feats make the logger's task wonderful; and the other to reveal the betrayals that represent to Le Sueur the shame of American history.

If, as one reviewer said, her history is "mildly eccentric," that is because in *North Star Country* Le Sueur concentrated upon the past of people usually omitted from history books of the time or pushed to the periphery of the page, away from the center and so ec-centric. In the thirties such people were called "forgotten men"; and as a writer whose literary views were shaped by the proletarian aesthetics of the thirties, Le Sueur believed that her task was to see them remembered, along with working women even more grossly forgotten. To those unspoken for in history books, silenced and anonymous, she would give a voice. Indeed, she considered herself their scribe, someone who continued the tradition of writing down words that otherwise might be evanescent and unheard. She listened for such words all her life. As a child she had heard the unheard stories of the immigrant farm women in the Midwest; as a young writer she

took down tales of women standing on breadlines and waiting in
relief stations; and as a reporter she would ask questions of usually
mute miners' widows and silent somber strikers. Always listening
and always writing for the ear, Le Sueur was essentially a folk writer
—for folk literature is oral. Like the recent oral histories rendered
by Oscar Lewis or Studs Terkel, her *North Star Country* should be
heard as well as read, and heard as a surge of unfamiliar voices:
those of immigrants, pioneer women, unnamed railroad workers,
farmers, traders, teamsters, millhands, miners, and the young soldier
called only Bud. Unexpected, sometimes cacophonous or antipho-
nal, their voices combine into a considerable and emotionally
unified chorus of those Le Sueur called "the nameless ones not
listed in old newspapers." These "work people" made America, Le
Sueur believed, and they were often unmade by the country that
needed their labor but found their lives expendable. Much that
these people have to say in *North Star Country* falls into regular
rhythms of hope and disappointment. The words of a Swedish immigrant woman capture this rhythm in two brief paragraphs:

> I came to America when lots of immigrants came because there was lots
> of work in America, because they were building then and talk of coal, iron,
> railroads, wheat, corn, digging, building, needing lots of laborers and you
> could get an education. . . .
> In America I was like drunk for years, a child coming every year, lifting,
> scrubbing, polishing, pulling, shoving, planting, chopping, birthing, the
> cold shooting into me, the child not born gnawing me, and famines, pan-
> ics, depressions coming and going.

Decades of history are summarized in the immigrant woman's
account that Le Sueur quotes in full: the slow building of a house,
the sudden coming of war and boys dying, and the quick loss of the
house in postwar bad times—"I cry to sell it because it's all I got to
show. / I like to go back there before I die."

For all its apparent looseness of structure, its fragmentation and
desultoriness, *North Star Country* achieves an extraordinary degree
of condensation. Each quotation and brief vignette concentrates
an entire lifetime and way of life, as well as an era of history. The
span of time the book covers is incalculable, beginning in prehis-

toric glacial ages and continuing into a future that is the book's prophetic vision. Like all of Le Sueur's apparent eccentricities, her treatment of time is strategic, serving a thematic purpose. Time moves exceedingly slowly to create in the North Star country, but man moves quickly to destroy: "The ice ages left the rich soil that has been depleted so quickly by man. . . . In a short space of time man has defaced and destroyed this earth." As quickly in the text as an immigrant's life in America is begun and ended, her house built and lost, her children born and dead, so quickly a nation moves through its paces. Its great land is created, then discovered, desired, and seized, then exploited, and finally trashed. Rich mines are exhausted, mountains eroded, forests denuded, rivers polluted, the air defiled. Le Sueur's story sounds startlingly familiar and modern, and explains another puzzling aspect of *North Star Country*, the seemingly disproportionate space it devotes to the history of the Plains Indians.

In the vast panorama of time that the book unfolds, the known interval of the Native Americans' occupation of the Midwest might seem brief, but to Le Sueur it was crucial as an epitome of the saga of exploitation that she was telling. Moreover, to her Native Americans were true environmentalists who understood that humankind and nature belonged together in a symbiotic relationship of mutual nurturing. Le Sueur's admiration for the Native Americans' holistic vision of life stems from childhood experiences among the tribes of Oklahoma, her mingling with children and women lovingly recalled in a late autobiographical essay "The Ancient and the Newly Come." There she tells how she first heard of Native American ceremonies and legends, of a long history when "antelope, deer, elk, and wild fowl lived richly upon the plains" and the mating buffalo roared, and of quick disaster, the genocide she would recount in *North Star Country*. Le Sueur's style in describing devastation shows her finding a way to keep her readers riveted upon events so appalling that they would wish not to know, not to read. She introduced statistics because they gave an illusion of neutrality, a kind of safety; but there is terror in her numbers. The decimation of the Indians was simultaneous with the destruction of the buffalo, an animal whose use to the Native Americans she had catalogued in its amazing detail. One must be terrified by the vision of seventy-five thousand buffalo stampeding "in a last instinct of escape" as they were being killed by five thousand professional hunters. In addition to seemingly neutral statistics, Le Sueur slipped in apparently innocuous asides, short parenthetical phrases the eye might pass over but then, in an obligatory double take, would return to and register to consciousness: "By the treaty, the articles of which were never fulfilled, the United States got possession—for a sum of money which was never paid—of nineteen million acres in Minnesota, nearly three million in Iowa, over one million, seven hundred and fifty thousand in South Dakota: in all, nearly twenty-four million acres of the choicest land existing on the globe." Repetition reinforces the power of the parenthetic remarks: "never fulfilled . . . never paid"; and juxtaposition enlarges the horror. For these astronomical figures, almost too large for the mind to encompass, are followed by others: "The Indians would now have ten miles on each side of the river, until that would be taken from them." Le Sueur's story of the decimation of the Midwest tribes moves rapidly to its denouement. With their land gone, their people slaughtered, their strength dissipated by whiskey, smallpox, and tribal humiliation, the Indians' desperate but futile insurrections leave them starving. As always, the details are minutely and excruciatingly graphic: "Starving Indian women with their children picked grain from the dung of the cavalry horses and marched two hundred miles in the dead of winter to the missions for help." Last seen, the remaining members of the once great Sioux tribe "were stoned as they were deported over the border."

In 1945, Le Sueur could not have foretold that Native American cultures would in time be recuperated and that native visions of the sacred oneness of all forms of life would be respected by a new generation of ecologically minded Americans. However, she could and did tell of a recovery from the devastation she had recorded in the North Star country. In the final section of the book she describes how erosion was being held back by terracing, how cooperatives had brought "new life" to Midwest villages, and how technology made farming, transportation, and labor more profitable and humane. Most important to Le Sueur, time in its recuperative sweeps reinvigorated the dream of American democracy, a native product of her region. For Le Sueur believed unequivocally that the seed of democracy had been planted in the Midwest as deeply and indigenously as the region's life-giving wheat and corn. The key passage of *North Star Country*, an incidental paragraph that seems to have strayed into the book two-thirds along the way, describes the seed's extraordinary vitality:

You can boil some seeds forty-eight hours; other seeds have been perforated, desiccated, put in a vacuum for six months, and then frozen. They lived.

Seeds have been put in glass bottles and buried for forty years, dug up, planted. They lived.

Seeds in the desert will lie for years waiting for a good season. Energy can be cramped in a tiny space, the shell hardens, life seems to be gone, the finest chemical test does not prove that the seeds are alive.

But they are alive!

The image of the seed, which emerges in all of Le Sueur's writing, reflects a lifetime spent in viewing prairies and farmlands, the seasons' eternal turning and renewal, the growth, withering, and new growth of corn and wheat. Seeds are buried, they seem to die and disappear, and then miraculously there bursts from them the blossoms of new life. *North Star Country* is thus an expression of Le Sueur's hope. Though it describes death—death by greed, genocide, extinction, and war—its subject is life, or more precisely, new life. Possibilities for a new life are, after all, the perennial American dream, which brought explorers, settlers, and farmers to a new continent and to a vision of how a society might be constituted and how a people, the common folk, might live. If Le Sueur looked beyond the vision to the violence of the past, it was to discover what lay buried and waiting to be reborn. She believed it was the idea and the reality of American democracy that she saw implanted in the history of the Midwest and in the story of her own as a prairie daughter. In affirming her belief in the future possibilities of democracy, Le Sueur implicitly paid tribute in *North Star Country* to her mother and stepfather, Marion Wharton and Alfred Le Sueur, whose lives she would recount in a brief biography called *Crusaders*. Educators, socialists, public servants, her parents made the growth of democracy their personal crusade. In their home Le Sueur heard many of the leading populists, labor organizers, public speakers, and radicals of her time tell their dreams of how the fruits of democracy would someday become available to everyone in America. Fittingly enough, *North Star Country* concludes with a section entitled "Stride On, Democracy." This Whitmanesque note reverberates in the fragment called "Cradled Hercules," which describes the giant of democracy taking on "new life." The word *new* becomes Le Sueur's final refrain in *North Star Country* as the long history of the Midwest leads to the creation of new means of movement—"new locks, new connections, new canals"—and the renewal of an old but perennial belief in "common and individual rights . . . [and] broader forms of democracy."

This is not to say that *North Star Country* ends easily on a note of unequivocal affirmation. Indeed, it cannot be said to end, nor need it have an ending since it is not a narrative but rather a concatenation of fragments—moments in history to which new moments will be added. Moreover, the conflicts in *North Star Country*, between those who further and those who impede the growth of democracy, can never be resolved. As Le Sueur sees it, resolution does not belong to the plots of history: they always interweave hope and bloodshed too intricately to allow a saga begun eons ago to realize an ultimate ideal. At the end of her book, current history sends the young men of North Star country to war. In a short vignette about Bud, now lost at sea, and his farmer father who has already lost four other sons, Le Sueur condenses a history of heroism, sacrifice, and slaughter that becomes recurrent as the father recalls how his "grandpappy" had lost *his* sons in the Civil War. Blood was shed earlier in another kind of war in *North Star Country* that Le Sueur depicted with an indelible clarity achieved by passion. In a preceding chapter called "Struggle" she had described labor wars that led to the nefarious events of Black Friday. During this "reign of terror," she had seen "a man stepping on his own intestines, bright and bursting on the street, and another holding his severed arm in his other hand." Out of the violence she had witnessed, which she wanted never to be forgotten, Le Sueur created a kind of prose folk ballad, its emotional impact intensified by incremental refrains. After the wounded were brought into strike headquarters on Black Friday, "The skirts of the women had blood on them. The floor of the strike headquarters had blood." A few sentences later, "A line formed . . . to give blood transfusions to the wounded."

Blood, blood, blood—words repeat, suffering and horror intensify, and yet life does not merely go on. Life prevails in Le Sueur's North Star country, for as she says, "the people are a story that never ends, a river that winds and falls and gleams [is] lost . . . turns to dust . . . [and] emerges to the sea. The people are a story that is a long incessant coming alive from the earth in better wheat."

All of the stories of wheat and grain set within the stories of *North Star Country* tell of survival, the result of creative American experimentation which made hardy American corn from Indian maize, winnowed wheat for the sturdiest grain, sifted through alfalfa for a strain that would survive. The secret of survival was always to find the best seed. Then at least "some of the grain will be good, some of the crop will be saved, some will return." With almost a religious fervor, Le Sueur was looking in *North Star Country* for the saving remnant—and she found it in her own Midwest. She believed that the incandescent moments of its tangled history could be searched out and saved and returned to the common people, the common reader, in order to shed light rather than blood. In *North Star Country*, Le Sueur's quest for a "usable" seed of the past ends in—or returns to—the dream of democracy. In all her writing, that dream has given life to her language, her faith, and her art. Since the seed belongs to the people, springs from their hearts, it has made *North Star Country* an American folk story that each generation can share with the next. This is why the reissuing of *North Star Country*, indicative of a revival of interest in all of Meridel Le Sueur's writing, is an important event.

Born in Iowa in 1900, MERIDEL LE SUEUR was brought up in Kansas and lived most of her life in Minnesota. She was an activist and writer whose books include *Salute to Spring* (1977) and *The Girl* (1978). She died in 1996 in St. Paul.

BLANCHE H. GELFANT long taught at Dartmouth College, where she was a professor of English and held a prestigious chair as the Robert E. Maxwell Professor in the Arts and Sciences. She is the author of *The American City Novel, Women Writing in America: Voices in College,* and *Cross-Cultural Reckonings: A Triptych of Russian, American, and Canadian Texts.* In 1995, the American Literature Division of the Modern Language Association awarded Gelfant the Jay B. Hubbell Medallion for distinguished lifetime achievement in the study of American literature.